Off Stage

Betty Comden

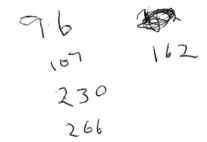

96
107
162
230
266

LIMELIGHT EDITIONS
New York

First Limelight Edition, September 1996

Copyright © 1995 by Betty Comden
All rights reserved
including the right of reproduction
in whole or in part in any form.
Published in the United States by
Proscenium Publishers Inc., New York,
by arrangement with Simon & Schuster Inc.

Manufactured in the United States of America

Library of Congress Cataloging-in-Publication Data
Comden, Betty.
   Off stage / Betty Comden
      p. cm
   1. Comden, Betty. 2. Librettists--United
States--Biography. I. Title.
ML423.C78A3 1996
782.1'4'092--dc20
[B]   96-2779   CIP MN
ISBN 0-87910-084-2

"The Donation" appeared in Wonders *(Summit*
Books).
"So Eat Your Heart Out, Elizabeth Taylor"
appeared in The New York Times
The first part of "Wanted: The Runaway Slave of
Fashion" appeared in Esquire.
"No More Fat Hair" appeared in Vogue.

An excerpt from Unholy Fools *(Viking), © 1969*
Penelope Gilliatt. Originally in The New Yorker. *All*
Rights Reserved.

Contents

Acknowledgments

I would like to express my thanks to Elaine Pfefferblit, my first editor, who insisted that what I was writing could be a book, and who made me believe it and do it; to Chuck Adams, my editor, who, with amused yet clear head, overcame my fears and thoughtfully saw the book through to completion; to my cousin Muriel Alexander Golden, who typed and corrected and gave me loving encouragement; to my beautiful friend Gloria Jones, the first to read the book, who told me she liked it and made me feel terrific; to Michael Korda for giving me the perfect title; to all the people in the book who enriched my life and gave me something to write about; and to Edith Fowler and Cheryl Weinstein for their patience and help.

To my daughter Susanna,
and in memory of
my husband Steve
and my son Alan.

Preface

This book is . . . well, picture Beaumont without Fletcher, Addison without Steele, Leopold without Loeb. I have had a lifetime collaboration and friendship with Adolph Green going back to, as we often say, the dawn of time, yet this book leaves out our equivalent of *The Knight of the Burning Pestle, The Spectator,* and the murder of Bobby Franks, the things we did together (such as the musical shows *On the Town, Wonderful Town, Bells Are Ringing, Peter Pan,* and *On the Twentieth Century,* to name a few; movies, among them *Singin' in the Rain* and *The Band Wagon*; and songs, like "Just in Time," "The Party's Over," and "New York, New York"). Didn't you always yearn to know all about Francis Beaumont at home without his partner? His personal life, his schooling, his children? What kind of tobacco he stuffed into the bowl of his long-stemmed pipe? His relationship with Beaumont *mère?* I want to express my gratitude to and my love for Adolph Green; without him my life certainly would have been different. He is truly "the man without whom . . ." He is also the man, among many, without whom these pages were put together. They contain some random memories, scenes from childhood, plus a reflection or two on things that happened in my personal life when I got older. On the last page of Edith Wharton's memoir, *A Backward Glance,* she wrote, "Life is the saddest thing there is, next to death." If I had read that when I was young—and I could have because I was sixteen when it was first published—I'm sure I would have been stunned. I had not had a totally merry childhood, but it was far from tragedy-laden. I would not have understood what she meant. I would not have believed it. Now I understand it and I believe it. Fortunately, I also believe there is a lot to laugh about.

Genesis . . .
in Brooklyn

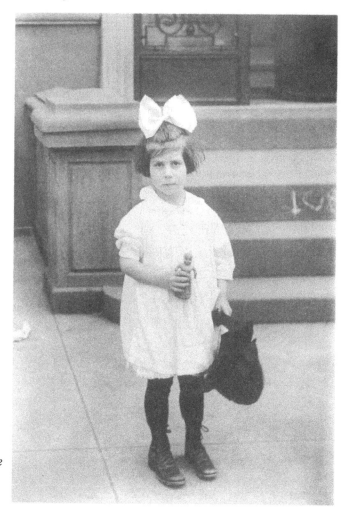

Five-year-old me, such a merry child, rejecting the pony just outside the frame, reluctant to pose at all.

Grandpa and Grandma on the porch of the house he built in Hunter, New York, when the good dreams helped push away the bad dreams of czarist Russia.

Grandpa with his grandchildren: my brother Nat, me looking snooty, and my cousins Muriel and Inez, in Hunter, where I spent my first seventeen summers, carefree except for math lessons.

Grandma and her sister on the kitchen steps in Hunter, shelling peas and talking about their men.

With my brother Nat. This picture is not a composite fake; he was really nice to me and taught me how to throw a ball.

My other aunt, Rose, who lived to 101 and never married. At ninety, lying naked in a hospital bed, she looked up at the circle of interns and doctors staring down at her and sang sweetly, "Getting to know you, getting to know all about you."

With "Fat" Aunt Celia, so named to distinguish her from my mother's slender sister. She was married to my father's brother Ezra, the owner of a stationery store that was pivotal in my life.

A tree and a girl grow in Brooklyn—both beautiful.

My mother and father the year they were married, 1912. Brother Nathaniel and I never saw their Riverside Drive apartment. We came later, in Brooklyn.

My mother (center) with her two closest friends, my aunt Celia, her sister (right), and my fake "aunt," Cal (left), who brought me a doll from Alsace-Lorraine.

The Children's Museum, across the street on Park Place, which I decided to honor by donating a precious doll.

Who said, "Her hair hung down her pallid cheek like seaweed on a clam"? My graduation from the Brooklyn Ethical Culture School in the green number I made myself. I'm taking orders.

Natalie the Flapper, married to my uncle David. On their honeymoon she played tennis in that wedding dress.

Graduation from Erasmus Hall High School. In the yearbook it says I made the Arista. Why not Miss Hairdo, Class of '33?

The Game of the Name

*T*here is a French expression, *"Il est bien dans sa peau,"* meaning literally, "He is well in his skin," meaning feeling comfortable and at ease being oneself—or as the song "That Old Black Magic" doesn't quite put it, "in his skin, loving the skin he's in."

I am envious of anyone in that state of grace because even at this late date, having reached the point when my *peau* could use a judicious taking in here or there, I am still not *bien* in it. Working hard at not discovering the reason for this, I nevertheless stumbled on a possible clue while visiting my then ninety-eight-year-old aunt Rose, who in the course of vague ramblings down a somewhat potholed memory lane started chuckling softly to herself about the day I was born. The farther back Rose's reminiscence, the more accurate, had been the general rule, so this vivid picture has a good chance of being the truth.

"You were brought in to your mother," Rose said. "Daddy and Grandpa were in the room and took one look at you . . ." She shook her head and sighed. I gather it was a look not of welcoming approval but of wild dismay.

"Well," Rose went on, "the nurse hadn't really cleaned you up properly." But is it not possible that in that fleeting second Baby Betty, still not cleaned up properly, her tiny eyelids stuck with the recent struggle to get into the world, opened her tiny eyes and caught that look? "Daddy and Grandpa adored you, as you know," said Aunt Rose, "but they did agree that to get you married they would have to find a Rothschild because they could never afford a dowry huge enough."

Is it not also possible that the tiny ears picked up that appraisal and that the tabula rasa of my equally tiny psyche recorded for all time the message "I'm-not-pretty-no-man-will-ever-want-me." Not the best start for *"bien-dans-sa-peau"*-ing. Not comfortable in my skin to begin with, a tot not oohed and aahed at in her stroller, my *peau* problem must have been enhanced by the question of my name. One's name is, after all, the label by which one identifies oneself. If it keeps changing, perhaps one's sense of identity keeps shifting about also. The birth certificate said "Baby," but I was officially named Basya after my paternal grandmother according to the custom of naming a child for a deceased relative. Basya means Daughter of God, *Ya* being one of the names for the deity, never spoken aloud except by the ordained. Yet somehow it was OK if it was only part of some female's name. The kids on the block did not know the exalted history of my name, and I was subjected to a good deal of the kind of unrefined torture only little children seem to be able to think up. Back then the nickname for a cow was Bossie, pronounced Bahssie, and on the farm toward milking time, a farmer was apt to stand at the edge of the pasture, hand held awninglike across his brow to shield his squinting eyes from the setting sun, and bellow, "Here, Bahssie! Hey, Bahss . . . hey, Bahssie!" I, now Basya, got quite a bit of bellowing from my peers in the sandbox. Finally, fed up to my tiny armpits, I approached my father and presented my plight with as much dignity as a puzzled and angry five-year-old could. He listened sympathetically. Rose was right: My father really did adore me and, following that first unfortunate look, made me feel loved and protected until the day he died when I was nineteen.

He said, "You can take any name you like as long as it begins with a *B*." Beaming, I ran down a list of possibilities, lingering awhile on Barbara and finally choosing Betty. The   19 adjustment to Betty was smooth on everyone's part, and only later did I have a little trouble convincing certain teachers that Betty was indeed a complete name and I was not now nor ever had been Elizabeth. There seemed on the surface no identity crisis at the time, and though shy and timid in my *peau* after my rocky beginning, I seemed fairly *bien*. But was I really, deep down?

This was only the first of a progression of name changes that would punctuate my life.

You see, there was also my last name. It was Cohen. But I knew from family evenings around the dining-room table that this was *not* my true name: It was the whim of a weary Ellis Island clerk who, upon hearing my grandfather declare his name to be Baruch Astershinsky Simselyevitch-Simselyovitch, rolled his eyes heavenward and wrote down Cohen. I knew I had been living under a false name. Other family members coming through immigration at the same time but through a different gate and past a different clerk had more of the luck of the Irish and wound up as Austin (not bad) or even Astor (wow!). The Cohens did not feel uneasy *peau*-wise, but the two youngest brothers in the family were not yet established in what they were going to do, and there were so many George Cohens and David Cohens that a movement was started to have the name changed. My father, the oldest and head of the tribe, was established as a lawyer and decided he would stick to the name the Ellis Island clerk had bestowed on him, but he urged his children—me, a fearful, aspiring theater nut, and Nat, a brilliant premed student—to make the change. Too many doctors Cohen and no actress Cohen. Probably none of this would have come up today, but it was 1936, and the drive away from the ethnic label and toward complete assimilation was not absent from their reasoning. My mother had arrived in this country from Russia at the age of six, and her perfectly modulated voice and beautiful diction made her seem more English than American. My father, blue-eyed and straight-featured, also spoke beautifully, only occasionally encountering a slight confusion when he hit a *v* or *w*.

But what to change the name to? It seemed positively

20

un-American to go back to Astershinsky Simselyevitch-Simselyovitch. My grandmother Basya's name had been Emden, a lovely name, but everyone in the family seemed unwilling to give up the initial *C*, so a combination was agreed upon: Comden.

So at nineteen Baby Basya Betty Astershinsky Simselyevitch-Simse*lyo*vitch Cohen became Betty Comden.

The name did nothing, however, to land me a job in the theater. There was a long period of humiliating and futile stormings of producers' and agents' offices, during which, on more than one occasion, my medical student brother had to hurl my flailing body on the bed and sit heavily on me until the hysteria abated. "If the producers could only see you now," he would say, holding my arms still and trying not to smile, "what passion!"

But the changes were not over. Around the same time I met a young god named Siegfried Schutzman. He was attending the Art Students' League and working for his father, and he was beautiful in every way. I did not know, until much later, of my father's and grandfather's prediction for me, but deep in my soul I wondered uneasily how this paragon could possibly want me. Yet he did, and we were married. And a brief six months later I was spending my time between shows at a nightclub learning how to knit, not tiny garments but scarves and mittens in olive drab for my soldier husband. Baby Basya Betty Astershinsky Simselyevitch-Simselyovitch Cohen Comden was now Mrs. Siegfried Schutzman.

But just as I was getting used to my strange new name, my husband returned from the war and announced that he wanted to change it. Its German-ness had made him suspect in an army of GIs out to "kill Krauts," and even as a kid it had given him a lot of trouble with his peers who did not appreciate the fact that his parents were opera lovers. How come his brother had been named just plain Carl? "Why can't I be just plain Steve?" he would ruminate. (His sister was named Isolde, but it's different for girls.) "And Schutzman isn't the family name anyway. I want my real name back," he announced. This was not another case of Ellis Island roulette but of misplaced gratitude. His father's very much older 21 brother had come to this country from Russia and was taken in by a kindly German family named Schutzman who treated him like a son, which caused him to adopt their name. When his younger brother (my father-in-law) arrived much later, it seemed only natural for him to do the same thing. Thus they embraced "Schutzman" and threw away their real name, "Kyle."

Suddenly   Babybasyabettyastershinskysimselyevitch-simselyovitchcohencomdenschutzman   was   Mrs.   Steven Kyle. Who?

I still harbor that "uneasy in my skin" feeling, and though it grows less intense with the years, it still hovers. That look of dismay the baby caught in her father's eyes, together with all its implications, and the endless variations of the label with which I identified myself to the world surely must have conspired to create one hell of an identity crisis.

Bien dans sa peau? Would going back to roots help me feel more *bien* in it? And how would it sound: "by Basya Astershinsky and Adolph Green"?

Lullaby of Wordland

*I*t is written that in the beginning there was the Word. In my own beginning, though I did not know at the time that my life's work would be involved with those units of language, words immediately fascinated me, and they have never lost their spell. Having grown up with a family of humans to listen to, it is not surprising that I learned to talk, read, and write. But how did Tarzan do it? I recall reading in the first Tarzan book how he discovered in Lord and Lady Greystoke's deserted cottage in the jungle a shelf of flat hard objects (books) that when opened revealed thin sections covered with what he called "bugs" running across their surfaces. I never fully understood how he figured it out and learned to read but, by George, he got it! A miracle. But perhaps no more a miracle than the secret code every lisping tot knows whereby when he doesn't want his mommy to go out, he doesn't say, "Home me mommy with stay," but somehow gets those bugs out in the proper order.

Early on at home, with radio in its adolescence and without the siren song of television to fill our hours, we played a variety of word games like Anagrams, Ghost, and my childhood favorite, Hangman, wherein you make dashes on a page to indicate the letters of a word you have in mind, draw a gibbet and noose, and ask your opponent to guess the letters. With each miss you draw an add-a-part body hanging from   23 the noose—a head, eyes, nose, and mouth, the body, each arm and each leg—until you hope he dangles there, strangled dead, while you shout with gleeful triumph. Words made great playthings then, and for me they still do. What's in a word? I remember finding out something surprising about certain words while on a streetcar ride in Brooklyn years ago.

The Tompkins Avenue trolley was making the turn from Empire Boulevard onto Kingston Avenue, where it would eventually get to our corner, Park Place. My mother, my nine-year-old brother Nat, and I, three years younger, were coming back from a Brooklyn Dodgers ball game at Ebbets Field. Dignified and reserved, my mother would take us to watch the team affectionately labeled Dem Bums because she knew her son worshiped them, but she would not allow us to say their nickname aloud. I went along, happy to go anywhere Nat went. The game was not memorable, at least not to me, but I mark that day as one of blinding revelation. As we rounded the corner we passed a wooden fence on which was inscribed the word FUCK in bold white chalk. I gasped inwardly, not in shock but in disbelief and astonishment. Glancing furtively at my family, I saw that my mother was serenely reading an Ethical Culture Society newsletter and Nat was staring idly into space, possibly replaying the game in his head. I wanted desperately to talk to him about what I'd just seen but knew this was impossible in my mother's presence; I would have to wait until we got home.

Safe in our ground-floor living room, while my mother went to take off her hat and start dinner at the other end of our long apartment, I grabbed Nat and blurted out what I had seen.

"What about it?" he said with nine-year-old superiority. It is not that I was shocked or didn't know vaguely what the scrawled word meant, but there it was, miles from where we lived, in alien territory.

"But that's *our* word," I said. "How come it was way over on Empire Boulevard?" I had thought the word belonged to our block, that it had been made up by my brother and the Pearlman boys from the apartment above, with the help of the Fitzpatrick boys from the basement below. They and some other lads on our street used to disappear down those basement stairs for what I assumed were discussions of a secret nature, sometimes making what I guessed was an obscene gesture, a forefinger slipped through an *O* formed by the other forefinger and thumb.

After recovering from his laughter, Nat revealed to me that the word—"our word"—was a very old one known by everyone wherever English was spoken.

"What about *shit*," I whispered thoughtfully, "and . . . and *cocks?*" I was vague about the second one. I knew the boys would ask me to repeat over and over again my kindergarten teacher's name, and when I said, "Miss Wilcox," they fell about laughing. So I knew it meant something and had almost decided it must mean "behind." It took me a while to sort that out. It was a big concept to absorb—that what I had assumed was our privately invented vocabulary actually belonged to the entire civilized world, not just to Park Place and Kingston Avenue.

Those same Fitzpatrick boys, the janitor's sons, no longer the co-inventors of great words in my eyes, were visiting Nat in our apartment one day shortly after the trolley ride. Nat had told them of a painting in one of our rooms, and his description had so inflamed them that they pestered him mercilessly until he agreed to let them have a peek. It hung on the wall in the small bedroom where our aunt Ethel was staying while waiting out the years until her suitor, our cousin Esaac, could get a divorce. She was out, so we slipped into the room and they started to stare. It was a woodsy painting in the Barbizon School tradition, a bosky knoll on the shore of a tranquil pool where sat a beautiful young woman, nude, her back to the viewer, her long gold-brown hair sweeping over her perfect shoulder and down one side, yet revealing the part she sat on, or what I figured they would call her "cocks." The boys stared a long time. They whistled quietly through their teeth. "I wish she'd turn around," said Tom, or was it John, wistfully. They stared some more. Suddenly, excited as if he'd come up with $E = mc^2$, John rushed to the picture, lifted it off its hook, and turned it around, looking expectantly for what he hoped to see. His look of disappoint- 25 ment when he faced the canvas and wood back of the frame is (as they used to say) etched forever on my memory. There was some disgruntled talk of my showing them my six-year-old front as consolation, but Nat would have none of that; however, he said it was all right if I showed them what the painting did (my "cocks"). Did she or didn't she? Here (as they also used to say) time has drawn a merciful veil.

One morning a short time before this, I had suddenly found that I could read. I had gone into the kitchen where my mother was opening the dumbwaiter door. Inside was ice. The iceman's horse and wagon waited in the street while the iceman used his tongs to pick up a block of ice wrapped in newspaper and put it in the dumbwaiter in the basement of our small four-story apartment house. In the kitchen above, my mother brought it up by pulling on the rope hand over hand. Money was placed on the dumbwaiter floor, and the iceman pulled it down as currents of cool air, smelling somewhat of coal, rose from the cellar.

While my mother was carrying the block of ice over to the icebox and putting it on the top shelf, my eyes happened to alight on the newspaper lying on the kitchen table. I had an epiphany. Letters, which up until then had been a jumble of unrelated, incomprehensible squiggles in a puzzle, suddenly danced into place. "Unwed Mother Abandons Baby," I read aloud. My mother looked around, astonished. "You can *read!* How wonderful you are!" In her embrace, joy was transcendent. I had done something wonderful! She was proud of me! She loved me! But my moment of triumph was immediately engulfed in a wave of anxiety. What does that mean, Unwed Mother Abandons Baby? I had a vision of a mother dropping her baby somewhere, down a dumbwaiter shaft perhaps. The "Unwed" part slipped right by me for the moment in my worry over the baby.

"What does it mean, Mama?" My mother, a quick thinker who had been a teacher before her marriage, was smart enough also to skip over the "Unwed" part, which would have been tough to explain to me since I, along with everyone else, knew you had to be wed to have a baby. But how to explain to a child on the brink of a terrifying discovery that such things can happen in the world, that indeed a mother could abandon her baby? This was a short hop from the unspeakable possibility that my mother could abandon me. Mama seated me on her lap and held me in her arms. Her brain must have been ticking away furiously.

"Do you remember what Miss Garrett was telling the class about last week?" she asked in a soothing voice. Miss Garrett was our nature teacher, a salty gray-haired lady who took us to the Bronx Zoo to ride on a huge ancient turtle and to Prospect Park across from the school to marvel at the buds on the trees in early spring.

"She was teaching you about certain birds, like the cuckoo, who deposit their eggs in another bird's nest and then that bird hatches the eggs and brings up the baby birds as her own with lots of love and attention."

I looked up at my mother's face, still fearful.

"It's something like that with people sometimes," she said, "so don't worry, the baby will be loved and cared for." She folded the newspaper away into the kitchen drawer behind me. "But what about your reading! When did it happen?" she continued brightly, switching the subject back to me.

"Just now," I said, beaming under her praises and quickly abandoning the already abandoned baby. I was still somewhat mystified and uneasy but decided to play my big moment and stifle the doubts. I ran down the hall to my room, brought a book back to the kitchen, and proceeded to read to my mother.

I read constantly from then on, but although not dyslexic, I still mysteriously read some things wrong. Nat received a present of the S. S. Van Dine murder mysteries, and I devoured *The Greene Murder Case* and *The Canary Murder Case.* But while discussing them with Nat, I found him laughing when I mentioned the detective's name.

"What did you call him?"

"Philco Vance," I said, of course.

"Philo," he said. *"Philo* Vance. No *c.* Philco is a radio." 27

He had to stick my head in the book to prove it to me, I was so incredulous. The great Mr. Vance never seemed quite the same to me after that. *"Philo"* was just ridiculous.

And the heroine of our favorite comic strip in the *Brooklyn Daily Eagle* ("Hairbreadth Harry" of the big shoulders and the overfirm chin) was a pretty blonde I called Belin-eye-da (rhymed with Ida). Again, my brother had to correct me by showing me the letter-by-letter spelling that was naturally Belinda. Where did I get Belin-eye-da? Where, indeed? From then on my heroine paled a bit for me with her mundane monicker. It just didn't fit her.

All children mishear certain things as they try to absorb all the new information bombarding them every instant of their unfolding lives. I am very fond of Jessica Mitford's mishearing "the final conflict" in the revolutionary anthem, "The Internationale," as "the fine ol' conflict." My mishearings had less to do with politics. The frilly thing my aunt Rose wore in the mornings or while preparing her toilette was a "boodwackap," later to be identified as a "boudoir cap."

I used to love to accompany my mother to the shop where we got elastic for bloomers and waist buttons to replace ones lost from some strange, now obsolete undergarment I wore, plus the requisite needles and pins and thread. One wall of the store was all shallow drawers filled with spools of silk and cotton threads in every color of the rainbow and every gradation in between; in one drawer all greens from the palest to the darkest forest shade, in another baby pink to deep magenta. I would spend my time opening and closing the easy-rolling drawers, drinking in the colors and occasionally moving my finger over a favorite spool to make it revolve. I told my mother how much I loved going to the "draggit" store. She took me outside and indicated the sign over the door. My mother never pointed. (I had learned to read.) The sign said KATZENSTEIN'S DRY GOODS STORE. Dry goods? How weird.

In spite of her interest in progressive education and the Child Study Association, reading John Dewey and the latest teaching theories, my mother was somewhat less than
28 candid when informing us about the names of body parts and

body functions. For some reason my parents decided to use Russian when discussing this area of life. My father spoke Russian, but all we children ever learned were some beautiful songs he would sing to us and the words for "one" and "two": *ahdin* and *d'vah*. So needing to go to the bathroom became needing to "make *ahdin*" or "make *d'vah*," causing no end of confusion among our little friends, early grade teachers, and parents of young peers. It's pretty lonely being the only kid on the block who goes to the bathroom in Russian. But my mother's sister Celia went along with these euphemisms, and her two daughters, my cousins Inez and Muriel—one a bit older and the other a year younger—used the same terms along with the attendant names for the parts of the body: *ba-part* (*d'vah* was quickly shortened to the slangier one-syllable *ba*) and the unisex *ahdin-part*.

This practice did not go on very long, as I recall. When we were a little older, my mother's honesty and sense of humor must have made her bite the bullet and give us the real stuff. I never cared much for the word *urinate*, but what can you do?

There were also numerous word restrictions. We were not allowed to say hell, darn, stink, or even belch. And when we were taken to see *The Vagabond King*, we all caught the patriotic fervor of François Villon but had to keep it somewhat in check. We would march around singing the "Song of the Vagabonds," but "Come all ye beggars of Paris town, ye lousy rabble of low degree!" lost some of its color when we sang "ye *lazy* rabble." And the incendiary call to action of the last line, "And to *hell* with Burgundy!" became less than stirring as "And to *heck* with Burgundy!"

Years later—oh, many, many years, when we were working on our first show, *On the Town*, and the song "New York, New York" was written—some deep inhibition from my past made me avoid singing the song to my mother. I was afraid she might disapprove of the phrase "a helluva town." It is true that for years the custom of the times made it necessary for radio and recordings to bowdlerize it to "heckuva" or "wonderful," and the same was true of the MGM movie. The definitive album made in 1960 finally used "helluva." When I   29 at last screwed up my courage to sing it to my mother, she loved it, "helluva" and all. She had changed. So had I, of course, but I did have a twinge of remembering what her disapproval felt like, and I hesitated to risk one of her black looks for saying the word *hell.*

What would she have thought if she had known I knew that word I saw from the trolley? It is hard for me to conceive that *she* had ever heard of it. I doubt that Tarzan knew that word, either. How could he have learned it in the jungle? Lord and Lady Greystoke would not have had a book in their possession with such a "bug" running across its pages. No, that would have to wait until many years later when Tarzan became Lord Greystoke and was sitting around with the guys one evening in his exclusive London club.

As for me, I'm still playing with words, and I did finally figure out why the boys on the block loved making me repeat my teacher's name—Miss Wilcox.

The Donation

*T*he doll was given to me when I was about eight years old by my aunt Cal on her return from a summer vacation in Europe. She was really a "fake aunt," as I would explain to my friends proudly: "not my mother or my father's sister but my mother's best friend from high school." Aunt Cal had begun taking her summer jaunts through Europe with my mother years before this, when they had gone on together from high school to the Maxwell Training School for Teachers and then into the public school system. My mother taught for several years in Brooklyn, then married, and as most young ladies did at that time, she stopped working to be a wife and mother. Aunt Cal remained Miss Seelman and continued teaching and traveling all her life, a teacher adored by her pupils—many of whom remained her friends long after graduation—and an inspired leader of young people at the Henry Street Settlement House.

I also adored her. She had white, white hair, always cut short, olive skin, bright eyes—blue, I think—that crinkled at the corners, and a quick, even smile. Her voice was low and beautifully modulated, and her speech patrician but not affected. When I was older, I realized that she must have had a profound influence on my mother who had arrived at Ellis Island from Russia when she was six, speaking no English at all. The cultured, reserved girls whose families had been   31

Americans for many generations, like Caroline Seelman and Mary F. Starkey, whom she met a few years later at the Girls' High School, became my mother's closest friends. She had sought the ones whose characteristics she admired and wanted to emulate. Her voice was low, too, and beautifully modulated; her diction was clear, her manner reserved, and her posture regal. When she sat in a chair, she always allowed several inches between its back and her own. Growing up, I was gently abjured from making unnecessary gestures, touching my hair and face after my toilette was considered finished, and indulging in emphatic inflections. My unusual mother, warm, loving, and formidable, was often, in the beauty of her composure, mistaken for an Englishwoman.

When Aunt Cal visited, she always wore something for me to try on and play with. She had many long chiffon scarves, mainly blues and greens in elaborate floral patterns, and strings of beads, lapis lazuli and silver, carnelian, amber, and my favorite, made of wood covered with crushed tiny beads in a swirling multicolored design. These I was allowed to appropriate for the length of her visit, and many were the undersea ballets and Arabian Nights tableaux my mother and Aunt Cal had to witness over the years. Sometimes her scarves became the billowing waves, and sometimes they were veilings to conceal my sacred face from the unclean in the marketplace. My father could not escape these theatricals, either, for sometimes Aunt Cal came to have dinner with my parents, and I was allowed to be the dinner floor show until they went off to the Philharmonic concert at the Brooklyn Academy of Music.

When I first saw the doll she brought me, I realized at once that it was something very special. "This comes all the way from Alsace-Lorraine," she said. "That is how the ladies dress there." The doll was about six inches tall but seemed larger to me at the time. Covering the entire top of her head was a flat black bow, stitched down the center like hair parted in the middle, the halves of the ribbon standing out stiffly on either side of the head. The bodice of her dress was black with a white lace insert at the throat, and the sleeves were striped in many colors. She held her arms close to her body, the hands disappearing somewhere under the bodice. The skirt was a round black satiny bell, broken in front by a tiny striped apron. The skirt was long, and if you turned the doll upside down, there were no feet or shoes, just the flat circular surface the doll stood on. What was extraordinary was her face. She was an old woman. The face was wrinkled and tan, the cheeks lined, the eyes realistically small and somber. I found her odd and beautiful. I had never seen an old lady doll, nor had any of my friends.

I did have other dolls, of course. On birthdays and Hanukkahs my grandfather would bring me a huge French china doll, so by this time I had a number of these gorgeous creatures with pink cheeks, long-lash-fringed eyes that closed when you lay the doll down, silky curly hair, and jointed bodies made of something very hard that hurt when you hugged them. They wore perfect starched dresses and underthings, little black buttoned shoes, and often a gold locket around the neck. On those special occasions Grandpa would appear with a long box and say solemnly that he had brought me a fish. It was a running joke, and we both knew it and enjoyed the ritual of pretended disappointment and revulsion, plus stifled giggles. Yet I remember always feeling a slight shudder of apprehension as I opened the box, which subsided only when I actually saw the little black Mary Janes peeking through the tissue paper at one end.

My other dolls were two soft, raggedy individuals, a boy and a girl named F'day and F'dunk, and a mottle-faced baby named Anna Katny. Not knowing the properties of the material from which her face was made, I had washed it with maternal thoroughness and soap and water, removing the paint and leaving her with a permanent case of the measles. But my little old lady doll from Alsace-Lorraine became my treasure. I felt privileged to possess her and treated her with deep respect. I could not cuddle her or presume to tuck her in at night, but I took her to the windowsill for an outing every day and stood her carefully in a special place on a shelf every night.

Our apartment house was directly across from a small park one block square. The long ground floor we occupied fronted on the street with what we knew, not as the living room or parlor, but simply as the "front" room. From there, going back along two consecutive hallways, were the rest of the rooms that looked out on an alley and, beyond them, a kitchen and tiny "back" room with a view of the backyard, complete with clotheslines, cats on a fence, and, from time to time, singers who would serenade in broken harsh voices until coins were thrown down to them wrapped in bits of newspaper. The park across the street had one long beautiful meadow marked with KEEP OFF signs. Sometimes my brother and the other boys on the block played stickball or "association," a form of football, in the gutter, and a cop would come, summoned by the old ladies from four forbidding stone houses that remained from better days among the somewhat newer post–World War I apartment houses with names like Joffre Court. The boys would leave the gutter, climb the park fence, and resume their game on the forbidden meadow; a genuinely frightening parkman, brandishing a stick, would come and chase them back into the gutter. Then the cop would come back, and there would be a lot of fast running.

I once saw a policeman confiscate a kid's baseball. If what ensued had happened to my doll, there would have been a juvenile cop-killer at large in Brooklyn. As the whole group, including me and a few other tolerated girls, gathered in a fascinated horrified circle, he took out a knife and carefully dissected the ball, first cutting the stitches and removing the two interlocking barbell-shaped pieces of leather. This skinning revealed a tightly compressed mass of tangled string that he flicked apart with the tip of the knife and scattered, seeming to fill the whole gutter with the baseball's intestines. Soon it all unraveled and fell away, leaving a tiny rubber center, the heart. This he flicked into the air with his thumbnail. We dispersed silently as from a funeral.

The other half of the park was composed of a hill, which was good for sledding in winter and rolling in spring, and the Brooklyn Children's Museum. This lovely Victorian edifice with its green-streaked oxidized roof was not only a museum to me but also a library, a theater, and a horror house. The library windows had faded cretonne window seats

34

where I could curl up on rainy days, first with Louisa May Alcott and Gene Stratton Porter, and later with Eliot, Dickens, and Twain. The theater was the auditorium, which showed historical movies on Saturday mornings; the one I remember best was a stately silent film about Alexander Hamilton. The horror house was the bird room. There were many nature exhibits, and it was in the bird room that I developed my lifelong fear of large birds from the gigantic all-seeing, all-knowing stuffed condor that dominated the main case, past which I would dash, breath held, eyes tightly shut, and heart pounding.

The wonderland of the museum, where I spent a great deal of time, was the doll collection. There were cases and cases of dolls of all sizes from all over the world and from all periods of history. They were stunningly arrayed in the native costumes of their countries and times, and some were arranged in dioramas and rooms furnished in detail to give them the perfect settings: Spanish, French, English, German, Portuguese, Dutch, Italian, African, Chinese, Japanese. I would stare long and lovingly at them, and could almost feel myself going through the glass to be with them. I knew what countries they came from, but I wondered how the museum had managed to get hold of them. I asked my mother, and she said she supposed the museum had people who traveled and collected for them but that most dolls had been donated by various citizens who wanted to share their possessions with everyone in the city.

The word *donated* rang in my ears. I thought it was beautiful. I became engulfed in noble feelings. I, too, would donate. I would share with everyone in the city. It would be a painful sacrifice, but I would make it. The poor dear museum, for all its great collections, had no doll from Alsace-Lorraine. But I had. There must be millions of little girls like me, I reasoned, and educated adults as well, who had never seen one and would never know how the ladies dressed there unless I donated my doll from Alsace-Lorraine to the museum.

I announced my intentions to my mother, who looked surprised and asked me if I was sure I wanted to part with my 35 doll. I stood tall and noble and said yes, I was sure. At the same moment I thought of the doll I loved so much and wished I could retract my reckless statement. If my mother felt any uneasiness about this, I did not sense it at the time. I spent the next few days until our appointment at the museum going through all kinds of conflicting emotions: joy, pride, sadness, regret, an impulse to mislay the doll, an impulse to run away from home with her. I loved the doll but truly felt it was the right thing to share her with others.

The day of the appointment came. I dressed carefully in my best dress, brown velvet with smocking and ecru lace collar and cuffs, and over it reluctantly my unattractive coat, leggings, and hat of brown chinchilla—not the priceless feathery fur but a sturdy bumpy woolen cloth made to last for several seasons. The precious doll was taken from her shelf, wrapped in tissue paper, and put into a shoe box. I whispered to her that I would come often to visit her and that she must realize she would now be able to bring pleasure and knowledge to thousands. Though trembling nervously when my mother and I were mounting the stairs to the curator's office, I felt the same warm glow of noble renunciation the "White Sister," as played by Lillian Gish, must have felt giving up her soldier lover for her vows. Sadly but proudly I handed over the box to the tall, thin-lipped lady who was the curator. She opened the box, turned back the tissue paper, looked at my doll, and said, "I'm afraid we can't accept this. You see, it's not really a doll at all. It's a pincushion." She poked a thin finger into the revered old lady's bell-shaped skirt, turned her upside down, and tapped the flat surface where there should have been feet. "It's a tourist souvenir, you see, sold by the thousands," she said cheerfully, handing it back to me.

I have no memory of going home. I do remember the waves of humiliation, rejection, and rage that rocked me into nausea. My mother tried to comfort me, saying, "Nothing's changed, dear. She's still as beautiful as she was, and now you can have her all to yourself again." But something had changed. When I took the doll out of the box at home and looked at her again, she seemed smaller, and I was embarrassed by the absence of feet and shoes and, indeed, hands. I

36

stood her on my dresser. I took a pin and tentatively stuck it into the stuffed bell that was her lower half. She did not mind. But I did. I grabbed my cuddly, raggedy F'day and F'dunk and, hugging them to me, curled up on my bed and cried.

The Flapper

The flapper came into my life when I was an overimaginative child waiting for something to happen in my life in Brooklyn. The most notable event so far that year had been the arrival of a new radio. In place of our old crystal set with its two pairs of earphones for a family of four, we now possessed a grand Atwater Kent cabinet model, topped with a separate loudspeaker that was shaped, I now know, something like a stationary radar transmitter. This exotic piece of furniture gave our dining room its center. It was hearth, pulpit, and stage, in front of which the family could gather nightly, my brother Nat and I lying on our stomachs on the rug, listening to "Amos 'n' Andy" and "The Happiness Boys," spellbound like the group of ancient Greeks in the reproduction of the famous painting, *Reading from Homer,* that hung in our parlor.

The day we were to meet Natalie the Flapper, our aunt-to-be, my brother and I were listening to music coming from our magic loudspeaker.

"It's inhuman," I moaned, "inhuman!" as the gorgeous music swelled. Nat tried to stifle his laughter. I closed my eyes tight, then falling limply against one of the oak dining chairs, pressed the back of one hand to my brow and asked faintly, "What is it?"

"Brahms, I think," my brother said.

"Inhuman," I murmured again.

Nat's laughter was uncontrolled. He was affected by music as much as I, but he was older and knew the meaning of the word *inhuman,* and the sight of me in my middy and drooping gym bloomers emoting to music was both familiar and hilarious to him. An hour before, I had been Charles-toning around the same dining-room table, eyes rolling, licking my thumbs and pasting them against my hips with a hissing sound to denote rising steam, in an imitation of Joan Crawford in *Our Dancing Daughters.* Only the brass chandelier hanging low over the center had kept me from leaping up and dancing on the tabletop like gyrating Joan.

Nat was accustomed to my changes of character and mood. I kept repeating "inhuman," and he kept laughing, although he understood that I was only trying to express my feeling that something beyond human comprehension was flooding the room with celestial light.

The music ended, and the announcer's patronizing voice informed us that Erno Rapee had just conducted the first movement of Brahms's First Symphony. In those early days of radio they often played only one movement of a work. As the next piece was being announced, I got up, insulted by my brother's derision, and sulked out of the room and down the two long halls to the privacy of the front room of the apartment. Nat shut off the radio and followed me. I glared at him, my lower lip extended in what was known in the family as my "pity me" or "oom-dah" expression. He said he was sorry, gently explained the true meaning of the word *inhuman,* and said if I'd promise not to tell anybody, he would show me something he had found in a drawer in the mahogany table.

What hit my incredulous eyes was a magazine cover picture of a half-undressed girl, crossed legs revealing rolled stockings, one finger crooked beckoningly as she winked out from under short red curls. The magazine was called *Pep.* Under it lay another, called *Secrets,* that had a cover picture of a blindingly handsome young man and woman wrapped in each other's arms, lying in a hammock under a golden moon. I covered my confused wild feelings with a loud giggle.   39

"Ssssh!" whispered Nat, checking for footsteps in the hall.

But our mother was in the kitchen at the other end of the apartment, nearly a block away. Solemnly and silently we looked through the treasures page by page, not believing we were actually seeing pictures of the perky breasts and rounded rumps exposed before our eyes.

"Natalie left them," he said. "She's the editor."

"Natalie!"

It came out somewhere between a shriek and a whisper. "We shouldn't be looking at them."

I started shoving them back in the drawer.

"No," Nat said. "Mom must have left them in such an easily accessible place so we'd be sure to find them. You know how smart she is. She probably wants us to see them and get over it."

I looked at the masthead of the lurid Street & Smith magazines (actually quite innocent by today's *Hustler* standards—anything beyond kissing, hugging, and desiring being barely hinted at), and, indeed, there was Natalie's name. "You know," Nat said, "Natalie's a flapper."

"I know," I murmured, "but I hear her hair is not like Joan Crawford's."

"There are many kinds of flappers," Nat said with careless worldliness.

Natalie was engaged to our uncle David, our father's youngest brother, and the announcement had caused a stream of agitated phone calls between various aunts and uncles, with our father, the virtual head of the family, trying to calm them. The oldest of nine brothers and sisters, he had arrived from Russia when he was eighteen, had become a lawyer, and had assumed this patriarchal position at an early age upon the death of his own father. He was judge, mentor, arbitrator, the voice of reason and sanity, the Solomon, the wise rabbi of the tribe.

Of course it was to our father that, singly and in twos and threes, my aunts and uncles came to express their objections to the marriage of Natalie and David. She smoked! She wore red nail polish! Worse than that, she was a Rumanian!

40

Being Russian, we were supposed to look down on Ruma-
nians for reasons obscure to me—both then and now. But
still worse, she was nineteen! She worked! And those magazines were filthy!

By the time David arrived that evening with his Natalie, the magazines in question were safely back in the drawer.
I remember, as Natalie kissed me, being lost in a cloud of
intoxicating perfume through which I sensed a tall, willowy
creature with blue-black hair parted in the middle and coiled
into a graceful chignon at the back of her neck. She was
wearing blue and green chiffon, layered one over the other
or all mixed together, I couldn't tell which. The chiffon hand-
kerchief points ended somewhere above her knees, which
were part of two of the longest, shapeliest, silkiest legs ever
built, tapering down to slim ankles and shiny high-heeled
pumps. I saw two dazzling rows of teeth and long Chinese-
red fingernails at the tips of slender fingers, between two of
which hung a lighted cigarette.

I gaped at Natalie with moronic open jaw, unable to
say a word and dying of hatred for my sturdy muscular legs,
my straight field-mouse-brown hair held back by a flat bar-
rette, and my bitten fingernails. I resolved to change all that.
At least I could do something about the nails.

My parents were gracious and welcoming, and in later
years Natalie told me how much she had feared that first visit
and how much their warmth had meant to her. With ease
and humor my father persuaded the rest of the family to
accept the inevitable and think of their younger brother's
happiness. Natalie was a working girl, which in those days
was still somewhat unusual, particularly after marriage. And
although the racy magazines she was involved in caused
waves of shock and disapproval all through the family, my
mother, whom I couldn't imagine even knowing about such
things, defended her. For a nineteen-year-old girl to get out
her own magazine was quite an accomplishment. Natalie was
proud of what she did and had no intention of stopping, and
my mother supported her position. Soon we learned that Natalie had been promoted and was doing glamorous things like
covering and reviewing opening nights of shows and movies

for other Street & Smith publications like *Silver Screen.* The tribe relaxed a little.

I was already picturing the wedding ceremony in our front room where, as a tot, I had witnessed the marriages of two aunts. Each time, the big green leather couch, brought from Riverside Drive where my parents had lived when they were first married, was moved out and in its place, in the bay of three windows hung with dark green portieres and ecru lace curtains, stood the wedding canopy. At the other end, near the door, was our upright player piano. As the bride came down the hall and entered the room, my father pumped away at the pedals and the traditional "Wedding March" sounded forth from the piano roll. I sat on his lap, filled with emotion, helping him (I was sure) to make the music happen; and if I had known the word *inhuman* at that time, I would certainly have been muttering it. I secretly hoped that this time I would be allowed to pump the pedals I could now reach, and "play" the march by myself.

I tried to stop biting my nails in preparation for the big event, which was held, as it happened, not in our front room but in a large caterer's hall. The excitement of this romantic occasion was so heady as to be nearly unbearable. I had given Nat cause for much laughter by acting out imagined scenes of how I would behave at the wedding, making up absurd conversations and ludicrous encounters that I fancied were the height of romance and sophistication.

A last look in the mirror before leaving for the wedding did not reassure me particularly, but my uncle David and my next youngest uncle, George, paid me extravagant compliments, admired my dress, and danced with me later at the reception. I wore a salmonish changeable taffeta creation, with a circlet of silk rosebuds and leaves entwined around my waist, a gold locket, white socks, and black Mary Janes. My two cousins had almost identical dresses, one mauvish and the other pinkish. As I look back, the ceremony is a blur, but Natalie remains a vivid picture: a white veil with orange blossoms cascaded over her glossy black hair and down to the floor, and her simple box-pleated white silk crepe dress ended at her knees. I thought she looked breathtaking, but my romantic nature was cruelly jolted by the news that her wedding gown was to double as a tennis dress on her honeymoon.

During the party afterward, I sneaked looks at her dancing and remembered what some dirty boy on the block had implied: that long legs were good for "you know what." I took stock of mine in contrast to hers and wondered forlornly how I would shape up in the "you know what" department someday. These thoughts made me wildly uncomfortable as they blended with illustrations from *Pep* and *Secrets.* Would Natalie and Uncle David be doing those unspeakable things? I tried to cleanse my brain of these polluting thoughts and concentrate on how thrilled and amazed I was that this modern goddess, this liberated nymph, this incredibly glamorous spirit of the new day had deigned to join our hopelessly conventional family.

It was 1928, and the young couple was doing the Charleston, happily unaware of where Wall Street was taking them and everyone else in the room. It was fortunate that modern nineteen-year-old Natalie had the guts and talent to make a real contribution to the family, who with the exception of my mother and father had not been eager to take her in. The years ahead were full of Rumanian jokes, but they became fewer and more good-natured: *Pep* and *Secrets* were forgotten as Natalie joined the ranks of the superb cooks and homemakers in the tribe. To me, David and Natalie's apartment was awesome in its chic Art Deco elegance (although I did not know that's what it was at the time), full of things I'd never seen except in movies: wall-to-wall beige-gray carpeting, glass tables, and lampshades with jagged silver arrows chasing across the pale green parchment.

After David's too early death, Natalie the Flapper became the sole breadwinner and the strong center of life for their two young children. She was also encouraging to me. Later on, when all my emoting to Brahms and improvising imaginary scenes of what might happen to me at weddings took shape as a desire to go into the theater, it was Natalie, through her many connections in the publications world, who arranged an interview for me at the Theatre Guild.

I met the Guild's casting director who told me to come   43 back when they were to choose the walk-ons for a play called *To Quito and Back* by Ben Hecht. I appeared on schedule, confident that I already *was* a walk-on in the play. We were herded into groups—more or less according to size, shape, and sex—and I remember my feeling of total disbelief when I stepped forward with my group and others around me were chosen. I was dismissed with a brisk "Thank you" and found myself out in the theater alley. I slunk home feeling I had somehow let Natalie down. Surely she would have stepped forward assertively, convinced them all that she was the perfect Ecuadorian peasant, and landed the job.

I called Natalie and reported what had happened at the audition. Although she was always most sympathetic and encouraging as I pursued my long, circuitous route to what I finally became, I felt that the efficient Natalie must at times have been a bit impatient with my progress—or lack of it. But she had tried to help me, and I remember.

Along the way, as the years passed, she cut her hair, curled it, and made it blond. Through her brother-in-law, my uncle Louis Astor, an executive in the sales department at Columbia Pictures, Natalie obtained a position in the Screen Gems division, where she coped deftly with the formidable Cohn brothers, Jack in the East and Harry in the West. But when the struggle became too heavy, this independent woman married again and happily slipped into many contented, comfortable years in Boston, still managing everything with her effortless skill and giving orders in her clear, strong voice.

My flapper aunt died in her late seventies, having survived a mastectomy, other cancers, two heart attacks, and a stroke. Up until very near the end she got out on the golf course and played what was just an echo of her original game, but even that echo was impressive. Thinking of those flashing legs and teeth, I can vividly reconstruct that afternoon in our Brooklyn apartment when David brought his Natalie to meet my parents and I met a new kind of "first": a nineteen-year-old woman who married, had children, and worked at a career in what used to be known as a "man's world." I guess Nat was

44   right: There are many kinds of flappers.

Bad Dreams

Returning, devastated and angry, from my visit to the Holocaust Museum in Washington, I knew that visions from it would always be with me. I can also relive my fear and bewilderment when, as a little girl, I saw my brother come home from school, crying bitterly because some boys from St. Gregory's down the block had ambushed him and, yelling racial epithets, had stuck pieces of ice in his ears—a minor episode in the long history of religious persecution. These are vivid memories, but I do not dream about them. My grandparents were not so fortunate.

Grandma died in 1932, and her bad dream remained with her until the end. My grandfather, too, had a recurrent bad dream, but all through his final seven years, until 1939, he had to wake from his nightmare alone. My maiden aunt Rose lived with her parents most of her life, tending them through their many illnesses with the help of her two married sisters and listening in the night for the sounds of trouble in the room next to hers. At the cry of illness or the cry for help, she would rush to the room. At other times she would be awakened by sad sounds from beyond their door, but she came to realize that there was nothing she could do. There would be an outcry from Grandpa, then muffled sobs mingled with Grandma's soothing words in Yiddish. Rose could not hear the words, but she knew what they were saying:

"Yudel, Yudel . . . it's all right. You had the dream again. . . . Forget. . . . Schluf, schluf."

Or it might be Grandma's cry breaking the night silence, and low whispers as my grandfather comforted her:

"It's nothing, Layee . . . nothing. . . . Your dream, Layee. . . . The dream. Go back to sleep. Schluf."

They both lived and died before the Holocaust, but their lives held memories of equal horror to them. Before it and since, Jewish history has been filled with a relentless, mindless procession of one man-made horror after another.

My grandfather suffered and survived the life of millions of Russian Jews in the shtetls of the 1870s and '80s. As a boy he grew up in the small Jewish enclave of Druskeniki, where life meant a routine of hard work, *cheder* (school), synagogue, and religious holidays punctuated by unannounced visits from the cossacks.

Rose, remembering what her father had told her, described how, when the warning wind of these impending visits swept through the community, the older men and women would frantically gather the young boys, including my grandfather, take up the heavy wooden planks in the middle of a section of the dirt road, lower the youngsters into the pit below, and hastily replace the planks. The little village would then attempt a look of industrious everyday activity. The cossacks, gigantic on horseback in their big uniforms with big boots, and swords, were usually out hunting firstborns, or second- or third- if need be. They would gallop into town yelling and brandishing their weapons, hooves thundering over the planks in the middle of the road and over the boys beneath. They would dismount and take over the tavern, where they would sing and drink to excess. Stimulated, they would burst out of the tavern and do a little window-smashing, fire-setting, pilfering, and terrorizing, and finally they would thunder back along the road and over the planks. One of the more imaginative ones might slow down and slip his sword down between the planks, and if it came up with blood on it, there would be wild shouting and laughter as they galloped off. The whole village was frozen in utter stillness waiting to be sure the sound of returning hooves was not heard.

Then the lone voice of a woman who had been hidden at the edge of town to watch and listen could be heard singing:

> *A mull hub ich gegangen in gruner wald . . .*
> Once I went into the green forest . . .
>
> *Die voglein hut gesungen, jung und alt,*
> The birds were singing, young and old,
>
> *Und vuss hut ehr gesingen?*
> And what were they singing?
>
> *Utt-a-zay . . . utt-a-zay.*
>
> *Und vuss ist "Utt-a-zay"?*
> And what does it mean, *"Utt-a-zay"?*
>
> *Utt-a-zay.*
> Status quo. All is quiet again.

Meaning, "All is as peaceful as before. It's safe." Only then could anyone dare to move or make a sound, and the desperate parents and neighbors would begin to pull away the planks to find out which child had been hurt and how badly. It was those thundering hooves and the plaintive echo of "Utt-a-zay" that haunted my grandfather's nights and caused him to reach for his beloved "Lay-ee" even after she was no longer there.

Julius Sadvoransky, my grandfather, married Leah Lubetsky in an arranged marriage after he had visited the bride's home and complimented the *colleh* on the dinner she had cooked. Referring to her already as the *colleh* (bride) was considered a good sign by her parents, and after she had unraveled a diabolically knotted mountain of twine without showing even a hint of impatience, there was obviously nothing to stand in their way. Julius, however, was impatient enough for two or more. Tall and volatile, he was in direct contrast to Leah, who was tiny and seemingly placid. Both had charm and also wit in two very different styles, and under Leah's diffidence there was spirit. There is a snapshot of my grandma sitting on the kitchen steps of the country house 47

Grandpa built around 1915 when grandchildren started to come along. She is facing her sister—two prematurely silver-haired ladies shelling peas and looking both serene and conspiratorial. Aunt Rose says they would sit for hours whispering like girls and then suddenly start laughing as they exchanged confidences about their men. Grandpa was prosperous by then, having slowly acquired pieces of real estate in Brooklyn until he owned almost a whole block. It was the block on which he had started out long before with a small tea and coffee store, above which the family lived: Rose, who was born in this country, and her two older sisters, my mother Rebecca and my aunt Celia, both born in Russia. The neighborhood was German at the time, and although some of the neighbors and storekeepers were warm and friendly, the A & P, which opened across the street, sometimes sent boys to pick up horse manure, an available commodity in the gutters of the 1890s, and smear it on Grandpa's store window. And Rose, a merry, birdlike little girl, would walk to school with spine erect, looking neither right nor left while other little girls and boys pelted her back with stones. The cossacks were here, too.

My grandma's lifelong nightmare was not brought on by cossacks or a pogrom directly but did result from the flight from persecution. Leah and Julius lived in a village called Sekulka after they were married, and soon there were two little daughters. Along with countless others, Grandpa felt the desperate need to get out of the crippling and dangerous existence of a Jew in czarist Russia and head for the "land that's free for you and me and a Russian lullaby." Today all is not exactly peaches and sour cream for Jews in what is now Russia again, either, but back then life was a true dead end, and persecution was rampant. So among the millions came my grandfather, alone. He would send for Leah and the two girls as soon as he had collected enough gold dust from those fabled streets paved with the precious stuff. He became a peddler of pots and pans in Kentucky and Pennsylvania. Carrying his heavy sack from door to door and along the roads from town to town until he could afford a horse and wagon, he earned his first American dollars plus a permanently asymmetrical silhouette, one shoulder lower than the other from the weight of his sack.

When the girls were six and four, Leah was sent for and set out to join him. She also carried a heavy load; a big bundle of belongings, a bag of food, and sometimes one or the other of the girls. As she trudged toward the distant town where she was to board the train for the first part of the journey, her long dress, trailing on the ground in back, dragged in the mud. She clutched the hands of the two girls while balancing the bundles on her back and shoulders. The living nightmare began. At the depot, swarming with more people than Leah had ever seen in her life or dreamed existed, she felt her children being wrenched from her by official-looking men in uniforms. As she cried out and tried to get to them, the children were being propelled toward a train and then were swallowed up in the pushing crowds. She was shoved roughly toward a different train, and as she cried and tried to explain what had happened, she was yelled at and shoved on board. She did not understand what they were trying to tell her, and she was sure she would never see her children again. After an agonizing time on the train, she arrived at a dock, and in a crush of men, women, children, old people, and bundles, she was herded onto a looming ocean liner and down into steerage. The boat whistle blasted. Her horror and desolation were complete. Then, in the next wave of human cargo spilled into steerage, came her little girls, Rebecca holding Celia by the hand. It was the vision of those two figures swallowed up by the crowd at the station and the sound of the boat whistle that made her cry out in the night for the rest of her life.

It was just a dream, as Yudel assured her years later when she awoke next to him in their comfortable bed with the beautiful sheets. But it had once been real. And that was just a dream, Leah would tell him, about the cossacks and the pit under the road. But it had once been real. Could it be real again? Grandpa and Grandma did not know that after they were gone it became real for new millions. While he was still alive, rumors started filtering in from Europe, but almost nobody believed them.

In a handsome private house on Union Street in Brooklyn there were nights filled with outcries, and sobs and moans, and nightmares. Millions of nightmares are out there. A moment must come sometime when a lone voice can finally sing out, "Utt-a-zay. All clear. All is peaceful. All is safe. Go about your life. Be who you are. Go on. No more nightmares. Utt-a-zay."

The Stationery Store

Although my father had desperately wanted his four younger brothers to go to college, as he had, and become professionals, my uncle Ezra wound up owning a small stationery store. When I was a child, this was thrilling for me because it gave me double joy: first, an exciting playground where a little girl could disport herself among the toys for hours, and later, because of the store's location near the Brooklyn Academy of Music, the chance for a slightly older girl to be taken to the opera.

Uncle Ezra, a small man with clear light eyes and a somewhat simian but cute face, was married to my aunt Celia Gordon (to distinguish her from Aunt Celia, my mother's sister). She was an enormously fat lady with delicate hands. Ezra adored her. They both loved music, classical and near classical. I remember when Fat Aunt Celia (you know how kind little kids can be) would take me to a vaudeville show. She would beam and clap as the card at either side of the stage changed to the name of a singer, and a piano would be wheeled in from the wings. I, on the other hand, would groan inwardly—"Oh, *no!* They're dragging out the piano!"—and brace myself for boring renditions of, probably, "The Italian Street Song" and "The Rosary." My aunt would listen as if in heaven, with moist eyes closed and dainty hands clasped well ahead of her chin on her ample bosom. She and Uncle Ezra 51 had no children of their own and loved to pet and spoil their many nieces and nephews, so it was an occasion for them when my brother Nat and I visited the store. For me, the place was magical.

My father, the lawyer, had an office in downtown Manhattan, but in my mind it could in no way compare to the glamour and excitement of the stationery store with its racks of little candies, shelves of serious bonbons, and cards, decorations, and toys. Even the stacks of different-sized looseleaf paper, lined and unlined, neatly piled notebooks with covers of many different colors, and boxes of pencils and crayons were wonders to behold.

When I visited, I was allowed the run of the place, but not before two rituals had been observed. First, Aunt Celia would take me into the little room behind the store where there was a table and chairs and a little stove, and she would prepare hot chocolate made with a bar of Nestlé's and garnished with fluffy, spongy marshmallows. After this feast I would have to perform. The performance was simply to write my name, address, and telephone number on a sheet of paper. I attended the progressive Brooklyn Ethical Culture School, and we did not learn to write script in the Palmer or any other method but were taught manuscript, each letter separate and distinct, the capitals twice as tall as the small letters. My aunt and uncle were enormously proud of this little girl who by the time she was five could write like a medieval monk. They would watch with awe as I performed this feat of calligraphy, enhanced by the use of a pen nib with a broad tip that made the up and down strokes come out fat and the horizontal ones thin and spidery. Every customer who came into the store was shown my handiwork, and I was praised, kissed, and coddled, and lifted high in the air by my proudly beaming uncle.

Once this ritual had been performed, I was allowed to play. I'd go from case to case examining each toy and doll, each set of doll dishes, even the boys' stuff like soldiers and boats. Everything looked tempting, but I never asked for any of it, knowing that on birthdays and holidays something wonderful would be forthcoming. One day when I was about six, before my opera-going days began, I pushed a sliding door along the wall at the back of the store where additional stock was kept, and next to the birthday candles of many colors was a box of birthday-candle holders, each with pink petals like little roses and a sharp pin at the bottom to stick into the cake. I had never seen anything so beautiful in my entire life. Some irrepressible urge came over me, and after looking around furtively to be sure I was not observed, I swiped two of the precious holders. Having no pockets, I had to clutch them in my hand. I remember being swept by a wave of guilt followed by billows of fear, but I could not put them back.

It was nearly time to go. Heart pounding, I pattered up one aisle of the store and down the other toward the little back room where my coat was hanging. Suddenly the massive form of my aunt loomed over me.

"Have you been having a good time, *tzotskeleh?* Mmmm, is that a face!" She bent over and squeezed my cheeks.

"How is my little *mozzik?*" asked Uncle Ezra, lifting me up and seating me on the counter near the cash register. "What have you got in your hand, darling?"

Feeling miserable and wishing I could crawl into the cash register and disappear, I opened my hand.

"I took them," I declared.

They looked stricken, bewildered.

"But why? You could have had anything you wanted in the whole store. You didn't have to take!"

They were devastated.

The realization that I had disappointed these two dear people who thought I represented the highest level of childom, plus the fear of jail, overwhelmed me, and I burst into racking sobs. These in turn set off my notoriously delicate stomach, and I threw up my recent treat of hot chocolate and marshmallows all over the cash register. It was a moment when I am sure Uncle Ezra and Aunt Celia were glad they didn't have children.

It was a risky business to take me on an automobile or trolley ride in those days. "She gets carsick, you know," I can hear my mother saying quietly, hiding whatever exasperation she must have felt when trying to decide whether or not to accept a nice invitation involving locomotion. When we did go, I traveled with my head in her lap, which usually kept my rebellious peristalsis in line. Once in an elevated train coming back from a Christian Science meeting with my mother, who had reluctantly agreed to attend at the urging of a friend, I was seated next to the window and, feeling a slight touch of malaise, put my head in her lap. To protect her beloved but mysteriously fragile child from the sun beating in, she covered my face with the *Christian Science Monitor*. An instant later a rock thrown from below smashed the window, and I was covered with shattered glass—or rather the *Monitor* was. Saved from disfigurement by nausea and Christian Science.

Uncle Ezra's cash register wasn't so lucky. During the messy cleanup I was banished to the little back room to wash myself as best I could. Left alone, I began to ponder my bleak future. Should I run away? Maybe join a gypsy band? Gypsy bands were around in those days. But who would I leave my dolls to? Eventually I was summoned out front, where things were more or less back to normal. The door to the street was wide open in spite of the freezing weather, and my aunt, mouth set, was spraying her toilet water all over the place. Slowly I walked the Last Mile to the counter.

"Betty," Uncle Ezra said. (No *tzotskeleh*, no *mozzik*, just my name, soon to be replaced, I was sure, by a prisoner's number.) "We're disappointed . . . very sad. . . ." He shook his head. My tears started spilling silently. I thought, "I'll never be allowed here again." Aunt Celia went to wait on a customer. Uncle Ezra and I waited in uneasy silence until she rang up a sale and returned.

"Uh, look," Uncle Ezra resumed, "write us a note . . . an apology . . . in your—you know, whaddya call it?—uh, manuscript. We'll keep it here, and we'll show it to you when you come. And I know you'll never do it again."

I think he felt worse than I did. He gave me a pad, a pen with a nice wide nib, and an inkwell, and sat me on some telephone books behind the counter. I chewed the tip of my tongue and thought and thought and finally wrote the following, words I recall because they were quoted from time to time:

Dear Uncle Ezra and Aunt Celia,
How are you? I'm very sorry I stole the pink candle holders. I will never do it again. I love you.

> With love,
> Your loving niece,

> Betty, the Bobbed-Haired Bandit

There was such a gangster, bobbed hair being enough of a novelty to make for a distinguishing sobriquet. I had opted for "wit" over sincerity.

My aunt looked grim.

"I don't like that! That attitude! Is that what they teach you at Ethical Culture? To steal . . . to be so . . . so . . . fresh!" If she had known the term "smart-ass," she might not have said it, but she would have thought it.

"Cele . . . Cele . . . she's clever . . . she's funny. I like that."

I loved Uncle Ezra. I made a pathetic peekaboo at my aunt, looking through my fingers. She probably wanted to kill me but she relented, and I was hugged and kissed and coddled and lifted high in the air and *tzotskeleh*ed—and not punished.

And that, dear children, is how your grandmother began her life of crime, which she soon gave up to start going to the opera, a transition made possible partly because my uncle Ezra knew Mr. Buckley, the manager at the nearby Brooklyn Academy of Music.

Today BAM, as it is now called, might be the home of the Next Wave in theater, music, and dance, but back then it was a bastion of traditional culture and genteel educational events. The Metropolitan Opera and the New York Philharmonic came to Brooklyn regularly, and it was there that I saw my first opera, *Hansel and Gretel,* and heard my first symphony concerts, conducted by Toscanini and Mengelberg. My mother had a yearly subscription for two to the concert series, given to her as a birthday present. If my father could not go, once in a while my brother or I would be chosen to accompany her to the thrilling top balcony seats close to the ceiling chandelier, a perch much more exciting, I thought, than those earthbound chairs on the orchestra floor miles below.

My second opera experience was the double bill of "Cav" and "Pag," and I can still feel my embarrassed disillusionment watching Maria Jeritza as the hapless Nedda, stabbed by her equally hapless lover Canio, fall feet up across the steps of *I Pagliacci*'s little stage and, well after she was dead, adjust her skirt over her legs.

The Academy of Music also showed travelogues with slides by Burton Holmes, and Admiral Richard E. Byrd came to speak after his Antarctic explorations.

Occasionally, when I went to the store, Uncle Ezra and I took a trolley to the Academy at matinee time, and he would look for Mr. Buckley. Mr. Buckley was an imposing dark-haired man, every bit "the manager" and rather handsome in his dark suit. He greeted my uncle as he stood with his hands clasped behind his back, surveying the lobby as it filled with that afternoon's audience. Most of the time Mr. Buckley would shake his head, and Uncle Ez took me out to have a milk shake. Although he often urged me to have an ice cream soda, neither wild horses nor indulgent uncles could get me to take even one swallow. I had not enjoyed my experience with a certain carbonated laxative, citrate of magnesia, and the thought of any "fizzy" drink made me physically ill. What finally broke the bubble barrier I don't recall, but by the time I was allowed to drink champagne, I did.

If we were lucky, Mr. Buckley would cock his head in the direction of the door to either the opera house or the concert hall, and my uncle and I would slip into some unclaimed seats, I shamelessly reveling in the glow of privilege. I was deeply impressed by the fact that my uncle knew a powerful man like Mr. Buckley and that through him I was able to see my first *Aida* and my first *Bohème.*

Uncle Ezra had given me a child's dream of endless toys to play with, my first brush with crime, a chance to go to the opera, and an introduction to the heady experience of knowing someone on the inside: of having "pull." I am sorry my loving, concerned, responsible father was disappointed, but I am selfishly glad he had absolutely no influence on the education of my beloved uncle Ezra who wound up running a stationery store.

So Eat Your Heart Out, Elizabeth Taylor

Stand back! One step further, and I will fling myself over the battlement! My body will be crushed out of the very form of humanity upon the stones of the courtyard below!"

Pulling herself up to her full four feet two inches, the eleven-year-old delivered her lines with flashing eyes and proudly held flat bosom. I was playing Rebecca in our seventh grade's dramatization of Sir Walter Scott's *Ivanhoe,* and the recipient of my disdainful rage was David Scheinart. Doing his twelve-year-old best to look villainous as the hateful Brian de Bois-Guilbert who had trapped Rebecca on the ramparts of the castle, he was advancing toward her to have his way with her. I loved doing this scene because I despised David Scheinart with all my heart. He had dared to have a crush on me and refused to understand that I did not, could not, and would not return his passion. He would moon at me across the schoolyard with his great dark eyes, leave love notes in my books that made me sick with embarrassment when I came upon them suddenly in class, and through a go-between had the audacity to present me with his junior lifesaving pin. My heart lay elsewhere. In fact, the very John Alden whom David had picked to give me the pin was the unknowing object of my love; unfortunately, he was already interested in the girl he would one day marry. This paragon, Herman Rottenberg, blue-eyed, freckled, and a bit on the pudgy side, was our Ivanhoe, and with enormous feeling I was able to play the scene where Rebecca nurses him back to health after he has been wounded.

"Thanks, dear Rebecca, for thy helpful skill," said Herman, lying on a pallet trying to look wan.

"He calls me 'dear' Rebecca," said I in a breathy aside, gazing out through the paper castle window, "but it is in the cold and careless tone that ill besuits the word. His warhorse, his hunting hound are dearer to him than the despised Jewess!"

Since there were only two decent parts for girls in *Ivanhoe* and more girls than boys in our little class of thirteen at the Brooklyn Ethical Culture School, our teacher, Miss Stebbins, was forced to resort to some fairly imaginative and unpopular casting. The role of my father, the aging Jew, Isaac of York, fell to Dorothy Becker, my best friend, and Wamba the clown to my other best friend, Theda Backalenick, neither of whom was particularly thrilled with her assignment. I, on the other hand, was so heady with joy at having been chosen to play Rebecca that I'm afraid I had little patience with their grumblings.

I did not know at this time, but Miss Stebbins had had a meeting with my mother to see if she thought I would have the stamina to take on one of the leading roles. I was very small and bony, and prone to respiratory infections, which allowed me welcome extra rest periods and unwelcome milk instead of orange juice for my mid-morning snack. But my mother must have told her that Sarah Bernhardt had been a skinny kid, too, because as history has shown, I did land the part. It was my first major stage experience, the only earlier one being in the second-grade Spring Festival playing "the first robin of." Rebecca was the "big time."

The beauteous Rowena was played by the beauteous Adele Pearle, and her guardian Sir Cedric was played, oddly enough, by one of the boys, Herman's cousin Kenneth Reiner. A warm family loyalty existed between the two. I recall a stormy session of our Student Council when Kenneth had been brought up on serious charges. The school building was actually two beautiful old Brooklyn mansions on Prospect 59

Park West, joined together so that the two staircases were almost adjacent, with a wall between, and although our population was small, to facilitate traffic it was a strict rule that one staircase was for going up and the other for going down, and woe betide the transgressor. Kenneth was accused of going down the up staircase, and the whole Student Council ganged up on criminal Ken, demanding blood. Suddenly Herman sprang up and with impassioned fervor sputtered, to the horror of the teachers and the delight of all of us, "Stop all this! The . . . the way you're attacking Kenny . . . he's got . . . about as much chance . . . as . . . as . . . as a . . . as a . . . mouse in . . . in a cathouse!"

There was a hush punctuated by stifled shrieks, and our faculty advisor sternly suggested that Ken not do it again and that we move on to other business immediately.

Kenneth became a law-abiding citizen and a dignified Cedric. But of course the casting did not take place until we had written our play. It was a class project in which everyone took part. After we had all read or reread the book under Miss Stebbins's guidance, we extracted the story line, examined the characters, and broke the book into sections for dramatizing. We learned how to turn prose into dialogue and how to construct scenes. All the class members contributed to the communal writing—my first experience with the dramatic form and with collaboration, twelve writing partners. Later on in my career I did cut down the number somewhat. On the last page of the book I found a sentence that delighted me. Scott had written that Brian de Bois-Guilbert came to a violent end, "a victim of his own contending passions." I wondered how we could best show that on stage and gleefully visualized David writhing in extremis and perhaps trying to tear himself in half like Rumpelstiltskin. I was disappointed to learn that Miss Stebbins felt we should not go into the future of the characters but end our play with the resolution of the plot—Cedric and Richard the Lion-Hearted restored to power and Ivanhoe united with Rowena, an ending I passionately longed to rewrite. I never asked Elizabeth Taylor how she felt about losing Robert Taylor in the movie version of a later day. I know I was loath to give up Herman.

Teaching by putting things into dramatic form was much in favor at Ethical. I remember one year the whole class dramatized the signing of the Kellogg-Briand Peace Pact. Each of us represented a different country. First we had to make a book in the shape of that country, containing a brief history, population statistics, map of the political structure, the topographical features, and principal products. It was not easy to get a great deal of written material into my book because I was Italy and had this long, narrow boot shape to contend with. On the day of the play itself we all marched solemnly into the library and took our places around a long table. "Mr. Kellogg" and "M. Briand" placed the treaty at one end, and we all came up in turn and signed it, vowing to "outlaw war as an instrument of national policy."

Considering what has happened in the world since the signing of the real treaty, not much was accomplished, but because of our dramatization, at least one child grew up remembering it vividly.

Dramatizing *Ivanhoe* took several months, and by spring we were ready. Costumes had to be improvised. Wooden swords were made in shop, and silver-painted cardboard helmets and suits of mail in art. And at home I feverishly searched my dress-up bag. This was a large pillowcase filled with old clothes of my mother's, which I often resorted to on a rainy afternoon, clunking down the hall in her old gray suede opera pumps with the curved heels and the cut-steel buckles, my small feet lost in the toes, leaving several inches of shoe flapping in back. With one of her big hats held on with hat pins and with a feather boa draped casually around my bony "wings" and trailing on the floor, I felt I cut a figure of the ultimate in sophistication. One time, having fallen in love with a picture of a shepherdess painted on a tray, I wanted to have a costume like hers and set about creating the bodice crisscrossed with black ribbon. I found a piece of lace in the bag that I thought would make an ideal bodice, cleverly cut two rows of holes in it, and threaded a pair of black shoelaces through them. Wearing this over a white middy blouse, a long striped skirt, and carrying an umbrella I hoped resembled a shepherdess's crook, I presented   61 myself to my mother. She blanched visibly and her dark eyes grew darker, but she did not scold me. She realized, I suppose, that this dopey little girl had no idea of the value of the lace, and if it had wound up in the dress-up bag, it was fair game.

For Rebecca I selected my mother's wedding dress of ivory satin trimmed with gold tarnished over the years. I needed only the overtunic, and with one panel of it draped over my head, I may have been scant competition for Liz, but I felt I looked exactly the way Rebecca should look. We gave the performance in a library near the school where there was a raised platform for a stage and doors at either end leading to a hall. The upper parts of the doors were glass, and I remember crouching low in the hall behind the door in order to remain unseen, then popping up suddenly on cue to make an entrance. In those distant days there was no peel-off tape, and the library had apparently forbidden us to nail, tack, or glue any cloth or paper over their precious glass-topped doors. Because of the modest size of our cast, the Saxon and Norman armies had to be merely suggested by a lot of shouting offstage (in the hall) by anyone who happened to be offstage at the time. The performance was a *succès fou,* but since we were on the Saxons' side, I should not use French. We were a smash. The audience of family, friends, faculty, and the rest of the students went mad. I remember the feeling of triumph I shared with my twelve collaborators, but even more vivid was the discovery, as an "actress," of instant love from the crowd. I recall one delirious uncle, elegant silver-haired Uncle Esaac, coming over to me, shaking his head in disbelief, and, his voice hoarse with emotion, predicting that I would be a star—if only, he added, looking suddenly dubious, I would grow up good-looking.

Recently, I received a letter from the University of Salt Lake City, Utah, saying they were attempting to raise money for their library by auctioning books that had been selected by various people, along with their signed letters explaining what influence these particular books had had on their lives. I chose *Ivanhoe.* I probably should have selected a book for the effect its contents had on me or one that afforded me a memorable reading experience, and I considered Strunk and White's *Elements of Style,* Stanislavsky's *My Life in Art,* anything and everything by Shakespeare, Noël Coward, Edith Wharton, and S. J. Perelman, but I found my mind traveling much further back. I thought of my superb teacher, Delia A. Stebbins, and of dramatizing and acting in *Ivanhoe* when I was eleven and how that experience might have helped point me toward the choices I made later in life.

I remember a scene in our play and in the book in which a knight at Prince John's court disparages the prowess of Ivanhoe, who is supposedly far away in the Holy Land. Suddenly a palmer in a hooded cloak (Ivanhoe in disguise taking a short breather from the Crusades) shouts out, "I say he is second to none!" Herman shouted it magnificently. Well, *"Ivanhoe* may have been just another movie to you, Liz, but to me—'Second to none!' " I shout.

Movies, Movies, Movies

*H*aving grown up on silent pictures, all my earliest images are in black and white, and of course, not knowing they would ever talk, we did not call them "silents," nor did we refer to them respectfully as "films." They were just "the movies." Vividly before my eyes, after many a decade, I can still see scenes from what must have been one of the first movies I ever saw, *The Magic Skin,* based on a Balzac story. A man is given a magic animal skin—mole, I think—and is told that he has eight (I think) wishes but is cautioned that every time he makes a wish, the skin will shrink, and when the last shrink is shrunk, his number will be up. He puts the skin in a frame and outlines it in black, and each time he makes a wish, the skin gets smaller. Greedily he asks for all the little comforts of life: wine, women, song, money, fame.

We keep cutting back after each wish to see the skin getting tinier and tinier inside the concentric outlines he draws. When we are nearing Fatal Number Eight, he is holding the last wee bit of skin in the palm of his hand, and he faces a dilemma. He has been a very bad boy. At this point the loving girl he trifled with and wronged (what did he do exactly? I wondered) has jumped off a cliff and is caught precariously in some kind of flimsy bramble bush that is about to give way. Facing doom himself, he must choose between having one last mad debauch and saving her life. (Didn't you always wonder why they didn't wish for more wishes?)

I won't tell you how it comes out because you might want to run out and pick it up at your local video mart (*The Magic Skin,* 1923) and I don't want to spoil it for you, but I recall a lot of soaring music from the organ and bursts of heavenly light on the screen. The point is that to this day I remember that poor guy's tormented visage more clearly than the faces of most of my relatives.

Many of my first images were imprinted inside my head at Loew's Kameo Theater on Eastern Parkway at Nostrand Avenue, a seven-block—four short, three long—walk from where I lived in Brooklyn. Usually I was inside the theater, but occasionally, on a summer evening, I was outside on its open-air roof garden. The sky would stay lavender for a long time, and I would fidget impatiently until it got dark enough to start the movie. Before the miracle of air-conditioning, relief from the heat could be found up there, but for enjoying a movie, this nine-year-old found it too exposed. You could see the people around you as well as the glow of lights from buildings beyond the screen, and you could hear the sound of the Nostrand Avenue trolley. Outdoor viewing lacked the magic of sitting in the dark where you and only you could be alone with those incredible creatures up on the screen, all of whom had beautiful voices you could hear only in your head as you read the titles. I remember seeing Dolores Del Rio in *Ramona* at the roof theater, and Douglas Fairbanks in *The Gaucho.* The latter contained two elements that left me disturbed and fearful, respectively: Doug wrapping his tango partner's lower body tight against his own lower body with his bolo whip, and a character completely draped in black cheesecloth, suffering from something called the Black Death, which allowed him to stick his finger in a candle flame and not feel it—obviously a character to be avoided. But he grabs hold of our Doug at one point and shortly afterward Doug also can put his finger into fire and not feel it, so he has to go up a mountain to a shrine in the woods and get redeemed before he is freed of his disease and can burn his finger just like everyone else. I'm a bit fuzzy on the details

65

today, but I think his redemption had something to do with the way he danced that tango. What I *am* clear on is that all my brother had to do was pantomime putting his finger into a lighted Friday night candle, and I would run shrieking from the room. After we had seen *The Bat,* he could throw the shadow of his hand shaped like a claw against the wall and get the same result.

The Kameo showed mostly MGM pictures, and there I saw my first Garbos as well as dramas like *The Doctor's Secret* with Ruth Chatterton and H. B. Warner. There was a Savoy Theater a few blocks farther away on Rogers Avenue; it showed mostly Fox movies like *In Old Arizona* with Warner Baxter, made well before he became the weary director of the musical show in *42nd Street.* Sometimes the family would venture forth to naughty, bawdy, gaudy downtown Brooklyn with its gilt-encrusted movie palaces, the huge Fox Theater, the giant Loew's Metropolitan, and the truly palatial Brooklyn Paramount with panels of ever-changing colored lights in the walls. There, when sound came, I saw Maurice Chevalier in *Innocents of Paris,* his first American film, and on stage Rudy Vallee and the Connecticut Yankees.

I had been taken downtown earlier to the Saturday morning movies at the much more austere Brooklyn Academy of Music where there was no piano or organ to underscore the changing moods on the screen. Instead, someone backstage simply put records on a Victrola in no particular order. A wild comedy chase might be accompanied by Chopin's Funeral March, and a death scene might be underscored by "The Italian Street Song," choices I found very disconcerting. I was particularly depressed by a piece of Victor Herbert's called "Pan-Americana" no matter what it was accompanying. One Saturday they showed a comedy with Karl Dane and George K. Arthur called *Rookies* in which one of them got into a suit of armor; you could see his eyes rolling inside the visor, and they kept playing "Pan-Americana" over and over again, giving eight-year-old me a lingering case of hopelessness and weltschmerz.

Quite a few things seemed to depress me in those days, Doctor. After I was in bed at night I could hear the radio playing down the hall in the dining room, where my father would be on the couch listening and reading. Or it might be Mary Kennedy, the new janitor's daughter called in to babysit for my brother and me. I'd hope against hope but knew that inevitably they would drift off to sleep. I could not bear the thought that some lady was singing or some fellow talking or playing the violin, and no one was listening. I felt embarrassed for the performers. It depressed me. The flickering shadow from the gas fixture on the wall outside my door did not help my mood, and I would get out of bed and tiptoe down the hall to the dining room. Sure enough, I would find that Daddy or Mary had fallen asleep, and no one was paying attention to the poor performers. Aching with shame for them and careful not to wake the inattentive sleeper, I would turn off the radio and go back to bed, relieved that I had restored the performer's dignity. The gas light flickered on. The lower part of the fixture was an electric bulb, but the top, the gas jet, was much cheaper to run and therefore could be left on all night. We were living on the cusp of change.

Another attack of depression would come on the few occasions when we invited some of the neighborhood kids to see a movie in our front room. We borrowed a projector but had no screen. Everything seemed all right until I saw that my mother had put up a bed sheet, fastening it to the dark green velour portieres with large safety pins. More safety pins held the portieres together to keep out the daylight. I don't even remember what the pictures were. I just remember embarrassment and depression because it was so makeshift. The fact that the kids watching the movie had a riotous time did not cheer me. See my study, "Things That Depressed Me When I Was Eight," two vols.

What never failed to cheer me, however, was going to a movie theater, and an entire weekend of moviegoing was the best. Happy is the child whose uncle owns a movie theater. My uncle Louis, later an executive in the East Coast office of Columbia Pictures, had a movie house on Whalley Avenue in New Haven. Never mind that New Haven is the home of Yale with its "Bulldog, Bulldog" and its Cole Porter. Say only this, it was the home of the Whalley. Every now and   67 then my parents, Nat, and I would go for a visit, and I was ecstatic. I remember sweeping into the Whalley without paying, to see the great double feature of two very grown-up sophisticated films, *God Gave Me Twenty Cents* with a siren named Lya de Putti plus *The Crystal Cup* with some hot current romantic team. One movie involved a pair of dimes, found on the waterfront, that happened to have heads on both sides, and the other was some marital problem play I pretended to understand.

Aunt Leah was one of my father's sisters and later, in my aunt's bedroom, I practiced slinking around like Lya, pretending to smoke a cigarette in a long holder, sure that Lya had a bedroom just like Leah's, with its apricot taffeta spread and curtains. I would receive imaginary phone calls from lovers on Aunt Leah's phone, which to me was the height of glamour, housed as it was inside a porcelain doll. You could get your calls only by separating her apricot taffeta skirt and reaching inside for the phone, a French phone, no less, the only one in my experience. To this day in pantomiming a telephone I am apt to use both hands, the right to grip the standing receiver and the left to hold the earpiece, which shows you how long a reflex can stay in your mind and muscles.

In my college years and those following, although I kept seeing many movies, I seem to have missed important genres, for example, the whole Bette Davis oeuvre. I caught up with *Now, Voyager* and *Mr. Skeffington* only fairly recently. The truth is, I was a dope and a snob, and I missed a lot. I was too busy going to art houses like the Fifth Avenue Playhouse, Little Carnegie, and World Cinema, purveyors of art and "furren" films. There I feasted on *Potemkin, Poil de Carotte, Sous les Toits de Paris, La Maternelle, Maedchen in Uniform,* and *Ivan the Terrible,* not to speak of *The Birth of a Nation* and *Intolerance.* I wasn't a total grind. I did catch Bette Davis in *Of Human Bondage* and *The Petrified Forest,* and of course I reveled in Charlie Chaplin, Buster Keaton, and Harold Lloyd from childhood on.

Movies impinged on my life as they did on everyone else's, dictating what one wanted to look like, what kind of apartment one wanted to live in, what clothes one wanted to wear. Once the Hays office was in there making the rules of conduct and morals for the movies, we all learned that if you did it before you were married or if you committed adultery, you would be dead by "fade-out" time. And married couples slept in single beds only, and even between married couples, embraces on couches were maneuvered so that one foot remained firmly on the floor at all times. Life did not imitate art in those matters, we all knew that. Before the code was in effect, Jean Harlow was able to live a sinful life in *Red-Headed Woman* in 1932 without retribution and wound up in the last shot alive, happy, and triumphant, surrounded by a circle of adoring men, and we all thought, "Wow!"

Three years later a movie came along that not only affected my life, it became part of it. *The Scoundrel* starring Noël Coward and written by Ben Hecht and Charles MacArthur opened at Radio City Music Hall, and my close friend Janet and I fell hopelessly in love with it and saw it repeatedly. We saw it so often that we could recite whole scenes from it, to the exasperation of many who did not share our obsession. I did not know it then, because I did not know them yet, but in the Bronx and in Boston, respectively, Adolph Green, my partner-to-be, and Leonard Bernstein, my dear friend and colleague-to-be, were separately discovering this movie in the same way. A few years later Steve, my husband-to-be, was also swept into this vortex by my enthusiasm.

The Scoundrel was the story of a ruthless, womanizing, brilliant publisher—modeled after Horace Liveright, I later learned—who is adored by women, admired as one admires a snake, and who behaves horribly to just about everyone he doesn't need for the moment. He is killed in a plane crash and is told while tossing in the ocean that he will never rest until he goes back and finds someone to cry for him. That is not an easy assignment when one realizes that a typical remark upon hearing of his death is "A slight interruption in Mr. Mallare's career of whimsies."

When we first saw the picture, we loved the first part, brittle and sophisticated, replete with elegant Hecht and MacArthur ripostes and witticisms that we repeated endlessly, but 69 we were bewildered at the change of tone after Coward died and the picture took on spiritual over- and undertones. In recent years, slipping into my dotage, dopey as that last part is, I have come to love it, too. The movie merged with my life through a scene between Coward and Julie Haydon, a young innocent poet with whom he has an affair. He takes her to a restaurant for dinner, a place called the Hapsburg House that was in the east Fifties and was decorated by Ludwig Bemelmans in trompe l'oeil style, everything three-dimensional painted flat on the wall. She says to him in her extremity of bliss, "I wish life could stay just like this . . . like that clock on the wall [painted], always twenty past two." (That may not be the exact line since, I am sad to say, time has eroded my once-total recall of the dialogue.)

I won't say the picture meant a great deal to me, but when Steve and I decided to get married, I insisted that our wedding lunch be held at the Hapsburg House. The fact that in the movie Coward soon dropped Julie and moved on to Hope Williams never cast a pall on my happiness. This is where I wanted to have my first married lunch. The wedding ceremony was at the rabbi's apartment, and only a few close family members were present. It was a small affair because we wanted it that way, never realizing the deluge of presents we were giving up. No matter. Afterward these dear, game, bewildered relatives were transported to what I thought was the most romantic setting in the world. We did not sit under the painted clock, always twenty past two, but were seated in a charming private dining room around a beautifully set table, which, to my astonishment, had a lovely pale green crepe paper crèche as a centerpiece. I was startled because I had not associated my getting married with having children, and it did take us eight years to get around to it. We had two. After all, the fortune teller in the movie who read the palm of Julie Haydon in that very place had foretold that they would be "verree hoppee" and that they would have "two cheeldren."

Some years later, when Leonard was married to Felicia Montealegre, and Adolph to Phyllis Newman, and both ladies

were puzzled and not altogether entertained by the references the three of us made to *The Scoundrel,* it was decided to hold a screening. A number of people were invited, most of whom had never even heard of the picture. We were bursting with desire to share our treasure with loved ones and could not wait to observe their radiant eyes and ears as the picture rolled over them. At every familiar line the three of us half-repeated it or muttered along under our breath, and rocked with appreciative laughter. (Steve was more moderate in his response.)

The event was a fiasco. It's not that they hated the movie, they just did not get it. Why the big craziness over this picture? It was impossible to explain. It had hit us at a certain moment in our young lives, showing us an urbane world of sophistication and wit that one did not encounter on the screen as a rule, or in our daily lives. The Hecht and MacArthur script and the flawless cast left an indelible impression. If I had been seeing it for the first time on the occasion of that screening, I'm sure I would have liked it, but it was too late in life for it to become the worshiped, strangely moving icon that an early image can be.

Just before my last visit to Leonard in the country, the summer before he died, someone had given him a videotape of *The Scoundrel,* and we watched it together. We were able to focus on the picture most of the time, but there were clouds hovering and our minds drifted now and then. At one point, however, we were suddenly brought up sharp. A line had been cut. "They skipped the Persian horse!" we hissed in outrage. Julie Haydon, visiting Noël Coward in his incredibly perfect penthouse where she is about to be seduced, is going around the room admiring all his beautiful possessions and stops in front of an antique figure. "I love your Persian horse," she murmurs. "It's so . . . Persian." Or is it *"He's* so Persian"? We were shocked that such a violation had been perpetrated. Then we laughed to think that we remembered and that we still cared.

These days I can get right back to the Kameo's roof garden minus the violet sky by simply turning on the American Movie Classics channel on my television set. They don't show many silents, but I did see Rudolph Valentino in *The Sheik* recently, and shortly before that *Wings* with Buddy   71

Rogers, Richard Arlen, and, in what we now call a "cameo" appearance, a totally unknown Gary Cooper, simply leaping off the screen at you. They show a wide range of early thirties talkies, many of them terrible, but to me they almost all have a certain fascination because of how the people looked then and the furniture they had, and what the streets and the traffic looked like. These are the very movies that so many of my earliest images come from. Maybe some six-, seven-, eight- or nine-year-old kids watching AMC today are receiving exactly the same images that filled my head so many years ago. Maybe there's some little girl somewhere being scared to death by her brother pretending to put his finger in a candle after seeing Douglas Fairbanks catch leprosy in *The Gaucho*. How weird, to be able to see that same ancient image that affected me so many years ago, sandwiched between MTV and "Wheel of Fortune."

Mother Wore Smocks

A new theory (*The New York Times,* Science, Tuesday) states that a baby even as young as four months old can do a kind of simple arithmetic. If you put one Mickey Mouse in front of him (it works with girls, too), then take it away, then put up another one, take it away, and then show him *two* Mickey Mice, he will look at them briefly and in a satisfied manner, content that you are telling him that one and one are two. You got it right. But if you complete the first two steps and then confront him with *three* of the famed rodents, he will stare for a longer time, and a faint furrow will crease his tiny brow. "You got it wrong; one and one are not three, stupid." This proves we are born with a built-in sense of numbers just as we are born with an innate sense of language. When we learn to count, we are only giving names to what we already know. Perhaps this is one baby who was born without an innate mathematical sense. Although I am somewhat older now, I am still apt to stare at numbers a long time, brow furrowed, not quite sure whether the answer is right or wrong.

When the "new math" hit the scene and my children came to me for help with their homework, I was completely bewildered and of no use to them, having been completely bewildered by the "old math" as well. The small progressive school I attended in those math-crucial years when it was still "arithmetic" did not give the subject a high priority. Creative work came first, things having to do with the arts and expressing oneself. In the middle of an arithmetic class I would often find myself slipping behind in my comprehension of the teacher's explanation, feeling like someone in the silent movies I used to see, desperately running behind a racing car, always unable to catch up. I would look at the nasty little Curtis test notebook before me, a pad with problems printed on each page and a transparent page in between for the answers. At the end of the class the completed test would be handed in to the high tribunal in the person of Miss Stebbins.

One morning, feeling particularly desolate and stupid, my serge bloomers scratching my legs, I had a daring thought. I went up to Miss Stebbins and whispered to her solemnly that I had a wonderful idea for a poem and felt an urgent need to write it immediately. She took the news calmly and sympathetically, and whispered back, "You may go into the next room, but be very quiet and come to me when you have finished." I tiptoed into the next room, a kind of annex to our classroom, shut the door, and sat down with pad and well-bitten pencil to begin creating. I don't remember what I wrote, but my feverish inspiration lasted exactly until the arithmetic period was over. I missed quite a few arithmetic classes that way, leaving a large gap in my knowledge of addition, subtraction, multiplication, and division, short and long, but with a small folder of poems by the end of the year. I squeezed by into the next grade because, dopey as I was with numbers, I caught on quickly to everything else.

I had entered the school with a few other five-year-olds when it was just a kindergarten. Every year they added another class, leaving us always in the highest grade. Very often the procedures the faculty felt had not worked on us were dropped, and the class following went through something quite different. We were the guinea pigs and proud of it, and we wound up somewhat spottily but interestingly informed.

My mother, ever devoted to progressive education, loved the school and had picked it for her only daughter because she admired its principles and those of the Ethical Culture Society that had started it. Years before, she had taught fifth and sixth grades in the public school system and was as crazy about creativity as the next one, but she knew that when it came to math, it was drill, drill, drill, and leave inspiration in the hall. She frowned on our math department (one teacher). The frown deepened as we approached the eighth grade, and although she knew an add-a-class high school was being planned, she was concerned that we might be flung into the dog-eat-dog world Out There with only a tenuous grasp of the decimal system.

One morning I walked into the classroom, and there was my mother in a green smock, chalk in hand, poised and ready to teach us math. This was not the traumatic shock one might have suspected. I was used to having her take part in school matters. Our teacher, a Mr. Paley at the time, warm and affable but slightly befuddled, stood by, and after my mother had taught several classes, he got the idea and took over his position with increased vigor, clarity, and sternness. And no one ever got excused to write a poem again.

But my mother had not waited until eighth grade to try to shore up the math education of at least one child, me. During the summers we were all at my grandfather's house in Hunter, New York, where, compared to our rather modest standard of living in our apartment in the city, we reveled in relative luxury. We had a tennis court on which, along with my brother, two cousins, and a raft of neighbors' children, I disported myself all morning long, with occasional breaks for drinks of crystal-clear water from Grandpa's artesian well. But throughout the fun I was ever tense, anticipating the tinkle of a bell from the house informing me that it was time for my math lesson. I dreaded the sound. I would shuffle back to the house where my mother awaited me, wearing a smock, and I would dutifully take my class, trying not to hear the pock-pock of the tennis balls.

My summers were partially blighted also by the necessity of returning to school in the fall with a completed "project." One year I collected leaves, made blueprints of them with blueprint paper and those simple frames you used to be able to buy, pasted the prints in a notebook, and labeled them in my neat manuscript. A few days before Labor Day there would be much cutting, pasting, and labeling to make up for weeks of neglect. Though I tried to ignore it in the early carefree days of summer, there it was, The Project, hanging over me the whole time. Another year it might be grasses I have known and loved, or wild flowers, types of fungus, unusual rocks, some with what one hoped were fossil remains, or a diary of constellations and shooting stars observed in the summer skies.

My mother was right. We Ethical Culture kids *were* thrown Out There. The high school was discontinued after the second year, and we all had to go to public schools and take state Regents exams to get into the junior year. I just passed the geometry Regents with a 65 but found out by chatting with my exam mates that I had failed to turn the last page where there were three problems left, which of course I never completed. I should have gotten an A for carelessness. I vowed to erase that terrible blot which lowered my stunning average by taking geometry over at my new school, Erasmus Hall. This time I got a 98. I lost the two points again through carelessness: The answer was pi to the first decimal point, and I wrote 3.2, knowing full well that pi was 3.1416 and that the answer was 3.1. Ah, some things you never forget. I have sometimes regretted my feeble grasp of math. I cannot blame it on the Ethical because others in my class turned out to be math whizzes. But as has been pointed out to me, my future seemed to lie in the direction of some kind of writing, not astronomy or the as yet undreamed of field of computer science.

My mother's involvement in school activities extended into other realms. In the spring or early fall of certain years there would be a class trip. When we were small, thirteen of us and two teachers would go off for a week to a place called Hudson Guild Farm, where we studied farm animals and nature around us in a lovely country setting. When we were a little older, we went to a camp run by Ernest Thompson Seton, the English-born naturalist, where we lived like Native Americans. To prepare for this, in art and shop classes we had constructed a large teepee of canvas decorated with Indian designs. This was shipped up to the camp, and we learned from Mr. Seton how to erect the long poles to hold the tent up and how to build a fire inside, leaving the flaps open at the top to let the smoke out.

In the evenings we would sit around the campfire and were told Indian tales and learned Indian songs, some of which roll around in my head to this day:

> Wah ta ho ta ho
> Wah ta ho ta ho
> Wah uta ho nahwee tama lo
> Wah uta ho tahhee man a lo
> Mya nah wee zumi tan a lo
> Mya nah wee . . . etc.

This Navaho hymn to the sun was delivered with right arm straight up and eyes on the sky. We girls made dresses of heavy muslin decorated with painted borders and fringes, which we wore with leather headbands and moccasins we had cut out ourselves from brown chamois and then embroidered with beaded designs. I loved choosing among the vials of different-colored beads and planning the designs to sew on the moccasins. At the campfire we would pass the peace pipe, but no tobacco touched our nine- or ten-year-old lips. During the day we went on hikes and learned how to make a trail through the woods, marking trees along the way so that we could find our way back to camp. Not knowing at the time that the politically correct '90s would have called us Native Americans, we thought we were living like Indians.

When the teachers felt they needed another adult along, my mother was a ready volunteer. I remember her in her smock at Hudson Guild and later at Bear Mountain. There we all lived in a great weathered wooden house with large porches on two levels. I have no idea what the educational reason was for being there. All I can recall is that on a few occasions during rest period all the kids would sneak upstairs to the attic to play kissing games. I stayed below and sat on my cot reading. After all, I was the only one whose mother was along. The thought of her popping up those attic stairs and surprising me in the middle of my turn at spin the bottle   77 was too much for me. I had a hard time handling her black look of disapproval. Recently I asked my brother what he and my father did while Mother was off camping. He told me that by age ten he had learned to cook and made the meals for the two of them. I never thought about this at the time and never heard any discussions between my father and mother on the subject.

My mother must have enjoyed those breaks from the routine of being a wife and mother and running the house. She was a woman who certainly should have gone back to teaching after her marriage or found some occupation other than her organizations to utilize her considerable talents and energy. But after all, my brother could not have been expected to cook all year round. Looking back, I'm glad my mother was home much of the time, as most mothers were during the '20s and '30s. She was there to greet me when I came home from school every day, to feed me, help me with my homework, and take me shopping and to other kids' parties. She told me that her mother had always admonished her and her sisters to take the smallest piece when sweets were passed around, but that is one lesson I could never quite master. Also, she was there to read to me and tell me stories.

There was the tale, for example, of the "House with the Golden Windows" in which a little girl who lived at the foot of the hill would look up at the beautiful house across the way from them up the hill. The house had windows that shone like gold and she bothered her mother a great deal by asking again and again why they could not live there. The mother went as far as to give up her home and move into the golden-windowed house, warning her child that they could never move back to the old place. As the excited child got near her new house, she saw that the windows were ordinary, like any others, and she cried out in disappointment, "But where are the golden windows?" The mother pointed across the way, down to where the light was hitting the windows of their old house. "There they are," she said. And the little girl saw that indeed the windows of their old house were shining like gold. But she could never go back there again.

Then there was the one about the little girl and the

apothecary jar. It goes like this: A little girl and her mother are walking along a cold snowy street in the dead of winter. They are very poor and the soles of the little girl's slippers are worn through, and she is wet and freezing and crying from the cold. But she suddenly stops when her eyes light upon a glorious purple glass jar in an apothecary's window. It is huge and lovely. The child beams with delight and says, "Oh, Mother, if I could only have that purple jar, I would be the happiest girl in the world!" The mother says, "I have only enough money for a new pair of shoes or for that jar. You will have to choose." Without hesitating the little girl says, "The purple jar!" She carries it home full of joy. Once in the house she sees that inside the jar is some dark powder at the bottom that looks like dirt, and she hurries to wash her precious jar clean. The dirt turns out to be purple dye that had been thrown in to make the jar look colored, so when the little girl puts water in it, the color washes out and she is left with a plain glass jar. She also has to spend the rest of the winter freezing and soaked in her worn-through slippers. I pondered over this a lot. Why didn't the mother tell the girl the dye would wash out? And why didn't she tell the kid to forget it and come buy shoes? I knew there was a lesson in there somewhere about making choices, and I think the story scared me quite a bit, as did the one about the windows. I also heard the one about the people going down into Hell and one of them being given a carrot to use to pull himself out. But when he kicks away the others who want to hang on and be pulled out, too, the carrot is yanked away from him and down he goes to Hell. I got that lesson, too. There were other stories, of course, beautiful ones where everything turned out great, but for some reason the ones with the dire warnings remain the most vivid to me.

My mother also told me stories when I was sick in bed, which, judging from a tiny diary I kept when I was seven, seems to have been most of the time. Apparently I was more at home than in school, coping with bouts of respiratory infection. Typical entries: "Sore throat. Stayed home from school today." "Still sick . . . stayed home." "Felt better, but they thought I should stay home another day." And when I   79 was afraid at night and couldn't fall asleep, my mother would stretch out at the foot of the bed, and sometimes she would sing to me, "Sweet and Low" or "Speed, Bonnie Boat" or the song her mother had sung to her in Yiddish, *"Allay loolee, kinderlach, allay loolee, puji-lach."* The gas light in the top of the hall fixture would flicker, and I would finally get to sleep.

My mother was there when at age ten I read *Jane Eyre* and reached the part about the mad wife in the attic and got so terrified I ran from the front room to the kitchen at the other end of the apartment, where I fell shuddering into her comforting arms. My mother was not a particularly cuddly woman, but she cuddled me then. In spite of her formidable aspects and her rather Calvinist code of behavior, she was warm and loving and protective, and ready to back me in whatever I did.

The first time she saw me perform with an amateur group, I had the role of a prostitute in Eugene O'Neill's *Ah, Wilderness!* Aunt Rose told me later that my mother had confided it had upset her, and she was relieved that my father, recently dead, had not seen what I had come to. All my mother said to me at the time was that I had given a great performance. I realize now she must have been made unhappy by many things that happened along the way, but she was always, as they say today, "there for me." And all my misery over math is forgotten, and what I like to think of is her teaching me about the magic of the number nine. You see, nine times two is eighteen, and one and eight are nine, and three times nine is twenty-seven, and lo and behold, two plus seven makes nine . . . and . . . Nine is an exceptional number, and so was my mom.

When she arrived here from Russia at the age of six, speaking no English, she was sent to school with her name and address pinned to her coat. After observing her for a short time, Mr. Bush, the principal of the school, P.S. 18, announced, "This little girl will graduate from school at the top of the honor roll." I have in my possession her medal, a gold disk hanging from a bar, which reads "R. Sadvoransky." One side of the medal says "P.S. No. 18, Feb. 8th, '95." On the other side it says simply "Honor." That was my mother:

She was loving, she set very high standards, and she lived her whole life with honor. I'm glad she never caught me playing spin the bottle, and I know she would be pleased to learn that today an accountant is adding up the numbers for her hopelessly un-math-minded daughter.

Daddy Called Me "Boobalee" (as in "Book")

When we heard his key in the front door at around six o'clock, my brother Nat and I would race down the hall competing to be the first to hurl ourself at our father, home from the wars at his small law office in downtown Manhattan. There was excitement every evening: Daddy was home. He usually was wearing a dark coat and a black bowler hat, and carried a newspaper under his arm. When April 15 came, he changed into one of those stiff straw boaters, which often left a ring across his forehead when it was hot, and on September 15 it was back to the bowler. My uncle Sam wore a panama, which I thought most peculiar. But back then every man wore some kind of hat. Women, too, would not dream of leaving the house without a hat on their heads. If you look at movies of the '20s and '30s, you will note that even if a distraught woman is rushing out of the house in some dire life-and-death emergency, she will stop to grab her hat off the rack and cram it on. A bareheaded woman equaled a "hussy," or worse.

My father, whose name was Leo, was a wonderful-looking man, I thought, of medium height and a somewhat stocky build, with blue eyes, slightly reddish hair, broad Russian cheekbones, a long upper lip, and a cleft chin.

I loved his low rumbling voice, especially when he called me "Boobalee" ("oo" as in "book"). I would sit on his lap while he pumped the pedals of our player piano, singing along to a Chopin scherzo. When it got to its signature phrase of three notes, he would sing out happily with the music: "Boobalee . . . Boobalee—dum *dah* da da da da dum!" The fact that his pet name for me just fit that musical figure never ceased to delight me. I felt Chopin would have been pleased, too.

My father loved music. We had a wind-up Victrola, and he brought home the basic records that every middle-class home of the period seemed to have, usually identified by the soloist's name as The Heifetz, The Elman, The Caruso, The Galli-Curci, The Alma Gluck. I knew the title of that one, "Whispering Hope." We also had The Chaliapin, and I knew the name of that one, too: "The Flea"—in Russian, "Bleh-heh." It was the story of a czar who kept a pet flea, and the song is punctuated with laughter from the singer, as Chaliapin tells how the czar lavishes a fortune on the flea, fitting it with costly garments and feeding it the best foods, while all around him the people starved and froze to death. I believe at the end the flea bites the czar and he swats it dead, and there is much sardonic laughter. Nat and I would go around the apartment singing, "Bleh-heh . . . ha ha ha ha ha *hah!* Bleh-*heh!* . . . ha ha ha ha ha ha *ha!*" trying to approximate Chaliapin's basso profundo.

My father understood the Russian. In fact, he spoke it but had no one with whom to converse because my mother, although also from a Russian background, did not speak the language. My father had come to this country at eighteen, and I am so sorry I never asked him enough questions; for example: How did you learn English? And learn it well enough to study law and become a lawyer? He would sing plaintive Russian songs to Nat and me, and sometimes of an evening we would gather around the dining-room table and he would read the stories of Sholem Aleichem to us in Yiddish, stopping to explain and half-translate enough so that we could understand.

As the oldest of nine children, my father was the head of the family, particularly after my grandfather died; he became mentor and counselor to all his siblings. When we had 83 family meetings or dinners and the boards were put in to enlarge the dining room table, it was usually a fairly jolly time, full of warm, self-deprecating humor and reviews of one another's faults, but never hurtful or acrimonious.

My father was on the board of directors of the Beth Moses Hospital in Brooklyn, and a group of his friends, mainly from the board, were the players in a pinochle game that took place at our house every few weeks. When I was little I would hang out behind his chair for a while, but when I grew a bit older I became very haughty about the game. I thought my father was so far above those other men that it was demeaning for him to associate with them.

A couple of them were very rich manufacturers, one was a doctor, and one a publisher—perfectly fine fellows, I guess, but to me, because they smoked cigars and their voices were loud and coarse, they were gross. How unfair that men of that caliber should make so much more money than my noble and gentlemanly father. I resented them.

At one point during the evening my mother and I would serve coffee and cakes while the men took a short break. I remember on one occasion I passed the cake and the coffee cups with great disdain, plunking them down with a rude abruptness and with my nose in the air, and then scooted out as quickly as possible. Later that night, after the game, my father took me aside and said, "I know how you feel about some of these gentlemen, but no matter what you feel they are guests in our house, and they must be treated with courtesy and good manners. Your behavior tonight was disgraceful. As long as you are in my house, you shall make my guests welcome and behave like a lady." He scolded me so seldom that this attack was a body blow. I had never felt so low. I resolved never to disappoint my daddy again. The next time the game took place I greeted each of the men with effulgent girlish warmth and served them decorously and with a smile. But I never changed my feelings toward them. I was an actress that night.

One of these men, who had a successful knit-goods business, lived in a huge house on the block next to us. It was most curious that in a neighborhood of small four- and five-story apartment houses there was suddenly a deep lawn with an iron statue on it, in front of an imposing edifice that can only be called a mansion. One of the daughters, Sylvia, and I were friends, and I was filled with awe and self-importance when I went over there to play with her.

Our games took place mainly in the kitchen, where we concocted unwholesome messes made of crayon slicings and pencil shavings mixed with water, which we called "gish-gish," no reference to the great sisters of that name intended. To get to the kitchen we had to walk through the living room, which I thought was the most beautiful room I had ever seen. The furniture was gold, with pink brocade upholstery. In the middle, among the elaborately carved couches and chairs, was an S-shaped loveseat. I fantasized lovers facing each other on the seat, very close and able to gaze rapturously into each other's eyes, with only a little piece of the S between them.

But perhaps the household was not as elegant as I wanted it to be. There were usually orange peels drying on the radiators. I noticed that this was true in many households because orange peel candy-making was all the rage. I suppose they sliced the peels, rolled them in sugar, and, voilà! I never liked it, so it did not distress me that my mother never took up this culinary pastime. I'm sure she thought it vulgar to leave orange peels on the radiators. Sylvia and I stuck to "gish-gish."

Even better than going to Sylvia's was a visit to Daddy's office at 299 Broadway. I did not know as a child that it was just the small office of a not very successful lawyer. It was glamorous to me. He had a clerk who made a big fuss over me when I visited. Maybe not many lawyers had female law clerks at that time, so perhaps among his other admirable qualities my father was prematurely profeminist. Jean, his clerk, was a smart, handsome young woman who let me play with the rows and rows of embossing stamps, trying to figure out what was printed on them—backward and upside down —and then putting a paper in the stamp, banging down on it, and finding the answer in raised letters on the paper. One famous day Nat and I went down to the office with our   85 mother for a special occasion. It was 1927, and Lindbergh had just flown the Atlantic to Paris. There was to be a ticker tape parade up Broadway and we were going to see it from Daddy's windows. I remember excitedly tearing up pages of old telephone books in the office—a few pages at a time, of course—and when the parade came into view, throwing the strips gleefully out the window to join with the thick snowstorm of paper already pouring out of other office windows and cascading down onto the cavalcade below.

I admired Lindy but had a secret crush on Admiral Richard E. Byrd, whose middle name, Evelyn, fascinated me. He had already been the first man to fly over the North Pole, but a few years later he became a hero by charting the South Pole for the first time. The rotogravure section of the Sunday *Times* was full of polar expeditions in those years, and I pored over them endlessly. I was thrilled to go to the Brooklyn Academy of Music to hear Byrd speak one Saturday morning.

Daddy later moved his office up to 1776 Broadway at Columbus Circle, which I thought terribly elegant, and I loved my visits there, which always included hot chocolate at Child's.

Perhaps more exciting than greeting Daddy at home every evening was going to meet him at the train station every Friday evening in the country. After a sweltering week in the city, "the men," my father and my uncle Sam, father to my cousins Inez and Muriel and married to my mother's sister Celia, would arrive at Kaaterskill Junction, a tiny station on a trunk line near Hunter, New York, where we spent the summer months at our grandfather's house. The two girls, Nat and I, my mother, and Aunt Celia, and sometimes my grandpa and my aunt Rose, would stroll through the woods en masse to meet the train. Hearing the chug-chug of the steam engine coming through the narrow notch a few miles away, and then the sight of the engine and the smoke puffing as it approached, was wildly exciting every Friday night of the summer. We hurled ourselves into our fathers' arms, and then we all walked back to the house, full of country and city news of the week. Monday mornings we would take them to the train to see them off to the city, in a contrasting mood of woe. Even on a blazing sunlit morning we would recite the refrain, "The skies are gray when my daddy goes away."

Daddy always brought us candies, including Peter's chocolate in round pastilles wrapped in silver foil which we would open and place in the sun to melt, and then have a contest to see which one of us could make the delicious treat last the longest. Uncle Sam also brought goodies. But he was a health food enthusiast ahead of his time and brought great-tasting fruit bars, bags of various seeds instead of sweets, and cans of maté, an herb tea from South America. I found him somewhat forbidding, but he was always nice to me, and adored Aunt Celia and their two daughters. He played the violin well and perhaps had wanted a career in music, but found himself managing his father's orthopedic shoe store. At one point we were all forced to wear the ugly things with turned-in toes, with the admonition that if we didn't, our feet would grow up crooked. We protested so much, however, that in time we were freed and allowed to ruin our feet as we saw fit.

Uncle Sam spent much of his free time in the cellar of the house in Flatbush where they lived, trying to find the formula for the varnish that was used on Stradivarius violins. He was sure it was the varnish that was the secret of the great unmatchable tone of the fabled instruments. When my cousins were a little older and beginning to date, a procedure he was very strict about, he was apt to pop up out of the cellar with two or three violins in hand, sit the young man calling on Inez or Muriel down, play each fiddle in order, and then ask him to judge which of the three instruments had the best sound, a trial by fire few of the young swains survived successfully. During the summer he would walk through the fields around the Hunter house playing snatches of the great works, but most often the cadenzalike section from Tchaikov-sky's Fifth Symphony. One summer when I was ten he brought records to the country of three Tchaikovsky symphonies, the fourth, fifth, and sixth, the Dvořák New World, and the César Franck D Minor, and I listened to them over and over again while reading through one of Nat's bar mitzvah gifts, a set of Alexandre Dumas. Forever entwined in my 87 mind is the Fifth Tchaikovsky with the characters in *The Three Musketeers* and *Twenty Years After*. I assigned themes to each of them and shuddered regularly when Milady's threatening music came along.

My father hoped my brother and I would play the piano well. Lessons were started on the old upright, and we would go over to our cousins' house to be taught by a Russian tyrant, brother of a well-known violinist, who sat next to us and kicked us in the leg to mark the beat. We later switched to a woman who lived on Grandpa's street, and we had to walk over there for our lessons. I, breathlessly afraid of being late, was always a step ahead of Nat, who ambled along relaxed, getting there just a step behind me. My father did not care for this teacher, I knew, mainly because she exhibited many mannerisms, body swoops and facial grimaces, but she was a good musician and at one point we were playing pretty well. By then my father had bought a thrilling huge Steinway, a parlor grand, one size smaller than concert. It was a used piano, and it had a glorious tone. It still does and is in my living room, having made quite a few moves in its time. Every living room I ever looked at had to measure up to the test: Will the piano fit in it? Like many kids, though we were both musical and loved music, we hated to practice, and I gradually stopped being able to play. Nat had the gift of being able to play by ear, and got good at pulling popular tunes out of the air, while he struggled with the first movement of the Mozart D Minor Concerto. He is still struggling.

Daddy was disappointed, I know. Why didn't they yell at us and *make* us practice, we ask ourselves now. What was this self-consciousness that made us ashamed that the neighbors would hear our mistakes through the door? I learned how difficult it all is when I had children of my own and the pattern repeated itself.

At Hunter, my father and my uncle would arrive from the stifling city and spend their afternoons (very often) indoors with my grandfather, playing a summer-long poker game. I loved to stand behind my father rooting fervently for him, while Inez stood behind her father hoping to bring him luck by placing a frog on his shoulder. Muriel, the baby, feeling that Grandpa was continually being taken advantage of by these younger men, would stand behind him, fingers crossed, praying that he would draw great cards. The sun would be shining outside in sweet air while indoors the room filled with my father's cigarette smoke and Uncle Sam's cigars, and our mothers would come in to shoo us outdoors to get the benefit of the country that we would have only until Labor Day.

At the end of the day in Hunter, I would sometimes sit on Grandpa's lap. Since I could do that on any weeknight and Daddy was there for only the weekend, I would creep up on his lap instead and watch the sunset, rocking in one of the big rocking chairs lined up along the length of the wide porch. Then I knew true contentment. Today, sometimes on a hot afternoon, I recall the picture of my father sitting near a window, sipping a glass of hot tea. He held a lump of sugar behind his teeth and sipped the tea through it, Russian style, holding his cigarette between his second and third fingers, deep in the curve where the fingers begin, also Russian style. Watching the perspiration form on his brow as he drank the boiling tea, I would ask him, "Why do you drink hot tea on a hot day, Daddy?" "It's the evaporation, Boobalee. It keeps me cool."

My mother was a good, loving mother, but my father was the one I preferred to have lie at the foot of my bed when I couldn't sleep, and he was the one I wanted to have wake me when I still had the vestiges of a cold because he would invariably say, "Don't go to school. Take another day."

I think he worried that I would never find a man to marry me and also that I was not assertive enough to get along in the cold, cruel world out there. I remember when I was around seventeen and had a date with an attractive guy I had met at a party. I was excited and took a long time getting dressed and made up, and my father said I looked wonderful. We sat in the living room, I poised for flight. Then began a period of waiting. The period got longer and longer. Daddy and I did not have much to talk about by then. When it got quite late, the awful truth made itself noisily evident: I had been stood up. Mr. Attractive was not about to show. I was 89 miserable and embarrassed. In an attempt to make me feel better, my father said, "That fellow doesn't know a good thing when he sees it. He'll be sorry." This only made me feel a lot worse. It was humiliating to think that my father was seeing me in this hideous moment of rejection. I ran from the room blubbering something like "Oh, what do *you* know about it!" and slammed my door.

My father died before I even met my beautiful Steve, a man with many of my father's qualities: kindness, humor, warmth, integrity. They would have liked each other, I think. As for the "assertive" part, I was just this unformed college student when he left me. He never got to see what wonderful things happened to me in a field where I must have shown some assertiveness to have survived at all. He did not know I would someday be connected with the theater and the movies. He would have liked that, too, I think—but not the nightclub part.

I learned a lot about kindness from my father. I thank him for that, and for my cheekbones and for my long upper lip and for calling me "Boob-a-lee" ("oo" as in "book").

Exodus . . .
into the Big City

Graduation from New York University. What a cocky stance! New home, new life, new name, new face, new sun in the sky! Actually, I felt I was walking on oatmeal.

With Steve, the summer we met. How incredible: This beautiful man came along, and —despite the predictions of my unmarriage-ability—

A brief four years later we were married, and a brief six months later he was drafted. Here I am visiting Steve on furlough in California. What *am* I wearing?

Steve, some time later, back in civvies, not having lost his looks.

A brief eight years after our wedding came the patter of tiny feet, first Susanna's, then, some three years later, Alan's. My mother in the garden behind our East Sixty-ninth Street house, with the carriage containing one or the other of them.

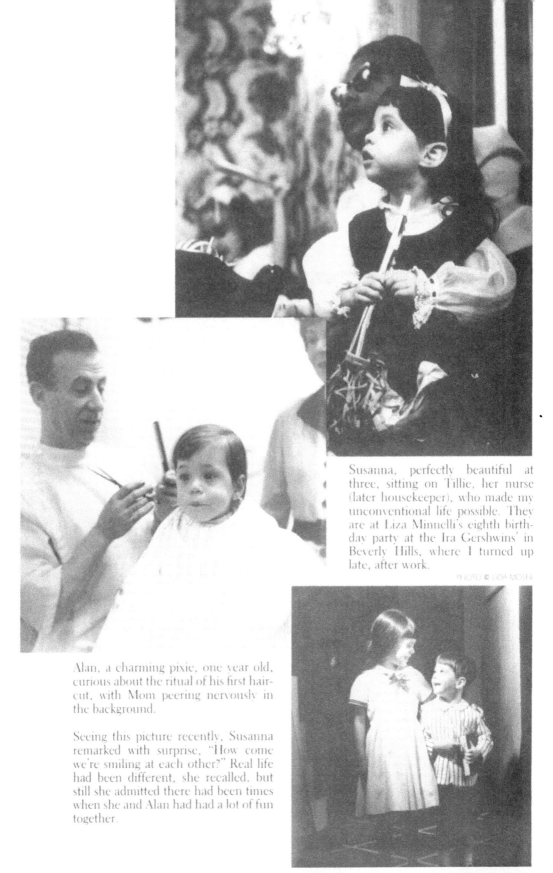

Susanna, perfectly beautiful at three, sitting on Tillie, her nurse (later housekeeper), who made my unconventional life possible. They are at Liza Minnelli's eighth birthday party at the Ira Gershwins' in Beverly Hills, where I turned up late, after work.

Alan, a charming pixie, one year old, curious about the ritual of his first haircut, with Mom peering nervously in the background.

Seeing this picture recently, Susanna remarked with surprise, "How come we're smiling at each other?" Real life had been different, she recalled, but still she admitted there had been times when she and Alan had had a lot of fun together.

Picture-book family in a house in Ossining rented for the summer.

Brother and sister on a bench, like Nat and me.

A serene moment with Steve in my dressing room after a performance. Steve loved the work Adolph and I did together and encouraged us to perform.

With Noël Coward. Little did he know, but years before we met and became friends, I had insisted Steve and I have our wedding brunch at the Hapsburg House, just because it was used romantically in a Coward film I admired, *The Scoundrel*. Try explaining that to your relatives.

TWO PHOTOS: LAWRENCE FRIED/THE IMAGE BANK

At the glorious twenty-fifth wedding anniversary party given for us by Adolph Green and Phyllis Newman, with an assist from Tom Guinzburg. Adolph is raising his glass, Jule Styne is across from us, and Lenny Bernstein and Betty Bacall are down the banquette apiece.

Steve and I in our private world in the middle of the party, wondering, "Where has the time all gone to—?" It was 1967. We had twelve years left to go.

The Great Profile

(Not the Story of John Barrymore)

*I*t wasn't grotesque. It wasn't gigantic. It wasn't even particularly long. No one ever pointed at my nose and asked, "When does the monument open?" as Cyrano suggested someone with imagination might inquire regarding his famous protuberance. It did have a bump on it. My family said it made me "distinguished looking." If there is anything a girl growing up does not want to hear, it is that she is distinguished looking. Pretty! Pretty! That's what she wants to hear.

"Distinguished" noses were not a rarity in my family. My mother's side abounded in them; my father's, however, was quite the opposite. My father had blue eyes, reddish brown hair, broad cheekbones, and a perfect, straight nose. It was obvious to me, when the genes were in there fighting for possession of my physiognomy, which side won, but what could I do?

For many years I did nothing about it but carry a large stone in my stomach. There are some early pictures of me in a brown velvet coat and tam, wrinkled stockings, and sturdy brown shoes in which I look moderately cute. But IT had not asserted itself yet. Still, I did not like having my picture taken. There is a shot of me in front of the stoop at 1054 Park Place, Brooklyn, the small apartment house that was my first home. I look miserable and angry. I recall that the photographer had come down the block with a horse, the point being to have your picture taken with the horse. I would have none of the animal and fought bitterly against the idea of preserving the moment at all. But I lost, and there I am frowning, my mouth a downturned crescent, fingernail-bitten hands desperately clutching a rubber doll, which like most dolls had a dear little nose. I did not. That shape shaped my life. Too much stress on looks? I agree. My general feeling of insecurity about everything made it of extreme importance to me. It's true my mother and father did not insist I wear a veil over my face when going out, as did the beautiful parents of distinguished-looking Edith Sitwell, who also had two depressingly handsome brothers to flank her like two great swans when they went forth. I had one brother, somewhat better looking than I, I thought, and he was nice to me and taught me how to throw a ball. Still, I lacked confidence.

As a student I excelled in everything but arithmetic. Was I compensating? Maybe, or maybe I was just smart. I was also small, skinny, and swift, and won all the girls' races on Field Day in Prospect Park until a smaller, skinnier girl joined the class. When I saw her pull ahead of me in our first fifty-yard dash, I realized she was also swifter, and somehow I managed to twist a thigh muscle, not seriously but just enough to allow me to fall screaming to the ground. I did get a big part in the class play, *Ivanhoe,* when I was eleven, but of course I was cast as the Jewish heroine Rebecca, not the fair Saxon Rowena, who gets the guy. That part went to pretty snub-nosed Adele.

In the getting-the-guy department, in my class of thirteen kids at the small, progressive Brooklyn Ethical Culture School I attended, there were a couple of boys I had known since we were all six-year-olds who liked me, and our school dances were no problem for me. Yet I remained troubled about my looks. My eighth-year graduation picture comes vividly to mind: It shows a smallish girl standing sideways but with her head swiveled around to present a front view in hopes of camouflaging the offending feature. We all had to make our own graduation dresses, and mine, I recall, was green organdy. Progressive schools did not respect the rule about white for graduation. My hair, medium brown and lank, hung straight down to the shoulder, where it sort of separated into points. My aunt Celia used to say of me, "Her hair hung down her pallid cheek like seaweed on a clam." Not exactly an ego-building description.

When the high school at Ethical was suddenly discontinued, I found myself at age fourteen flung into the giant teeming world of Erasmus Hall, where there were forty in a class and the halls and entrance arches were agog with boys and girls engaged in social discourse and myriad mating games. The snickered motto attached to Erasmus at the time was "You go in with a diploma, and you come out with a marriage license." Not *me*. I went in with a diploma and I came out with a diploma.

My first term there, I was so frightened I would lower my head into the pile of books hugged to my missing bosom and rush past those wildly sophisticated, attractive, chattering, giggling, and guffawing fellows and girls lounging around the Arch (the main entrance on Flatbush Avenue) and hold my breath until I got into the hallway. I didn't feel so good there, either. Compared to the halls at my little school these were overwhelming, filled with turbulent traffic as the student body with mature beard stubble and bouncing breasts thundered from classroom to classroom. Fortunately, a close friend of mine from Ethical was at Erasmus, and we had lunch together daily, were in some of the same classes, and also joined the poetry club. Bea did not seem as terrified as I, but then, she was a big blonde with an acceptable nose.

On one of my desks I found a profile scratched into the wood with a sharp pen. It was the kind of profile I had been wistfully drawing from an early age: high forehead, wide-set eyes, rosebud mouth, and in the center a straight little nose tilting ever so slightly upward, a shade retroussé. I know that Amy March in *Little Women* wore a clothespin on her nose in hopes of making it more elegant by curbing its retroussé tendencies, but I loved that little tilt. There was a name, "Martha Glenn," scratched next to the profile, and by some wild coincidence I found out in later years that she was an old girlfriend of my future husband's, and she had

98

scratched her self-portrait on her desk. It was her profile that inhabited all my doodles.

Today I look back fondly on Erasmus, but to be truthful, I know that in the two years I spent there I was never truly comfortable except perhaps during the after-school poetry hour run by a stern, splendid teacher, Miss Weirich. Once a week I would rush there to read and write poems. We studied all the various forms of verse and read our own attempts at them aloud. I remember a ballad I wrote that got printed in the *Erasmanian.* It began

> Some years ago in Surrey shire
> There dwelt a wench not comely.
> "Alas," she sighed, "how came I thus
> To be so very homely?"

Does this seem just a bit "on the nose"?

My ballad proceeded to relate how this ill-favored creature asked a witch to find the remedy, a potion perhaps, to cure her condition. Little did I know that a few years later I would seek out my own witch, in the form of a plastic surgeon.

I would not say I was wildly popular with the boys during high school. I had some suitors, but never the kind I yearned for, needless to say. I saw my old school friends, went to a few football games in an attempt to whip up some passionate involvement in the rivalry between Erasmus and its arch-enemy Manual Training, and then there were the temple dances. These were not as exotic as they sound, no tinkling finger cymbals, ritual drums, veils, incense, or hands and wrists like whirling fans. They were simply Saturday night dances at the local temples: Union Temple, the Shaari Zedek, on my corner, and the Jewish Center.

Somewhere along the line we had made the venturesome move from 1054 in the middle of the block to 1078 on the corner of Kingston Avenue. My bedroom window faced the side entrance to this place of worship, the secular side, and many's the Saturday night I knelt with my chin on the windowsill watching the golden lads and lasses go laughing into the dance. In Hebrew, Shaari Zedek means "Gates of Righteousness," but to dateless me it must have meant the gates to laughter, love, and romance, and I felt left out. Lest I break anyone's heart, including mine, with this bathetic image, I hasten to add that one could attend these affairs without a date. I just didn't have the guts. Pity must now give way to exasperation, which I imagine my parents felt more than once.

Before my two years at Erasmus were up, I made Arista, had been mistakenly asked to join the Newman Club, a Catholic organization, by a very nearsighted student, played on the volleyball team, I think, wrote a lot of poems, swam the required length of the pool, and graduated with a dizzyingly high average. In spite of this accomplishment, by early summer Barnard had rejected me. I can't blame that on my profile; I've seen worse-looking Barnard girls. There were dark mutterings of "quota" around the house. I was disappointed, of course, having planned a broad liberal arts curriculum with no goal in mind (teaching, perhaps?), and now what was I to do?

The family fell into its set routine, and we all went off for our yearly summer stay at Grandfather's summer house in Hunter, New York. My grandparents, aunt, uncle, their two daughters, my unmarried aunt, my parents, my brother, and I had been going there every summer of my life. Early in July my mother, who had been quietly furious at the Barnard rebuff, showed me a brochure from N.Y.U. with little commedia dell'arte figures prancing on its cover. It told of the School of Fine Arts' Dramatic Arts Department. I had done some acting at Ethical—we had dramatized everything from social studies to science experiments—and I was famous from one end of our apartment to the other for my kaleidoscopic moods, and I had thrilled to our occasional excursions across the bridge to go to a Broadway show, but it had never occurred to me that I might go into the theater professionally.

I applied, I waited, I conquered, and soon I was hugging my books against my now discernible bosom while riding the subway all the way from Brooklyn to what we who lived in the provinces used to call "the City." I thrived on the fare in the Dramatic Arts Department, but, realizing that I was getting only "Hail-Theseus-our-renowned-Duke!" parts in the affiliated Washington Square Players, and sneakily admitting to myself that I might want to be an actress someday, I became more and more aware of my profile. What if I changed it? I wondered. Would that enhance my chances for a life on the wicked stage? Could it change my entire life? I began to grind my teeth at night, but the teeth of the frustrated grind slowly and this all took time.

At the end of my sophomore year I was eighteen and determined to break the pattern of going to Hunter with the family and doing nothing. I would get a job. Although the Great Depression is what I had been living through, I have not referred to it because I am dealing here only with my own personal great depression. But, in brief, life during that generally disastrous time was not much different for us from life before it because we had never been up on any heights to come crashing down from. By the time summer came I had gotten a job through a friend at a children's camp in Monticello, New York, as the arts and crafts counselor, qualifying by having done some sculpture from time to time and having taken a crash course at Dennison's in "What You Can Do with Crepe Paper."

Summer brought me to an incident that propelled me uneasily toward the decision to do something about IT. Camp Winston was coed, and I found myself successful with several boy counselors—"playing the field," I think we called it. One of these fellows was dangerous, I thought, maybe evil. Up at the lake one night, fully clothed, he climbed on top of me, also fully clothed, and after a kiss said, "You think as far as a kiss, while I think as far as intercourse." Although I was already eighteen, I was horrified. I rolled him off me with the excuse that I had to check on a couple of "sailors" (bedwetters) in my bunk. Horrified though I was at the time, I was thrilled when in the fall, well after camp was over and glorious night encounters like ours were supposed to have been forgotten, he called me for a date. The evening remains a blur except for its last moment. He saw me into my vestibule, 101 turned my face toward his, and as I was swimming in anticipation of a kiss, he stared at my face, took his index figure, pressed hard on the bony bump on my nose, and then left.

No big deal, really. I just wanted to die. I wish I could say that I got magnificently angry and brushed him out of my thoughts like the crumb he was. But no, that stone in my stomach just got heavier.

There was a girl named Beverly in some of my classes at N.Y.U. She was out of school for a bit, then came back with a new nose. It was new and smaller, but unfortunately it still looked as though she could use an operation. Beverly thought she looked swell. An open, hearty girl with pretty legs and a big chest, she smoked incessantly and spoke with a strong New York flavor. She was casual, undefeatable, and never seemed to care much if she became a good actress or not. She left school and started making the rounds of the offices, and although we were never close friends, she turned out to be significant in my life. She started nagging me about calling her doctor and having my nose done. I avoided the discussion as much as possible and quickly lost the name of her doctor. I just knew I could not do it, and even if I might, I would never go to *him*. What if, I asked myself, it turned out like that? I was sure my parents would not hear of it anyway, particularly my father, who, I am happy to say, thought I was not only smart and talented but also attractive. At least he made me feel that's what he thought. Having a better nose would just be gilding the lily, tempting fate. And an operation was expensive.

Summer was coming again, and I found myself not yearning for Camp Winston. I planned to look for a different kind of job, but early in June my father died of angina, at fifty-four. I had been away for a moribund weekend with a fraternity brother of my brother's from Cornell who was visiting his own brother at Penn State. My date behaved toward me very much like a fraternity brother. On my return I found Daddy in the hospital, and although the year before he had retired because of his condition, I never thought of him as really ill. It was a shock to find him at Beth Moses where he 102 had been on the board of directors since its founding. When we were small, the phrase "board of directors" used to reduce Nat and me to helpless laughter, a childish mystery I have never solved—some silly pun on the word "board," I suspect. Sitting at my daddy's bedside, I felt sad and guilty at having been away. He was no longer conscious. We never spoke again. I know this was a catastrophic loss for my mother, but she was always very controlled and never let her emotions spill out. As a result, much of what was inside her was unfortunately hidden from Nat and me. I think it would have been better for all of us if she had opened up and shared her grief, but, loving as she was, that was not my mother's way. I was devastated at the loss of my warm, kind, affectionate, understanding daddy and must have been more overt in my feelings because I remember getting furious at a young man who took me to a concert at Lewisohn Stadium six weeks later when he berated me for daring to be still sad. He said it spoiled the evening. I wonder what kind of warm, understanding daddy this sterling fellow turned out to be.

The summer proved to be a time of big changes: First, we moved to "the City." Arriving in Manhattan from Brooklyn, I felt like a kid from a small town clutching her straw suitcases and staring up at the Big Town for the first time. It was madly glamorous. On Park, Madison, and Fifth avenues ladies wore hats and gloves, and I felt I was in a movie. Mother and I had picked out an apartment on East Seventy-fifth Street near Cornell Medical School, where Nat was in his second year, and it was a short subway hop for me down to N.Y.U. Of course we could have lived in Greenwich Village, handy for me, but the boy going to be "the Doctor" got the consideration due him.

The building we moved into was brand new, not quite completed, and our apartment had a sunken living room (very new in those days), down two steps, and an iron railing along the foyer and bedroom level. It is sad to note that in my father's lifetime, with his struggling law practice, we could never have afforded this move, but with his death there came the insurance that he had kept up through years of denial and hardship. He had provided us kids with our fully-paid-for years of higher education, plus what I felt was a glamorous, if 103

not quite finished, apartment in the heart of dazzling, sophisticated Manhattan. I *knew* I was in a movie. I wasn't sure
what kind, however, when on the first night, because of the
as-yet-unsealed holes around the risers, I saw a huge rat climb
up into the kitchen. My screams rivaled those of Louise Fa-
zenda in *The Bat.* The picture may have been silent, but
those were the loudest screams I ever heard.

The second big change that summer was my name.
No, I did not get married. My father had urged Nat and me
to change our name from Cohen to Comden, the name two
of our uncles had chosen, and we decided to follow his suggestion. We have the legal papers to prove it. It was supposed
to look better on a marquee and to facilitate my name getting
up there in the first place, but I don't recall being deluged
with a wave of wild offers ("Back! Back! All of you!") just
because I became Betty Comden.

The third change was my profile. It seems the time
had come. We could afford it, Mom said, and she did not
disapprove. Nat was uneasy, particularly when I felt too shy
or ashamed or whatever to discuss the matter with anyone
other than Beverly and perhaps get the name of another doctor. No, I recklessly decided I'd go to the one name I knew in
spite of the constantly warning evidence of Bev's face. I don't
recall much of the event itself, but Nat, the doctor-to-be, was
present in the operating room and told me later that he nearly
fainted as he watched the scalpel start slicing his sister's face.
Today plastic surgery is as common as root-canal work, and I
can think of several other slices I might have considered.
After all, Ruth Gordon had her bowed legs broken and reset
to improve her chances in the theater. Like Michael Jackson,
I could have kept cutting, pruning, and rearranging my facial
garden, but I stopped there, settling for just a simple nose
enhancement. At the time it was still a fairly unusual thing
for your average N.Y.U. student—or anyone else, for that
matter—to do.

After my confinement there was a period of bandages
and black and blueness, but the Grand Unwrapping, fraught
with fear, uncertainty, apprehension, anticipation, and
104   dread, turned out to be a rewarding event. IT really looked

nice—not delicately sculpted, to be sure, but the journey down my nose from bridge to tip was smooth and uneventful.

In the beginning I spent quite a bit of time, mirror in hand, admiring it in the medicine chest mirror or in the three-way folding one on my mother's dressing table, making up meaningful and flirtatious conversations, and I blessed the fine, sure, clean hand of Beverly's doctor. I guess in plastic surgery as in anything else, you win some, you lose some. I was thrilled. I knew I looked better, even good, and I enjoyed the newfound ease of flashing my profile proudly, head up, chin held high. But the complete transformation I yearned for in personality, approach to life, physical confidence, and social ease did not happen. There was no instant magic. The inside lagged behind the outside, and even at this late date it hasn't caught up. In many ways my innards have remained quite the same, and I am still trying to believe the picture I seem to present. There is a faint feeling of yes, it's a straight nose now, but isn't it a fraud, a phony? Does that make me a fraud, a phony? Now that I have gone public with my dark secret, will people who generously have said there is a hint of Garbo in my looks see instead a hint of Margaret Hamilton in *The Wizard of Oz*? You can separate the nose from the girl, but can you separate the girl from the nose? I am obviously still trying to.

At N.Y.U. I didn't get any better parts in the affiliated company, the Washington Square Players. And after graduation, out in the competitive real world, my new face did not bring me the deluge of wild offers I'd hoped for. ("Back! Back! All of you!") True, with typical, canny planning, I made my rounds of the producers' offices with two outrageously stunning friends and felt as much like the Dormouse as before. Nor was I deluged with men, men, men. ("Back! Back! All of you!") I guess somewhere inside lurks that frowning little girl clutching the rubber doll, not wanting to have her picture taken.

Despite these negative thoughts I believe I did a good thing by giving up looking "distinguished," and I recommend changing whatever makes you unhappy if you can and are willing to take a few risks. There was no miracle for me of a 105 completely transformed person, and the witch from my ballad about the homely girl from Surrey shire might have been a better witch than mine, but what happened did change my life. Just a couple of years later I was embarked on some kind of theater career, although the theater at first was a nightclub, and I got up to perform in front of people with more confidence than before. And around the same time I met a marvelous man who would think I was beautiful and would love me and marry me for life. There is no way to prove it, but I have to feel that my road would not have been the same without that scary hour under the ether that changed my face.

A number of years ago I was interviewed for some oral history project, and I remember being asked to list the people who have had the greatest influence on my life. I named my parents, my brother, my husband, my partner, and a very few terrific teachers. Then I named two girlfriends. One of them, Shirley, now called Lee, taught me four chords on the piano in the key of C and the key of F, which made it possible for me to write some of the numbers for our early nightclub act, the Revuers. The other was the girl called Beverly, who pestered me so endlessly about my nose. Thanks, Bev.

Not Quite
Woman of the Year

*L*ooking in a closet for a nice tray I could use for serving a few drinks, I came across a silver one that had writing on it proclaiming that it had been given to me by the Alumni Association of my college at N.Y.U. as part of a "distinguished alumni achievement award." I remembered the other part, a lovely bowl, but ungrateful alumna that I am, I had forgotten about the tray that went with it. I had always referred to that as my Woman of the Year award, but I realize I had glorified it a bit. Too many movies. Now, ten years later, I am about to receive, at this writing, New York University's Distinguished Alumna Award. One step closer to "W of the Y," the whole university, not just a college.

But what college had I graduated from? When I entered N.Y.U., I had not planned to graduate from the School of Nursing, but it seems that is what I did. Having enrolled in the Dramatic Arts Department, I was working toward a bachelor of arts in the School of Fine Arts down at Washington Square. Those grim gray palisades uptown at N.Y.U. in Washington Heights may have cast their shadow on the rippling Hudson and on a lot of young males, but not on any females. Girls—or women, as we are known today—were not admitted uptown, and I never set eyes on that lovely, leafy campus until graduation day.

In the School of Fine Arts I majored in dramatic arts 107

and English, with French, history, philosophy, and a few other electives thrown in, but was surprised to learn halfway through that my school had been transferred to the School of Education and I was now working toward a bachelor of science, which required me to take some education courses, mainly in teaching remedial speech. I rather missed the ring of "School of Fine Arts" and "bachelor of arts," having associated science with test tubes and retorts, ohms and amperes, which had given me some trouble in high school. Now I was working with darling kids with cleft palates who broke my heart, and striving to correct lateral emission, explosive plosives (p's and b's), and dentalized t's and d's on my way to a teaching license. Surely if I had gotten one, I would have fallen into the trap of becoming what I did not want to be, but some brute instinct led me to take two credits too few to qualify, thus sparing afflicted children the inept ministrations of an ungifted teacher.

My mother had a moment or two of thinking it was rash of me to cut away the safety net of a teaching career, but she rallied. In fact, it was she who suggested the dramatic arts program when Barnard didn't want me, and she never wavered in her support of even the strangest things I wound up doing, like going home by subway at three o'clock in the morning after working in a Greenwich Village nightclub. At any rate, I graduated from the respectable School of Education, or so I thought. Nearly thirty years later, I received a letter from SEHNAP—a group? a school? a pill?—at N.Y.U., which wanted to hail me as a successfully functioning alumna. It turned out that the Dramatic Arts Department had been shifted over to, or rather was under the motherly umbrella of, the School of Education, Health, Nursing, and Arts Professions—hence, SEHNAP.

It wasn't easy to get teary-eyed from nostalgia with the other old grads over this acronym, but of course I was happy to be honored as long as it did not entail taking any nursing courses. I had had my one taste of that in high school where, at Erasmus Hall, one term of nursing was a requisite for graduation. We learned how to make a bed with a patient in it, working with a dummy that was either called Olive Oyl or just

108

looked like Popeye's lady love, long and skinny, with a tangled topknot glued to her skull. Luckily, we never got to work with a real live girl or fellow, especially when we were learning how to give a sponge bath in bed. I have since been the recipient of expert and kindly care from professional nurses who have dotted my life, and I respect and admire their skill and am indebted to them for their expertise and warmth. I am proud to have my dramatic arts and me lumped together with them under one banner from here to eternity, unless they decide to move my department yet another time—to the School of Agriculture, perhaps.

The event honoring me was a curious mixture of elements. David Oppenheim, dean of the Tisch School of the Performing Arts and a longtime friend of mine, said some lovely things about me, although he was not from SEHNAP. The Tisch now covers all the functions of a performing arts school curriculum, preparing students for active life in the theater and encompassing everything we had had in the little old dramatic arts department of bygone days, whereas SEHNAP—or, at any rate, the AP (or Arts Professions) part of it—trains people mainly to teach theater and to run and administer theater, theater education, and music programs.

Also present, in addition to Dean Oppenheim, was Marian Primont, the radiant redhaired actress who had acted with the Washington Square Players while I was still in school and who joined the faculty years later. She remembered me as a substitute Third Witch in *Macbeth,* from the old days when she would come down to take part in the productions, a gorgeous Rosalind, Viola, and Portia. This group, connected with the Dramatic Arts Department, rehearsed and played in the seventh-floor auditorium of the Administration Building, recruiting the best of the students to act in the classics—Shakespeare, Shaw, and Sheridan—and inviting certain professionals as guest artists: Margaret Wycherly as Lady Macbeth; Whitford Kane as the gravedigger in *Hamlet,* a role he played with many of the great Hamlets; and actor-comedian Hiram Sherman, a terrific Bottom in A *Midsummer Night's Dream.*

The director of this company, and head of the school 109

as well, was Professor Randolph Somerville. An actor himself, he inspired the whole department with his great knowledge and almost missionary zeal. The courses were enthralling to me; acting, voice, mise-en-scène, fencing, history of the theater, folk song, makeup, and Shakespeare combined with a liberal arts program.

Our acting class was made up of all girls except for two men, one of them Herb, so incredibly handsome I could hardly focus my sixteen-year-old eyes on him. Our teacher, John Koch, paper-thin and bony, resembled Gielgud a little and was most exacting. To train our ear, he started by giving us a reading of the sentence "Do you see that bee?" The word *bee* started high up on the scale and swooped down about a fifth at the end. You were treated with patient tolerance if you started at the bottom and emphasized the word *bee* by flipping it up. He then taught us how to sit down on a chair onstage: You walked until you were facing the chair, stepped with one foot slightly under it, then pivoted gracefully on both feet until you were turned around and your backside was in place to be lowered into the waiting seat without bending your back or looking at the floor. And there were rules about gesture: "Always gesture with the upstage hand so you won't hide your body from the audience."

I remember going uptown to see the great Gielgud in *Hamlet,* appearing at the same time as Maurice Evans in the same play on another street, and whispering to a classmate in shock: "Look! He used his downstage hand!" How come he was so brilliant in the part? On the day we had fencing, the yells of *"en garde,"* "lunge," and "parry prime" rang through the seventh-floor halls. That floor was our headquarters, and visitors from other planets would often be startled to see what appeared to be an ancient figure with a hideously wrinkled face and long gray beard come bouncing out of the ladies' room on its way back to makeup class.

I took extra voice lessons from a young man who had finished school and came back to do some tutoring and to work with the Washington Square Players. He tried to get me to find my fundamental tone, and I believe I am still looking for it. He took me out a couple of times and gave me a little

110

red leather–bound copy of *Henry V,* along with a lovely poem he had written comparing his crossing under the East River by subway to get to Brooklyn to Leander swimming the Hellespont to be with his Hero. He is now a well-known critic, and I dare not reveal his name because he might have to review something of mine one day and, well, you know how it is, dredging up racy stuff from over fifty years ago. . . . My lips are sealed. He knows who he is. I nearly fainted every time he arranged for me to read for the professor. Somerville was formidable: tall, with tufts of reddish hair framing a balding head, penetrating eyes under reddish tortoise-shell glasses, and an intimidating mien. I always lost my fundamental tone completely when I read for him, and it is no wonder I never got much further in the Washington Square Players than minor parts.

I went off to college every morning on the IRT subway. I recall I once told Groucho Marx a fact about those days, which for some reason he relished: I would stand on the subway, which was always jammed, with my stomach sticking out, cradling my books against it, trying to look pregnant so someone would get up and give me a seat. Ah, those were gentler times. It would never work today. (As I recall, it rarely worked then.) One late afternoon riding wearily home I looked down the row of straphangers, and there was the Incomparable Herb, hanging a few straps away! A spasm of anxiety shook me. Would he acknowledge my presence or not? I dared not hope for either, but he made his way down to me while I tried to look not pregnant but winsomely desirable. Then, oh miracle of miracles, he got out at my station! He lived a block away from me in the new, big, swell apartment house on the corner! He asked me if I'd like to come over later and listen to some new records, to which I replied as casually as I could that I'd see, then dashed over there right after gulping what we called supper. He had some new Duke Ellington records. And even though he told me he had just had a fight with his girlfriend and was lonely (they made up, of course, and eventually married) and we never shared another evening, I'll always remember hearing that wonderful Ellington tune, "As Long as I Live," for the first time while looking 111 at his beautiful face. He never looked ugly, even as an old man in makeup class. He would have aged well, I know, but sadly he died young, after a successful career in children's television.

Our mime class was presided over by Professor Mitchell, a huge man with John L. Lewis eyebrows and a deep voice. Demonstrating how simple it was to arouse emotion by summoning up something sad, he would close his eyes, murmur to himself, *"Absalom, mon fils, mon fils, Absalom,"* and tears would course down his mountainous cheeks. I would try to think of something sad, like never dating Herb, but it didn't work. He would exhort us to "come alive!" in acting. He said, "Just before you go onstage, bang your wrist on the proscenium." I tried it. I came alive all right. It hurt like hell, and I went on biting back my tears.

The professor's wife, Jocelyn, birdlike with big, staring eyes, and Wallace House, a gentle, talented man, taught us folksinging. Each of us had to buy a cheap guitar and learn the three basic chords in the key of C, to which we added two or three more as our skill improved. We accompanied ourselves singing songs of all nations, in all languages, memorizing the words phonetically but never really learning what we were singing about. I remember an Italian air about a girl who didn't want to marry a shoemaker, and a Russian one about Dunya, who was being urged to do something or other, I'm not clear what. There was even a song in Finnish.

The folk song group headed by Mrs. Mitchell and Mr. House had a full repertoire they performed in concert, and we were encouraged to learn those songs and seek others in songbooks in the library and bring them in to sing for the class. The performing technique seemed to involve lots of arched eyebrows and knowing smiles, as if the contents were in some way vaguely suggestive of hijinks of a hilarious nature, possibly involving sex.

Professor Somerville required us to take elements of stage design, and I think I can still draw a floor plan and make an elevation from it. And a year of logic was required to try to get us to think clearly. A good idea, no matter what field 112 you might wind up in. I think I can still construct a syllogism:

at least I know one when I see one. By the time I was in my junior year I had added to my repertoire at the Washington Square Players the Third Witch in *Macbeth* and the Gentlewoman in the same play, and nearly got a shot at the Player Queen in *Hamlet.* I was not exactly a star. In class it was Sibyl in *Private Lives*—oh, never the glamorous Amanda—and in makeup class a growing proficiency in making crepe-hair beards, an essential for Third Witch.

And there was Shakespeare! Shakespeare! Shakespeare! Professor Somerville read the plays aloud to us, and in the evenings there were the performances by the Washington Square Players of many of the plays in repertory. Whatever disappointment I may have felt originally at not going to an out-of-town college, like my brother, who was premed at Cornell, I quickly realized I was delighted to be right here in The Big City. The theater was here. My friend and classmate Janet and I bought standing room as often as we could and thrilled to the D'Oyly Carte Company night after night in every possible Gilbert and Sullivan operetta, and later to all three programs of Noël Coward and Gertrude Lawrence in *Tonight at 8:30.* And sometimes we would sneak off to see the explosive, thrilling work of the recently formed Group Theatre under the leadership of Harold Clurman. *Waiting for Lefty* and *Awake and Sing* excited us, but, loyal to our classical education, we felt the thrill of guilt as well, like a Catholic reading books in the Index.

Looking back, I am glad Barnard turned me down. I would never have received the beautiful silver bowl and tray SEHNAP gave me. But before it was placed in my hands came the finale, a piece of entertainment put together in my honor that baffles me to this day. A group of Irish girls from the organization dedicated to the preservation of Gaelic appeared in traditional costume—white blouses, full skirts, embroidered vests, and flower circlets adorning their plaited hair —and sang ancient Gaelic songs, followed by clog dances that they performed charmingly. While I was pondering the relevance of this sweet entertainment to my definitely non-Celtic background, they clogged their way into the climax, a group rendition of "Singin' in the Rain" performed to the 113 accompaniment of an instrumental recording that sounded as if it had been waxed just shortly after Edison had made his landmark discovery. I was both pleased and puzzled. In accepting the bowl, I thanked my lovely Hibernian serenaders and then tried to sum up what my education at the School of Fine Arts–School of Education–School of Education, Health, Nursing, and Arts Professions had meant to me. I said I thought I had received splendid preparation for whatever I wound up doing. I had studied the classics, and the classics provided one with high standards. The emphasis had been on Shakespeare, Shaw, and Sheridan. What better background can one have? And maybe the Gaelic entertainment was relevant after all: Two of those classic playwrights were Irish. In keeping with the spirit of the occasion, I sang the Finnish song I remembered from folk song class, and then we all went out for a Chinese dinner.

Scenes from
One Couple's Marriage

Steve said I looked like a big doll, lying there with my red cheeks and my stiff, black, false eyelashes. There was not enough time between shows at the Village Vanguard where I was performing to take my makeup off and get it back on. What time we had was spent dashing around the corner to my cousin's apartment, slipping me out of my costume, losing ourselves in each other, then back into the costume and back to the Vanguard. Love was on the run throughout a great deal of our courtship, and when we married, I was working in a nightclub that had a two o'clock show, from which I got home around four. And Steve, an artist, was managing his father's underwear factory in Queens, where, in order to unlock the doors by 8:00 A.M., he had to leave the house by 7:00. To one degree or another our whole marriage was something like that. Yet when he died in 1979, Steve and I had been married thirty-seven loving years. Am I sagely giving the recipe for a successful marriage? It was successful for us, that is all I can say. I wouldn't necessarily advise any other two people to try it.

We met on the tennis court at my grandfather's house in Hunter. It was Labor Day. I had spent July and August at a summer theater connected with N.Y.U. and was making my annual visit to the place I had once spent every vacation since babyhood. While doing walk-ons in Shakespeare on the 115 lawn of Hofstra College in Hempstead, I had been bombarded by letters from my cousins Muriel and Inez, still loyal to Hunter, about this incredible-looking guy who had been coming over for tennis. My brother Nat had run into a high school friend on the main street and had invited him to play. The friend explained that he had a bunch of cousins in a family enclave past the opposite end of town from where we were, and they all played tennis. Five of them came. When I walked on the court that day, The One was there, hammering staples into the tape that was used to line a tennis court in those days. He was everything they had promised. We met. There was an informal family party at their end of town that weekend. I went. So did he. I wore the wrong dress. Nothing happened.

The following year my brother's friend, the cousin of The One, turned up at our New York apartment with a few of his cousins, and there he was again. I had the incredible nerve to issue an invitation to all to come see me in an excruciatingly bad play I was performing in with a group of hopefuls, in which I played an eleven-year-old girl who became pregnant. My brother told me later that they all came, including The One, but they all drifted away into the sweltering night before it was over and I never heard a word from him.

During that summer while I was away at a theater in East Hampton, something told me to pursue. Heaven knows I was not being pursued. I wrote to him, telling him I had not really committed suicide at the end of the play but had merely jumped offstage into a pile of mattresses. My smart, funny, adorable letter elicited no reply. That Labor Day weekend I again made my pilgrimage to Hunter, and there he was. And then it happened. We had a date. We went to a roadhouse on a country road and danced and drank applejack. I had never met anyone as beautiful in all my life: tall, black hair, hazel-gray eyes, incandescent smile, and a surreal sense of humor. I tried to find some poetic description in Shakespeare that would do him justice, but none came close.

There was some mix-up the next day when he and his family left for New York City, and he didn't come to say good-116 bye as arranged. I felt a message was getting through to me, so I went to a Columbia-Army football game in a chilly rain with someone not nearly as beautiful and came down with severe bronchial pneumonia that put me to bed for several weeks. I did not know until later that he had called many times during this period but was told I was too sick to talk. He thought I did not want to see him. A misunderstanding. But, dear children, it all got straightened out, and on January 4, 1942, a brief three and a half years or so later, we were married.

He was an artist, and when we first met he had been studying at the Art Students' League, but then he had to help out, and later run, his father's business, as noted previously. By then there was a war on, as we used to say, and six months after our wedding, he was drafted while I was working in a club with the group, the Revuers. At the beginning he was stationed in the East, so we got to see each other, and I learned how to make shoulder pads for my handsome soldier-husband's rifle practice. He was transferred to San Francisco, and then, by a wild stroke of luck, he was moved to the desert south of Los Angeles just as our act got an engagement in the desert that *was* Los Angeles. We were able to be together from time to time when he was on furlough.

One weekend when he was stationed in Indio, deep in the desert, he called me to see if I could meet him halfway in Palm Springs. He was in the Engineers. Army personnel were not supposed to be stationed there for very long periods of time because it was unbearably hot, 140 degrees, and nothing but a truck to crawl under to get a few inches of shade. But he was so good at what he was doing, teaching camouflage to army personnel going off to the North African campaign, that they kept him there a long, long time. It was September and I thought Hollywood was hot when I got on the bus, but when I got out at Palm Springs, the air hit my face like a mat of steaming cotton batting. Gasping for air, I squinted around and saw loping toward me my adored sergeant, purple-faced with sun exposure, grinning, and yelling, "Hey, isn't this great! It's so cool up here!"

We were separated often and for long periods of time, and he was in the army for four years. It was a heart- 117 wrenching time brimming with anxiety and worry—waiting for letters, desperate when there were delays, periods of black-outs, secrecy, and unremitting loneliness.

I wrote to Steve every day, and he wrote as often as he could. Along with everyone else I wore tan leg makeup as I adjusted to not having nylons, sugar, shoes, and meat. There were blackouts at night whenever there were air-raid drills announced by frightening sirens. The New York streets teemed with servicemen on leave or just ready to embark. Sometimes I'd think I saw him in the crowd, and even though I knew better, I'd run and look.

At one point when I was visiting him at Fort Belvoir, Virginia, we discussed my becoming an army wife and living with him wherever he was stationed. He wouldn't hear of it. He knew it would be a horror for both of us and that the ache of separation was something we would just have to endure until the world came to its senses and the conflict was over. Later, when he got out of the army, we faced the other con-flict—between my work and his work—and how to manage our lives, individually and together.

He came back from overseas with a bad spinal disk problem. I had rented a new apartment with an elevator be-cause our old walk-up was too difficult for him to maneuver, but when we moved in, the elevator wasn't working. In fact, nothing worked quite the way I would have liked it to. I had hoped he would resume a life of art in some way, but the war had removed his interest and he no longer felt the desire. Steve was very gifted, as I would see from work he had done before he met me.

Walter Chrysler, Jr., had admired what he did and had sponsored a caricature show, of which I have only the brochure but none of the drawings. Chrysler also commis-sioned him to do portraits of his horses. Steve had an extraor-dinary sense of color, something like perfect pitch. He could look at a color and match it exactly without having a sample with which to compare it. He had a strong sense of composi-tion, and . . . well, he was through with it, and too bad.

With my closest friend, Janet, and her husband we started a business called Americraft that employed artists and craftsmen, all of whom were veterans. It was both store and workshop, with beautiful silver jewelry and leather things made at worktables right in the store itself. I took some time off to help get things started, then economics prodded us and I was off to Hollywood to do a movie. Thus the years of wrenching good-byes and ecstatic reunions continued. Having a business partner, Steve was able to have some time away from New York and be with me out of town with a show or out on the West Coast. A lot of pain and a lot of joy. No children yet.

A mere eight years after we were married we had a baby daughter, Susanna, born beautiful with long black hair and huge dark eyes. My plan had been to have an instant family: twins born with a three-year age difference, but I was told that was not possible. Three and a half years later came Alan, looking like a pixie and instantly funny and odd. I used up a whole living-room floor of our house for my work, meaning that most of the time that part was out of bounds for everyone else. I realized that my kids did not come home to the smell of Mommy's freshly baked bread but to the click-click of Mommy's typewriter in a house where they were always being reminded: "Sshh, Mommy's working." Later we moved to a bigger house, and Mommy had a workroom. The separations continued, and there were reunions on the coast or in a Boston hotel, or I came in for weekends.

Whatever unconditional love is, we seemed to have it. Steve admired what I did and knew what a life like mine entailed, and managed to live with it. But at all times he retained a strong sense of who he was and was his own man. We were deeply, closely happy with each other and about each other. Sometimes I think that such a closed corporation makes it harder for children to have their own full place. When asked how I managed my life, "having it all" (to use the expression that later flowered with the women's movement), I used to say somewhat vaguely that there were problems which never got solved that you just had to live with. Whatever that means.

Two months before Susanna's first birthday I had to go out to MGM with Adolph to write what became *Singin' in* 119 *the Rain.* I rented a house, and the plan was that as soon as he could Steve would come out with the baby and her nurse, a certain Miss Van Vlack, who had worked for some of the "best" families and periodically let me know it with a loud sniff. They arrived, and the next day we had Susanna's party. She looked enchanting in her pink-and-white dress, going from one to the other of us, crawling and poking about inquisitively. My mother, Steve, Adolph, and I were having coffee with our birthday cake, and Miss Van Vlack excused herself to have a little nap. Susanna was just at the point when she was about to walk and loved to pull herself up to a standing position to see what was on top of things. Suddenly she stood up by grabbing hold of the table, and a cup of scalding hot coffee toppled down all over her body. She screamed and kept screaming. We tried to get her clothes off, but they were sticking to her skin. She was in agony. In horror I called the one person I could think of who would know the right doctor: Lee, Mrs. Ira Gershwin.

The doctor came quickly, but the poor baby never stopped screaming and relief came only when he gave her an injection, making her instantly quiet, no longer in pain. He gently removed the clothes, revealing that she was burned from her neck to her legs. We wrapped her up and took her to the hospital where she had to stay for ten days with her little arms strapped down. She was behind a glass-topped door, through which we could see her from the hall but were not allowed to enter. We visited and tried to make contact through the door as often as they would let us. It was a nightmare. We had all been right there, just inches away from her, yet it had happened.

At the hospital I became known as the mother of the little girl who whistled. At a very early age Susanna had somehow mastered the art of whistling, twisting her puckered little lips to one side and producing a flutelike sound. It was very funny to see, and she amazed and amused the hospital staff while her agonized parents pressed their faces against the glass door.

Finally she was healed enough to come home. The burn covered a large area, but there was only one severe spot

120

just below her ribs and over the years the keloid scar about the size of a silver dollar faded away. All through her childhood it added to her self-consciousness. When we got home, she recuperated swiftly, but the child who was on the brink of walking didn't want to. She kept crawling. I should have understood that having had such a trauma she would be most fearful of being adventurous or curious about anything. Yet, as she kept crawling, I felt impatience rise and was unhappy that while most kids her age were walking, she was not. She would sit for hours contentedly bouncing up and down in a little canvas swing. Although she could not walk, she got around on the ground at an alarming rate, zipping across rooms and lawns with one knee bent, pushing herself along like a diminutive human scooter. Why was I so anxious to have her walk, knowing what she had been through? I'm sure my disappointment communicated itself to her in some way.

By the time she was two, she was walking. One of her favorite pastimes was listening to records. The most often played were *Tubby the Tuba,* the Mozart G Minor Symphony, and her favorite, *Peter and the Wolf.* She played it over and over. One day when it was on, I paused for a moment in her doorway, watching her busy with her dolls. The narrator on the record got to the point where he said, "Just then, some hunters came out of the forest." I heard Susanna say quietly, "And some didn't." Soon this statement became folklore among family and friends, so much so that when Leonard Bernstein was making a recording of *Peter and the Wolf* and got to the part where the hunters come out of the forest, he stopped, peered at the text, and asked, "Where's 'And some didn't'?"

Susanna's imaginary friend, Mrs. Lionface Burdsgurds, visited her often and perhaps helped her start making little books for Steve on his birthdays. They were colorful, beautifully drawn pictures of Steve as a small boy, always in a sailor suit because I told her one of my first dates with Steve was a masquerade for which he dressed as a sailor. They were stories in which he had different adventures, struggling to give up smoking or walking our dog Paris, and were done cartoon-style with the dialogue in balloons over the charac- 121 ters' heads. She was an imaginative, very bright, and witty child, but she was timid and unsure of herself. What did not help this condition was the arrival of her brother Alan.

Susanna and he did not get along. They fought. Since my brother and I had always had a close relationship and to the best of my recollection never fought (his recollection, too), it seemed logical to me that my children would feel the same way about each other. Dope. No doubt my mother worked skillfully to see to it that my brother and I liked each other, and I just expected it to be that way and was chagrined and appalled when I saw the rivalry and the sometimes bitter fighting. But I was protected. Steve and Tillie, our children's nurse, did not tell me half of what went on, and I was—more often than not—not there to see it. They did not want to bother me because "Mommy was working."

When Susanna broke her arm, I was not told about it and did not know until I came home weeks later. I was terribly upset. I told Susanna that had I known I would have flown right in from wherever the hell I was, but I doubt if she believed me. It was hard for her not to know whether or not I would be around when she wanted me. Today we happily remember the lovely times we did have together. I was not great at sitting in the playground for more than an hour, but I read to her a lot and, at bedtime, sang to her whatever favorites she requested, from the Nightmare Song from *Iolanthe* to "Neverland" from *Peter Pan.*

When she was about two and a half, I took her to the theater where a show of Adolph's and mine was running to watch the last few minutes from the back, trying perhaps to illustrate what "Mommy's working" meant. Thus far she had only listened to records. She was dazzled by what she saw and heard. When the curtain came down and the conductor started the exit music, she struggled out of my arms, ran down the aisle, tapped him on the shoulder, and said to him, "Put it on again." That was such fun for me, but the everyday problems that came up bewildered me. I felt there was some secret formula of child-rearing that I could never discover.

Susanna began to feel the competition with Alan, and 122 it hurt her. (I know that kind of pain in a small way. I performed for many years next to the blond, brilliant Judy Holliday.) Alan was willful and hard to handle, but remained ever charming. When asked once what he wanted to be when he grew up, he said, "I'm going to be a nonconformist just like everybody else."

He was a brilliantly gifted artist. I have a great pen-and-ink drawing he did at eleven of a Beatles' audience of hundreds of wildly ecstatic faces and bodies and arms and a couple of brassieres thrown up onto the stage. Al Hirschfeld, our neighbor, marveled at his work. Alan received a lot of praise and admiration, and his future looked bright.

But the light began to fade as Alan began his tragic descent into addiction. Yet through it all, the loving closeness Steve and I felt for each other never diminished. I loved so many things about him that were different from me. He had a real gift for living, for enjoying himself. He had an "up" approach to life in contrast to my "down" attitude. I worried a lot. Even in my relaxed facial expression, all the lines pointed down rather than up. Sometimes my children would ask me anxiously, "Is anything wrong, Mom?" Surprised, I would say, "No. Why?" And they would tell me I looked as if I were angry and displeased about something. I must say I remember that expression on my mother's face.

Steve never looked like that. He had wonderful outlets for his feelings. He was a fine tennis player and played often and well. And he was a skillful gambler and loved it. A very high stakes poker game went on over the years with a group of friends in a much higher financial echelon than we were, but by the end of the year Steve usually came out far ahead, with lots of extra winnings. The poker game, a rotating one, was sometimes held at our house. The children would say good night to the players around the table, and then the next morning when the kids got up, the group might well still be there to wish them good morning as they trooped off to school.

Americraft remained a modest enterprise, and at one point when I was going to the coast so often, we discussed opening a branch in California, but that never came to pass. As time went on it became more and more apparent that we 123 would continue to be dependent on what I, in my more lucrative field, could bring in. There were tensions, of course, and fights, but there was a kind of resignation, a realization that the financial pressures combined with my undeniable desire and need for work would continue to shape the pattern of our lives. Steve loved what I did, and admired it, and always wanted me to go on with my work. He was always there for me to discuss my work with, and his judgment was perceptive, creative, and helpful. That was the man I was married to.

The other factor in our marriage was the man I was *not* married to, my partner Adolph. The fact that I worked with a man caused confusions and questions, I know, in the minds of many who viewed our lives from the outside. But to the three of us, everything was perfectly clear. Many people thought Adolph and I were married to each other. They still do even though by now he has been married to Phyllis Newman for more than thirty years. Confusion still reigns. I always say as long as we are not confused, everything is all right.

Of course, it was not easy, my being with Adolph so much of the time and having him so woven into our lives, but somehow we managed. Steve was secure in the knowledge that it never was or could be a romantic complication. It has been every other kind of complication.

Steve won his first bout with pancreatitis but not the second. One evening in September 1979, Steve and I were having dinner with our old and true friend Tom Guinzburg and a new girlfriend of his. We were such close friends at that time that when we rented summer places in the country, we would always ask each other, "Which should be Tom's room?" That night we had a delicious but heavy dinner with a large amount of wine. Tom's daughter and a class friend of hers were interested in the Maharishi, the guru of Beatles' fame, and after learning from his daughter that the Maharishi would be at Carnegie Hall the next day, Tom wanted to see what he was like, and we all decided to go. Steve was not feeling well, and no wonder.

Earlier that day we had gone to an overelaborate bar
124 mitzvah of a friend's son, followed by a monster lunch at a

Madison Avenue restaurant that to this day I cannot pass without feeling angry. Steve and I were upset because the boy's mother, a lovely woman and tennis friend who had died a short time before, had not even been mentioned. I was not happy watching Steve eat some rich dish *en croûte* in the middle of the day, knowing we were to dine later with Tom.

The morning dawned unseasonably hot and sticky. Tom called to say he and his girlfriend had decided not to go, and we agreed. But as the time for the event neared, I told Steve I was curious and wanted to see the famous guru but that he should stay in and rest. To my surprise he wanted to go, and even though I could see he was not feeling terrific, I could not persuade him to stay home. At Carnegie Hall there was a mob around the doors, but the girl we knew pulled us inside and there we sat among the faithful. The dark-skinned, long-haired, rather wonderful-looking man came out, and I found it hard to follow exactly what he said or why it was inspirational. But when it ended, our friend encouraged us to go backstage where the guru was receiving. She said the most meaningful experience was to meet him, and perhaps his touch would make Steve feel better.

In the Green Room we joined a group sitting in a circle on the floor. The Maharishi spoke to each one individually. Someone had told him about Steve, and he put his hands on Steve's brow. We tried to savor the "meaningful experience," but it was hot and stuffy and I knew we should never have come. Why did we? Why didn't we leave and just go home? These questions still haunt me. I am in no way denigrating the Maharishi, a holy man who has helped many. It is not his fault that what ensued was pure disaster for us. We got into a cab, and it was still warm and muggy. I dropped Steve off at our house and went on my accustomed weekly visit to my very old aunt Rose, living alone. But as soon as I arrived, something told me to go right home to Steve. When I got there, he looked very gray and was in pain, and I knew it was another attack of pancreatitis. But it was Yom Kippur Eve, and I could not get a doctor who knew his case, a situation that persisted all through the night. They were all at temple. I got Steve to the emergency room and kept trying to get his 125 doctor or any of the ones who had treated him the last time and would recognize his condition, but all in vain. Years later one of the doctors, who had transferred to another hospital, told me he had gotten my message on his machine but in my frantic state I had forgotten to leave my unlisted number, and he could not call me back.

Susanna joined me at the hospital where they took forever testing Steve and asking questions. A nice young doctor who was substituting for others who were at the Yom Kippur service finally came, but he, too, did not recognize what was wrong. The intensive care unit where Steve should have been was full, and again, although I know some of the people in charge, even the president, I could not reach them. Steve was put in a room with three others and was very, very sick. Susanna and I spent the night there curled up on the floor, watching and calling floor nurses when we thought something looked worse than it had been.

Seventeen days later Steve was dead. If he had been in intensive care, would that have made a difference? If it had not been Yom Kippur, would that have changed everything? The questions still persist. At one point I asked Leonard Bernstein's doctor, Kevin Cahill, if he would come and evaluate the care Steve was receiving. He very carefully examined the records and observed him, and told me all that could be done was being done.

As people gathered at the funeral, Cy Coleman played Steve's favorite show tunes, and Lenny, Adolph, Tom Guinzburg, and Cousin Muriel spoke. Betty Bacall read a poem, Isaac Stern played, and Tillie, by then our housekeeper, cook, and a member of the family, radiantly affirmed her faith by telling us that she loved Mr. Kyle and knew she would surely see him again. Our close friend Sidney Bernstein, head of Granada Television in England, arranged to have a beautiful book printed for me to have and distribute, preserving all the loving, sometimes funny words spoken that day, and noting everyone who participated. A friend at *The New York Times,* Arthur Gelb, asked me for a picture of Steve and had it published along with the obituary notice.

126   I remember Joe Fox, an old friend who for years had

invited us to the tennis quarter finals at Forest Hills, telling me what a heart-stopping shock he had while having coffee outside Fouquet's in the bright Paris sunlight, opening the *International Herald-Tribune* and seeing Steve's face on that dark page.

As arranged, people came back to our house from the service, but not long after, they drifted off gradually to continue their own lives. And I was left to continue mine —alone.

From my long, long years of experience I have no thoughtful, wise, helpful things to say about marriage in general. I wish I did, but I know only about one couple's marriage. I said earlier that it worked, it was successful for us, but I wouldn't advise any other two people to try it. Maybe I should say I would not advise any other *three* people to try it.

Numbers . . .
My Friends
(Old, Hot, and True)

With Adolph Green.
We started our
friendship and
working partnership
in 1938, and are still
at it.

HANS NAMUTH

For Betty
with Love
on our 25th
Phyllis
Adolph

Opposite, top to bottom:

Adolph Green with his beautiful wife Phyllis, the best thing that ever happened to him.

Lenny and his lovely, elegant wife, Felicia, staring adoringly at each other outside their country house in Fairfield, Connecticut. Death came much too early for both of them.

With Leonard Bernstein, at some event or other. Our never-ending closeness began in 1939. He was a genius at friendship as well as everything else.

With Lenny in Salzburg, where he was conducting. He wrote on this picture "Dearest Betty, Can you show me (in Braille) the road to Salzburg? Love, Lenny."

This page, top to bottom:

Lauren Bacall (Betty) with her son, Stephen Bogart, snapped at a birthday party for Susanna (down the row), back of one of those houses I rented in Beverly Hills while out there doing a movie.

Bacall posing on the tennis court at our rented summer house in Ossining. She could play, too.

Years later, Betty Bacall and this Betty, happy that our friendship survived the experience of working together.

James Jones with his wife Gloria, a couple fiercely loyal to each other, and to their friends. From their wedding day in Haiti on, we remained close, and now, alone without our husbands, Gloria and I cling.

Penelope Gilliatt, brilliant eccentric writer and splendid friend, with her daughter Nolan, visiting Steve and me in the country. One of the few moments she wasn't writing something.

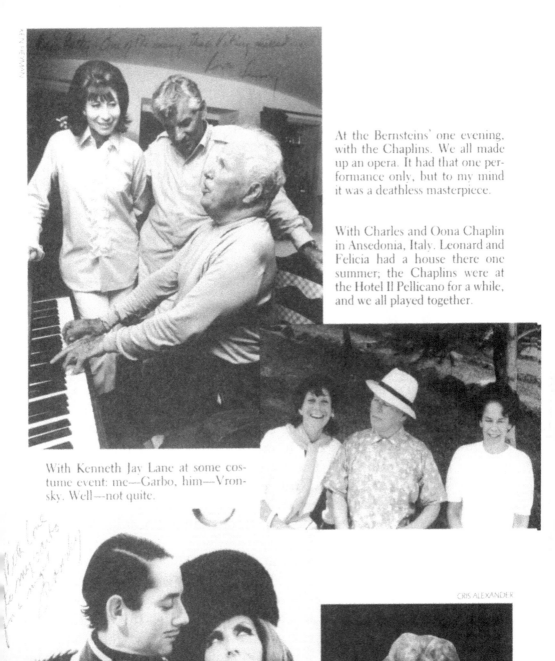

At the Bernsteins' one evening, with the Chaplins. We all made up an opera. It had that one performance only, but to my mind it was a deathless masterpiece.

With Charles and Oona Chaplin in Ansedonia, Italy. Leonard and Felicia had a house there one summer; the Chaplins were at the Hotel Il Pellicano for a while, and we all played together.

With Kenneth Jay Lane at some costume event: me—Garbo, him—Vronsky. Well—not quite.

CRIS ALEXANDER

I know it is only the wizardry of Cris Alexander and his camera transforming workaday me into that goddess Garbo, but I can't help loving this picture. I also know it is presumptuous of me to include her in a section about my friends, but, after all, I did meet her once.

The Adolph Green Story:
Now It Can Be Told

*M*yth hath it that Pallas Athena was not born like any of your everyday gods or goddesses; she sprang, they say as they accompany themselves on the lyre, full-blown from the head of Zeus. The mythic character in my life, my partner Adolph Green, it seems to me must have sprung full-blown from his own head. There is no other head quite capable of having done the job. Only his head has the antic, manic imagination and offbeat creative erudite-plus childlike originality to conceive of such a person. I can just hear his head making him up:

"How's about I jump out like this . . . tall, blond, bland, grand, and NAH!" The head shakes with fierce rejection. "How's about medium, dark, Hungarian, with a Hapsburg jaw and lots of assorted teeth . . . and I'll study music and literature and the cinema and . . . NAH!" Again the head shakes violently. "I'll just absorb it all, sort of osmosis-wise, simply by listening and reading and watching and just being, and I'll store it all away in here along with stuff like the succession of the heavyweight boxing champions of the world, the famous old Yankee lineup, the great comic strips, and vaudeville acts and songs like 'I Wish That I Was Born in Borneo' (I'll store that right next to Satie's "Gymnopédies"), and my body will be like Michelangelo's David and"—the head snorts dismissively—"NAH! Who needs it? . . . It will be spare and strong with a well-turned leg—two of them, in fact—and they will be able to lift me into the air to great heights like Nureyev, and I will have an easy rhythmic saunter like—dare I say it? What the hell!—like Astaire, so that some critic one day will write of me, 'A dancer of rare comedic grace,' and somewhere early on I'll meet a girl, and we will be on the same wavelength and will have a big career together with nary a thought of romance, let alone marriage. And I'll have a voice like Placido, and . . . NAH! PLEASE! but it will be loud, very loud, but sometimes surprisingly tender and good on ballads, and I'll know acres and acres of poetry and miles and miles and miles of art, and I'll know every piece of music ever written, and I'll be able to sing it, replicating a full orchestra if need be, and I'll know the director and stars and cast, down to the last extra, of every movie ever made. And, listen, so I may get depressed once in a while *(once in a while!!!????)*, but here comes the best part: I'll be funny. I'll be able to make people laugh. I'll be witty. I'll say things in an unexpected way, spontaneously juxtaposing odd thoughts and words, giving them a kind of surreal twist, and . . . and . . . NAH! that's not the best part. The best part is I'll marry the most beautiful, gifted girl in Jersey City and all the rest of the world and have two smashing children, one who'll graduate from Harvard and one from Brown. And WOW! No one will believe such a creature could exist, but I *will!!!!* I *will!!!!!* Here I come, ready or not!!!!!!!!!!"

(Stage direction: He springs full-blown from his own head.)

I have written about Adolph before, and it is always a tough assignment trying to get it just right. I have said that when I first met him he was "fat, unkempt, and wore his galoshes rain or shine. Now trim and slender, he is the picture of sartorial elegance. Whereas the line 'Where did you get that suit? Adolph Green's tailor?' was once said with a guffaw of derision, it is now pronounced with hushed, respectful awe." And another time, quite a while ago, I wrote, "Adolph is a man who reads while crossing streets. It is no uncommon sight to see him weaving his way across Broadway at Forty-fifth Street in the crush of matinee traffic, all the daily papers 135 bunched under one arm, the *Saturday Review, Atlantic Monthly, Life,* and *Paris-Match* slipping from under the other, an ash-trailing cigarette drooping from his lips, head deep in some book or periodical as brakes screech and drivers swear. Oblivious, he shuffles across engaged in leisurely perusal of anything from *A Skeleton Key to Finnegans Wake* to this week's grosses in *Variety."* The British had better look to their laurels and even their Hardys. Adolph Green gives new meaning to the word *eccentric.*

It is harder to write about him now because time is being mean to him. It is tough to imagine anyone or anything that would be willfully mean to Adolph, but his vision is degenerating: he can barely see and he cannot read. It breaks my heart. I have a feeling, though, that the power of that extraordinary mind inside the head that (I stand by my theory) invented him will pull him up again into a Nijinsky-like leap and that hitting the ozone up there will clear his eyes up, and he'll be, as we used to say, back at the old fruit stand. To quote from an early essay in my A.G. collection: "A long time ago deep in dreamland at 3:00 A.M. my dear husband Steve, now gone, and I were apt to receive a phone call and sleepily make out Adolph's voice murmuring in shocked surprise, 'Oh . . . you're asleep,' followed by 'My God, is it *that* late? Well . . . then . . . I won't . . .' He was forlornly wandering the city to pass the hours till morn in search of a welcoming candle in the window. A lonely man. Eventually we would be sure to sigh and say, 'Come on over.' " At least he is not alone now. He has Phyllis. Adolph married actress/singer/writer Phyllis Newman in 1960. In addition to her smashing looks and talent, she is a very funny woman, and the two of them spend a good deal of their time keeping each other laughing.

Steve and Adolph used to enjoy each other's humor a lot, making endless games and contests, some of them continuing fitfully over several years. There was one called "What would you eat for a million dollars?" at a time when a million dollars meant something. One dare was "Would you eat this electric toaster, wires and plug and all?" Another typical challenge: "For a million dollars would you eat Mike [a friend's large, friendly, hairy dog]?" These proposals were considered solemnly and argued over, pro and con. My children found Adolph entertaining, too. As a baby, Susanna would laugh gleefully at a slipper Adolph insisted on wearing even though the sole had almost completely detached itself. The sight of him flapping it at her would send her into gales of laughter. Perhaps that is not such a good example of his wit, but how about when someone was talking about the poet he always referred to as Walt Whiteman and Adolph whispered to me, "The King of Grass." Some of our references are now so old and arcane that perhaps an explanation is necessary here. Paul Whiteman, a jolly, stout bandleader with a tiny mustache, used to be known as "The King of Jazz," and Walt Whitman, the poet, wrote . . . oh, well, you had to have been there or at least alive and conscious at the time.

I remember when Adolph and I were in London riding in a cab along the Embankment and we hit a sharp bump. The driver, in heavy cockney, apologized and then went on to explain that there was a metal medallion in the middle of the road marking the fact that the Romans had originally built it. That thought launched him into a tirade: "How about that," he exclaimed. "Those Romans invaded our country! They occupied England! Can you imagine! Romans!" As his neck reddened and his voice rose in nationalistic outrage, Adolph said gently, "Aw, let bygones be bygones."

Adolph and I have lots of old, outdated references and phrases we have mutually piled up over the years. There is a kind of radar between us, knowing what the other is thinking based on stuff we have both read or heard or shared. I remember a time years ago when Adolph walked in silent and gloomy. I looked at him and said, "Eva Le Gallienne?" He nodded glumly. Maybe no one else would have known what this exchange meant, but the actress Eva Le Gallienne, splendid woman and founder of the Civic Repertory Theatre, had written a book about her life up to then called *At Thirty-three*. Not exactly a best-seller, the book had not been read by many people other than the two of us. I was telling Adolph that I knew why he was depressed. It was his birthday, and he was thirty-three. Facing up to our present ages, was it possible 137 to be depressed at thirty-three? Of course. You can be depressed when you are five. I did not know Adolph when he was five and I was two. That happened about eighteen years later. And today we can still make each other laugh. He can still amuse, surprise, even astonish me with his knowledge, his insight, his compassion. Out of that Fernandel-shaped head (Fernandel: a French actor with an Adolph Green-shaped head) sprang, full-blown, a most unusual man. Adolph, my friend, don't change partners, for God's sake—just keep dancing.

Clinging to
Leonard Bernstein

After returning home from my late-afternoon visit with Leonard on October 14, 1990, I called the apartment to find out if it would be all right to see him again in the evening. His sister, Shirley, answered and told me that he was dead. That was impossible. I had just been talking to him, and anyway, we were all sure Leonard would live forever. I knew he had time and room for everything in his vast canvas of life: music, of course, voracious reading, friends, parties, tennis, fast cars, care for the whole world, family, word puzzles, games, conversation, teaching, love, laughter—everything but death. There was so much of all the above he still had to do. I had been sitting on the side of the bed as he lay there, his beautiful leonine head looking diminished and his lids heavy from illness, and for no reason at all we were reminiscing about an old (1938) number my partner Adolph and I had written for our act, the Revuers, having to do with three movie psychopaths. I could remember only a few random lines of it, but Lenny, drawing on the prodigious reference library of his head, rattled off the whole thing without hesitation, verse and all.

I was astonished at that feat of memory, dragging out from between, let us say, Mahler's Ninth and Keats's "Ode on a Grecian Urn" some lyrics from a long-defunct nightclub act. But I should not have been surprised. Magic of that kind 139 was like breathing to him. We were laughing at both "The Psychopaths" and his remembering it when I left. I did return in the evening, but the apartment, so elegantly and warmly assembled by the beautiful Felicia, gone twelve years, was changed. The whole world was forever changed.

Along with our professional relationship, Leonard and I shared a long and close friendship. Our families were often together on occasions like Christmas Eve and Leonard's birthday in August. Steve and I would go up to Fairfield, Connecticut, for the birthday, and later, after Steve died and I had little family life, Leonard made sure to include me in their other celebrations as well, like Thanksgiving and Passover. I became a kind of honorary Bernstein. One August there was an especially huge inundation for the Fairfield birthday party, and a few of us had to be put up at inns around the neighborhood. When Lenny found out that I had spent the night in a hotel, he was so horrified that he decided I must have a permanent room of my own somewhere in his establishment. When he converted a building on his grounds into a pretty house for his older daughter Jamie, her husband David, and children to come, he also designated one spot as forever "Betty's Room." So if all things fail me, I know I'll always have a room to run to.

I not only have a special room, I have a special name. Quite a while back he started calling me "Beddim," a two-syllable sobriquet that, when pronounced by him, seemed to have at least three and a half syllables in it, with perhaps a hint of *y* before the *im*. He loved acrostics and sent me one on my birthday in 1988:

> _B_rilliante, vivace, sempre presta
> _E_, qualche volte, di pin in pin mesta
> _D_a capo, l'islesso (ma meno marcato)
> _D_al cuora al cuora, si stessa la dato.
> _I_'ve said all these words and I'm glad that I said 'em!
> _M_y dear, there is none so deserving as
> BEDDIM!

I don't know Italian, and to this day I am not entirely
140 sure what it says, but I decided to assume it was something

very nice. But I don't hear the name Beddim anymore. Occasionally another Bernstein, Shirley or Alex, may use it, but sad to say it is fast fading out of our language.

When my son Alan died early in 1990, Leonard, who had loved him and marveled at his drawings, gave me this acrostic to read at his service.

> Alan, I've missed you these
> Long years of knowing and half-knowing.
> An ink drawing born of your suffering great is
> Near me on the wall. God rest your soul.
>
> Clingingly,
> Lenny

I love "clingingly." I once said, when we were all together with several friends and realized how long we had known one another and how precious our friendships were, that we must, whatever happened, "cling" together. Leonard loved the thought and the word *cling*. I remember the night of the day President Kennedy was shot. Steve and I, and Adolph and Phyllis rushed over to Leonard and Felicia's where in our shock and sadness we all took whatever comfort there was from not being alone but with dear friends we could "cling" to.

There were also happy occasions to celebrate, like birth. I was the first in our close group to have a baby. At the time, Lenny, Adolph, and Judy Holliday were unmarried. Judy, the superb stage and screen actress, had begun her career along with Adolph and me in a group called the Revuers. Lenny, already our friend, had played for us occasionally in those early days, and all four of us had remained closely connected. Now Steve and I were doing this pioneering thing, having a baby. One of our rewards, outside of our exquisite baby girl, was that Leonard marked our daughter Susanna's arrival by composing a piece for her. He would dedicate a short composition now and then to someone dear to him, like Aaron Copland, and he would call it an "Anniversary." Susanna's "Anniversary" is a poignant, lovely air, and I 141 have the manuscript and the recording. The theme turned up in the ballet *Facsimile*. I also have the manuscript for a twenty-five-second piece he wrote for Steve and me on the occasion of our twenty-fifth wedding anniversary. The haunting "Lonely Town Pavane" from *On the Town* is dedicated to me, and an arcane fact little suspected by the army of archivists now categorizing every note Lenny wrote is that "Peter, Peter" from his *Peter Pan* was originally "Betty, Betty."

Recently someone surprised and puzzled me by saying Jonathan Schwartz had played something on WNEW called "For Susanna Kyle," which turned out to be Lenny's "Anniversary" for my daughter with words by the widow of Charlie Parker. Complicated, but it keeps our lives entwined.

Lenny's gift for living made occasions small and large at his house joyous and often very noisy. One Christmas we had a long carol session around the piano, with him conducting and singing lustily in the voice that was the only gift not granted him. How he wished he had been blessed with a beautiful singing voice. He gave out the parts to "The Twelve Days of Christmas," and he was both a stern and laughing taskmaster as we fumbled and missed cues and generally fell apart.

The evenings often bubbled down to a few folk around the table playing anagrams, a game he hurled himself into with ruthless competitiveness even against his children. They were all brilliant and verbal and needed no coddling in that department, however. It was a noisy and sometimes expensive game since each time a word was formed, or stolen, or a mistake was made, dimes were paid by all the participants. Words and fortunes were won, or lost, or changed in one heart- and earstopping instant. We also played cutthroat "charades," dividing up into two equally ruthless teams. And on Thanksgiving afternoon, weather permitting, there would be the tradition known as "The Nosebowl," a touch football classic not to be equaled even by the Kennedys. I will never forget the heady moment when to everyone's surprise, particularly mine, I caught a long pass and made a touchdown on that hallowed Fairfield lawn. I felt I had won the Olympic gold medal plus the Pulitzer Prize.

For Lenny's sixty-ninth birthday I went to Salzburg where he was conducting and had the fun and excitement of being around for several days. It is fortunate that I checked the schedule before taking off for Munich where Harry Kraut, Lenny's manager, was to meet me. I had planned a day flight to arrive in plenty of time for what I assumed was an 8:00 P.M. curtain for my first concert. On closer peering I learned that the concert was at 11:00 A.M. I left the night before and found that black tie was the accepted dress. All the ladies turned up in the blazing August sunlight in long gowns and sparkling jewels, and the men in dinner jackets or dressy Tyrolean gray with lederhosen, a bizarre vision in the morning. But the music was glorious.

There was a celebratory lunch afterward at the Goldener Hirsch, at which Leonard arrived half an hour late, so besieged was he at the stage door by backstage visitors and crowds that followed him down the street. I stayed near Lenny's villa in a carriage house at a charming inn and walked the few steps to his place for lunches and visits. On the twenty-fifth, his birthday, there were three celebrations: a lunch at the picturesque hunting lodge of the Princess Wittgenstein, a reception at the consulate, and a party at night given by Deutsche Grammophon. Lenny was constantly apprehensive at the possible arrival of Kurt Waldheim and tried to figure out what he would do if such an appearance materialized. It did not, but Lenny was not thrilled to learn that the day after his birthday lunch the Princess had entertained Waldheim in the same fashion. He was not happy being part of the same club.

James Levine was there as well, conducting opera and recitals. It was a joy to watch the two of them, Leonard and James, the silver head and the dark, tightly curled one, bobbing close to each other as they discussed music, drank, ate, and laughed. The best part for me was attending Lenny's orchestra rehearsals. I sat behind the orchestra's last row of musicians, facing the conductor as they did. I could watch his face and hear his instructions. They were rehearsing Mahler's 143

Fifth Symphony in which one movement is a sublime kind of meditation.

They played a short section and Lenny stopped. I thought it had sounded beautiful. Then Lenny started explaining some things to them, speaking individually to some of the musicians. It was the Vienna Philharmonic, so he spoke to them in German. Then they played the passage over again, and I could hear the difference between what I had thought could not be improved upon and the kind of perfection I was then hearing.

Lenny conducted two concerts. On the evenings he was not busy working, we went to the opera that Levine was conducting. I heard *The Abduction from the Seraglio*, Strauss's *Capriccio*, and most memorably Schoenberg's *Moses und Aron*. Lenny told me he had heard it only once before and was not sure how he felt about it, that it might be rough going, and we might want to wander out at some point. We sat there totally mesmerized and deeply moved. The prologue was a brief reenactment of Kristallnacht with Jews hunted and cemeteries and synagogues defiled and destroyed. Onstage through the whole opera there was a menorah, overturned and broken, lying on its side. During the Golden Calf scene, they ingeniously used the arms of the candelabra to construct the golden horns of the idol. At the end Lenny turned to me and, visibly shaken, said that that was the opera he wished he had written.

In the middle of that week of glorious music and great times with Leonard, I took a day and went to Dachau, quite nearby. My companion was a young German assistant of Lenny's who lived in Munich and who had visited Dachau often. He knew every detail about the infamous place, and I was impressed and heartened to find a young German so involved, so caring, and so horrified at what had happened. There are pictures from that visit that will never leave my mind's eye. Walking out through the gate I remember saying to myself, "*I can walk out of here.*"

At the end of the stay we all saw Leonard off to the airport, headed for his next conducting stop. That was his sixty-ninth birthday.

In 1988 I spent Leonard's seventieth birthday with him in Tanglewood, where I took part in the immense gala given in his honor. He seemed tired, not at all pleased with being seventy and hearing his age repeated so often. It had been going on all year, since the day after he turned sixty-nine, that he was turning seventy, as if everyone and everything was pushing him toward that landmark birthday. He wanted no part of it.

I was in Fairfield the Christmas before Lenny died. I had gotten ill with the flu, and Shirley nursed me as I lay upstairs in his bedroom while he was in Europe taking part in the dismantling of the Berlin Wall and conducting the great concert from Berlin. I was just well enough to creep downstairs and watch that extraordinary performance with the family; I saw that he looked tired and ravaged, yet magnificent. He did not live to see another Christmas.

So often since his death I have thought of something or have seen or read something I wanted to share with him, and I have an impulse to go to the telephone. It would be nice to be able to do that. Or to laugh at a joke. Or listen to him reel off lyrics no one else remembers. Or bask in the warmth of his larger-than-life personality and charm. Or to feel his caring. He did take good care of me even to the point of providing me with the lifetime room in Connecticut. He helped me when I was having difficulties with my children. And he spoke at Steve's funeral. Whatever sort of whirlwind volcano he seemed on the outside, on the inside he could also be kindness and consideration itself and a loving friend. In fact, genius that he was in so many things, my genius friend was also a genius at friendship.

Snapshots of Bacall

I have an early '50s snapshot of Lauren Bacall sitting outdoors on a folding chair at my daughter Susanna's third birthday party, held on the lawn behind one of those strange houses I would rent in Beverly Hills while out there to write a movie. With Betty (Lauren) is her three-and-a-half-year-old son Stephen Bogart, and she is pregnant with her daughter-to-be Leslie. She looks beautiful in a cool summer dress, and one can sense that here is an arresting personage. Looking at her as she is today, we can see that, as in Cleopatra's case, "age" and "custom" have been unable to "wither" or "stale" her essential qualities.

Later that year when Leslie was born, after staying with Betty at the hospital as long as they would let him, Bogart came over to our house for a celebratory dinner with a few friends. I am quite sure I served stuffed squab with black currant sauce because he claimed to like that. Actually, he never ate much of anything. Dinner at the Bogarts' home when there were just a few folk was usually served on trays in the cozy tweed-upholstered den, where companionship and having fun were more important than ritual and food.

Celebrating one another's children's birthdays was a big activity out there. These revels were often quite elaborate, 146 and I was inclined to get fairly hysterical about them. For me this must have come from that old feeling of not giving as much of myself to mothering as I did to movie-making. Betty certainly had her problems managing her home life and her career, but she has always been level-headed and sensible, a glorious combination mixed in with all that glamour and sensuality. In her early years with Bogart there is no question that he and the children came first. My excessiveness can hardly be blamed on Hollywood, the land of excess. I did the same in New York.

There was a party store on Rodeo Drive in Beverly Hills, and there I purchased not only miles of crepe paper and streamers, plus hats, balloons, paper plates, and toys, but I also booked a whole variety show. Out of my terror that the children might have an unscheduled moment or two and that all uncontrollable juvenile hell would break loose, I ran a very tight ship. When the children arrived, fifteen or so, with mothers, fathers, nurses, they were greeted and given favors and told where to pile Susanna's presents. Then, before they had time to lounge around and get into trouble, or even to talk to each other, I enthusiastically and briskly herded them out behind the house where rows of chairs had been set up facing a raised area sheltered by the extended roof. That is where the snapshot of Betty was taken. I could see her shaking her head at me indulgently as I dashed around. Parents were invited to join the kiddies, but some preferred an indoor drink and canapé, having been subjected to these spectacles many times before. Show time! First a clown miming his delight at the children's presence and getting the occasional laugh, then a magician pulling rabbits out of hats and coins out of children's ears, then trained dogs doing acrobatics and getting rewarded, and then, lest there be so much as a tiny pause before the eats, a nice young woman, "good" with children, led them in songs and little games as attention was starting to wane. Just as my panic was about to rise, there was a merciful signal from the kitchen, and the kids were promptly led into the dining room for refreshments. The birthday cake, blazing with candles, was brought in, grown-ups balanced martinis as they cut cake, spooned ice cream, and mopped little mouths, and Susanna looked radiant. My 147 child's shining eyes and the knowledge that this party would soon be over filled me with the first euphoria of the day.

Steve, who had come out to California for Susanna's birthday, saw my first relaxed smile of the afternoon and came over with Betty to assure me all had gone well.

"You know you're crazy," Betty growled. "Why don't you leave the kids alone for a minute? They like to talk to each other and play a little." I just could not take that chance.

I had first met Betty and Bogie about five years before that when they were expecting their first child, Stephen. Adolph and I were in Hollywood writing a movie at MGM. We saw them at parties and had some dinners together. Shortly after, they met Steve, and our friendship continued on one coast or the other. We lived in a small town house in New York, and they would come to dinner and we'd have coffee downstairs in the playroom in our "finished" basement. Steve was a superb outdoor cook (he even got a review from Craig Claiborne in *The New York Times*), and sometimes we would have dinners of huge hot dogs, specials, on toasted buttered buns, followed by steak cooked on the grill in our garden, and served with french-fried potatoes. Why don't we eat that way anymore? I know why, but my stomach and my soul stir with longing when I dare to think of how much fun it was.

At first the Bogarts lived in a small house in Benedict Canyon. Then they moved to a gorgeous estate in rolling, luxurious Holmby Hills, which Betty decorated with her customary splendid taste and expertise. There she either started or continued her collection of the myriad silver boxes, paperweights, and other carefully chosen objects that surround her in profusion to this day. They had another home, their yawl, the *Santana*. It was more Bogart's, really, since sailing was not Betty's favorite sport, but she was a good hostess on the water as well as on land, and I have a snapshot of us all on board to show that she was.

Bogart liked me. I don't know why. He said he liked my "cat face." Of course his wife had the greatest "cat face" of all time. And he had a little act that he repeated often. He
would come up to me at a gathering, bringing me a drink or

starting to sit next to me, and then he would see Steve and pretend to be puzzled or annoyed. "Who is this guy?" he would mutter out of the corner of his Bogart-type mouth. We would all laugh. I know it doesn't sound particularly funny. It wasn't. Even if you were there. But I can't help it—his attention flattered me.

Betty and Bogie were terrific together, but then came the time there was just Betty. Steve was not able to go out to California when Bogart died. I went and Adolph went. We had visited him at drink time in the den, where he sat gallantly receiving during his illness, Betty arranging the succession of friends' visits with grace and humor and letting us know when it was time to get the hell out. Back in New York we heard that he had stopped going down to the den and then that it was all over. Betty was beautiful in black at the funeral, sitting with her two picture-book children, four and seven, facing the model of the *Santana* with bravery and seeming composure. Back at the house, upstairs in her dressing room, she let loose with a well-deserved volley of rage at the Florists' Association, which had angrily turned on her for asking the public to send contributions to the American Cancer Society instead of to them. She was packing for a short trip she had been urged to take. I can see her selecting things abstractedly from her beautiful, orderly closets, filled with a rainbow of silk shirts and matching pants, a wall of color the length of the room.

The summer of the year after, when she was preparing to move out, she brought the children to stay with us while she got settled. Our children were nearly the same age—Steve and Susanna, Leslie and Alan. We had a big, sprawling house in Ossining for the summer and, sadly dislocated as her children must have felt, they had companionship and managed to keep occupied and reasonably happy. I have a snapshot of the four kids on the Ossining house steps holding Susanna and Alan's cats, Clem (from Clemenceau) and Veronica (from the Archie comics). Betty came to collect her brood and became the New Yorker she has happily remained.

All through her marriage to and parting from Jason Robards and the advent of her new son Sam and her big 149 success on the stage in *Cactus Flower,* we found ourselves good friends, and finally the friendship was put to one of the toughest of tests possible, working together. She starred in the musical *Applause,* for which we wrote the book, and joy was uncontained when we all won Tonys together. Working with her, I was impressed by her professionalism, her boundless capacity for hard work, her good humor, and her talent.

Today Bacall is strong and independent. She is a good businesswoman and knows her rights. She quotes Bogart as saying, "All you owe the audience is a good performance," and she does not suffer intrusions on her privacy gladly or silently. She has always been politically aware and active, and many were the Adlai Stevenson rallies we shared with her and Bogie. She toured all over with Adlai. Later she was impassioned about John Kennedy, and still later Bobby, and has always taken an active stand on issues she believes in. She has strong opinions on just about everything and lets you know them, and she can be a tough critic.

She still has her unique beauty, tall and tawny, fashionably chic yet casual, her voice sounding as if she has just awakened from the big sleep, her long eyes still able to give "the Look." I heard her say in an interview once that the look happened because she was so nervous on her first picture, she trembled, but discovered if she held her head down and looked from below, it steadied her. I doubt if she trembles much now, but what is so endearing is that in spite of the smoky sexuality she projects, there has always been a humorous, mocking tone to it, and even an underlying girlishness. Many widows of famous men go through a period of eclipse once their renowned husbands die. Betty was a movie star in her own right when Bogart died, but she still suffered a time of confusion and loss of identity and had to fight for her own place and her own recognition. She achieved all that on the stage in *Cactus Flower, Applause,* and *Woman of the Year,* and in many pictures and TV appearances that continue in profusion. She is a person of deep family feeling, "grappling" her children and grandchildren to her heart with "hoops of steel," and she can be counted on by her friends for loyalty and devotion, warmth and practical assistance in good and bad times. I asked her if she would read a poem at Steve's funeral. I know this kind of "appearance" is nerve-racking for her, but she loved Steve and came through with a perfectly beautiful reading of Conrad Aiken's "Music I Heard with You." And recently, when I was hit by another dreadful blow, my son's death, she arrived full of love—and with enough Chinese food for an army for a week—to comfort me, my daughter, and my other close friends who were gathered around me.

I have snapshots of her singing at our twenty-fifth wedding anniversary party and at her East Hampton home, and she looks great in all of them. As far as I can see there isn't a bad angle or even a second best angle, even as the years advance and she has four grandchildren's birthday parties to go to.

Whatever she is doing, shooting a Robert Altman film in Paris, hosting an important benefit, or insisting in her unmistakable deep contralto on TV that you have "some Royal Caribbean coming," or just calling me up on the phone to say hello, I know I have a very glamorous friend.

Keeping Up with the James Joneses

At a table in a meeting room at the University of Texas in Austin, I was poring over an exhibition of the work of the author James Jones. There were original manuscripts, letters between Jones and his two editors, Maxwell Perkins and Burroughs Mitchell, exchanges between him and Norman Mailer, first praising each other's work and then later arguing, photos of Jim with the stars of the movie *From Here to Eternity*—Montgomery Clift, Burt Lancaster, and Deborah Kerr —plus other Jones memorabilia. I was there with my friend Gloria Jones, his widow, and a few others from the East who were traveling together with another friend of ours, Marshall De Bruhl, as he toured with his book about Sam Houston, *Sword of San Jacinto.* Knowing that Gloria Jones was coming through, the Harry Ransome Collection at the university, which houses the literary works of many, many great authors including Keats and Joyce, had put together this display in her honor. I walked around the table, handled the manuscripts and letters, and looked at the face of the young Jim Jones. I was moved.

We had met in 1957 and had remained close friends until his death in 1977. Now, in unlikely Texas, I thought back to our meeting and our relationship, and remembered them with pleasure and sadness.

It all began when the owner of the Oloffson Hotel in

Haiti showed my husband Steve and me to our cool, shady room and said, "You know who got married here this afternoon? James Jones." Roger Koster, a French-Hungarian ex-*Life* photographer turned innkeeper, was accustomed to having literary and theatrical personages at his hotel—there was even a John Gielgud suite in the annex. After *From Here to Eternity,* the big smash war novel that launched his distinguished career, Jones's second book, *Some Came Running,* did not meet with the same critical acclaim .

As I later heard it, the story was that Jim, wondering what was wrong with those goddamned critics, had gone to New York where he looked up Budd Schulberg and spent a few days and nights with him, holed up on Budd's living room couch, the two of them talking Books and Life until the wee hours. Budd, unclear about Jim's intentions (not toward him, but in general), asked him what he wanted to do, to which Jim replied that he wanted to find a girl. He hastened to add that he was not looking for a girl for a night or for a fling but for *The* Girl—for life. Budd asked what kind of girl he envisioned. Jim said he thought someone blond, with a good figure and a sense of humor, intelligent, and not shockable; someone who would not mind his uninhibited language but who would in fact talk the same colorful way he did. Budd said he knew just the girl: blond and witty, she had even written a book she never did anything about, and her language had been known to empty elevators. To give an idea of what she looked like, recently she had been standing in for Marilyn Monroe who had been in New York shooting a movie. Her name was Gloria Mosolino. A date was arranged, they had a few drinks and hamburgers at P. J. Clarke's, and three weeks later they took off for Haiti where they got married.

Steve and I met Jim and Gloria that day, and it was quadruple love at first sight, an affair that lasted many, many years and is even now continuing with a sadly reduced cast: the two remaining widows, Gloria and me.

In Haiti the four of us did everything together. We drove high into the mountains, black and mysterious, where we could see little flashes of fire dotting the darkness and 153 hear the constant muffled rumble of drums. High up on one mountain was a kind of oasis run by the Barbincourt Rum people, where one could stop and taste a hundred different kinds of rum, which is fine as long as you have a driver. We took in the usual tourist-trap voodoo ceremony, complete with whirling headless chicken and unguents sold in cold cream jars. Mostly, we lay around the pool and talked and laughed. But we had arrived the very day of the plebiscite that brought "Papa Doc" Duvalier to power. Roger and his beautiful Haitian wife Laura were apprehensive about what lay ahead and had already learned that some journalist friends of theirs were in trouble. Nothing seemed to dampen the gaiety around us, however.

We met a Russian-French-Jamaican who invited us to come over to where he was building a beach, not far away. Beaches in Haiti were virtually nonexistent at the time, and he was laboriously carting sand over to this delectable spot, where he hoped to build a hotel. We had to cross a body of water to get there, and for this purpose we rented an outboard motorboat, and merrily set forth. The location was stunning, and so was his wife, Future Fulton (in her leopard-spotted bathing suit), who had been a showgirl in one of Adolph's and my musicals. We had a delicious time on their island and, as the afternoon sun waned, started out for the Oloffson. Along the way the water began to get rough, the motor failed, and the boat sprang a leak. We kept frantically bailing out with Steve's shoe and banging on the motor with the heel of Gloria's sandal, getting it to sputter enough sporadically to carry us a few yards farther before conking out again. We didn't think we would make it, but the heel of that sandal worked miracles and finally, exhausted and scared, we arrived home. We were friends already, but once you face death by drowning with someone, the bond somehow becomes even stronger

When Steve and I had to leave for the next part of our trip, Round Hill in Jamaica, we vowed to meet the Joneses in New York, never to part. Jim, of medium height, powerfully built, with a large, great-looking head set on a short neck, rough dark blond hair, and the sweet smile of a baby, pos-

sessed a wardrobe consisting of two pairs of jeans and some

work shirts. He appealed to Steve, whose wardrobe by anyone's standards was quite spectacularly stunning, to get him
outfitted, and with the help of one Morty Sills, Jim developed
into the well-dressed but still craggy-faced, gravel-voiced, and
quick-to-explode author about town. He was charm itself and
held his liquor well, but at some point things sometimes got
pugilistic. He loved poetry, particularly Yeats, and read it
aloud beautifully, and he was always either writing or preparing for the next book.

The Joneses' decision to move to Paris left us desolate,
but we made plans to keep seeing each other. Gloria gave
birth to their daughter Kaylie in Paris, and knowing she could
not have any more children of her own, a couple of years
later she and Jim adopted a beautiful French boy they met in
Jamaica. (Kaylie, an author herself now, has written charmingly of her relationship with her adopted brother Jamie in *A
Soldier's Daughter Never Cries.*)

We visited the Joneses in Paris where they occupied a
whole house on the Quai d'Orléans, on the Ile St.-Louis opposite Notre-Dame. Jim's office was on the top floor; Gloria's
bathroom, a floor below, was zebra-striped and had a Cleopa-
tra-sized bathtub. Their place had no name, but what was
going on there was kind of a salon with international writers
passing through for heady evenings of talk and drink, cigarette smoke and sometimes poker. Anyone planning to be in
Paris was told to look up the Joneses, and when anyone had
a question about anything—where to go to live, love, or shop
—the advice was always "Ask Gloria."

A number of years and a couple of Chanel suits later,
they took a house in Jamaica for a year. Jim was writing a
book, *Go to the Widow-Maker,* which involved the islands
and skin diving, and he wanted to work in that atmosphere.
Through the years he and I kept up a steady argument about
his use of four-letter words in his books and how many I
thought could be tastefully allotted to each book. We laughed
about it, but the talks were basically serious and of course I
never won my arguments. I wasn't making a moral judgment;
I just felt the over-repetition of those words diminished the
strength and grace of his writing. He teased me and accused 155

me of being prissy and schoolteacherish, and uneasy about things sexual. There is a character in *Go to the Widow-Maker,* with some of those qualities.

In spite of this, he would often ask me to read sections of his work in manuscript and seemed to value my opinion. When the book was assembled for publication, the Joneses rented a house in East Hampton, and one afternoon Jim gave me a chapter to read. It was a description of a man's experience skin diving, going into the depths and playing among the beautiful undersea creatures and foliage. It captured the man's euphoria and otherworldly feelings with great lyric power. I was drifting dreamily into the poetic beauty of this passage when I came upon the closing sentence: "Then he sat on the floor of the ocean and masturbated." That's my Jim.

Steve and I visited the Joneses twice in Jamaica. The first time, Gloria met us at the airport with little Kaylie, then a blond cherub of two. She looked up at me. I smiled down at her angel face, overcome by its beauty, and the first words out of her mouth were "Fuck you, white lady!" What had happened was that the day before, Gloria, with Kaylie in the car, had been stopped on the road by a band of Rastafarians, Jamaican natives who wear their red hair in long dreadlocks and who do not care for Caucasians. They surrounded the car and yelled racist imprecations, terrifying Gloria, who somehow had the guts to step on the gas and speed away. But an oft-repeated phrase of theirs stayed with little Kaylie, who thought it would be an appropriate greeting for the next white lady she saw.

The house was right on the ocean at a place called Lilliput. The Joneses' bedroom was at one end, then a living room and kitchen section, then an open patio, and past that, our room, which jutted out over the water. The noise of the waves was deafening, making conversation possible when close in bed but impossible while moving around and dressing. One evening we were preparing to have dinner at Round Hill, the elegant enclave of "cottages" built near a central hotel building. Getting ready silently, I lip-read that Steve

156 thought I looked pretty good in my blue-and-green silk dress

and jacket. Then we joined Jim. Gloria entered in a deep V-necked black silk little nothing, giving new meaning to the expression "drop dead looks." If I had not loved her, I would have been seething with envy. I was anyway. She was truly a golden girl, gorgeous figure and legs, bright yellow hair, and the kind of sexy upper teeth that jut out just a little but not too much.

Steve and I spent quite a bit of time at Lilliput with the Joneses' English friends, Sir Bruce Tuck, his sister Tuckie and her husband Nigel. The two men were partners in real estate, and Sir Bruce was the kind of Englishman who pronounced my name, the simple two-syllabled "Betty," as if it had at least five syllables: "Bi-yeh-eh-uh-tyeh." Jim would sit up with them talking and drinking until dawn, and although I liked them enormously, I would often wonder as I slipped off to bed exhausted at three, what on earth they found to talk about for the rest of the night.

Preparing for his book, Jim had been taking skin-diving lessons and had become quite proficient. (I don't think he had time to take up the sport at all when he was in the army at Pearl Harbor in Hawaii.) As soon as we arrived in Jamaica, Jim arranged for Steve to take skin-diving lessons at one of the hotel pools, and after a couple of sessions with mask, tank, and flippers, diving to the bottom of a swimming pool, he was deemed ready for the big time. Steve was excited and eager to go, and with my heart in my mouth, I admired his crazy bravery. The four of us went out in a boat with all the equipment, and somewhere out in the Caribbean Jim found the spot he liked. He stood up all equipped with his gear, said to Steve, "See you down there, kid," and went over backward into the sea. Steve stood up and did the same.

It is a terrifying thing to watch someone you love go over backward into the deep for the first time. Gloria and I looked at each other in silent terror. A few seconds later Steve was clambering aboard, tearing off his mask and gasping. There was some little thing he had neglected to do, but no amount of tear-stained pleading on my part could keep him from masking-up immediately and back-diving in again. Gloria and I sat in silence. After a few minutes Jim came bobbing 157 up and asked for the underwater camera, then disappeared again. An agonizing amount of time later they both surfaced, to the joy of two not-yet-thank-God widows. Steve was euphoric. He had loved it. He said there had been a scary moment or two when the back of his tank caught on a tough castle of coral, and he could not move. He thought some monster of the deep had him in its clutches, but fighting vigorously and swearing underwater, he got free and floated away. He was idly flippering about and enjoying the beautiful quiet with his fellow undersea companions when he noticed Jim nearby and hailed him in friendly fashion. Jim, camera in hand, nodded, and then went up to the surface. Steve followed. He learned later that Jim had gone back for the camera because he had seen a shark right near Steve and wanted to get a picture of it. I refused to let myself ponder the implications too much. Steve was back in the boat, a dripping, happy man. That was enough.

The second time we stayed with the Joneses in Jamaica was over Christmas, with our children. Small Kaylie was there with her nurse Juditha, and we all had a spectacular time, swimming, going to beaches, boating, sightseeing, eating, and drinking. It was a joy to view Jim and Kaylie from the back, walking down the beach—their shapes identical, one tiny, one big, large blond heads and short necks on broad shoulders, then tiny hips—her little hand in his big one as they marched down to the water.

The household was run by a Jamaican cook/housekeeper and a man friend. Or should I say it was run into the ground. When Gloria arrived about a year before, she had been furious at the attitude her English friends displayed toward the native population, calling Bruce and Nigel racist empire builders. Passionately, she tried to educate them, exhorting them to change their attitudes and extolling the virtues of The People. As time went on, however, and she began to notice the disappearance of some of her belongings, the dwindling of her food supply, as well as stunning discrepancies in the household bookkeeping, her militant manner started to fray a bit around the edges. By the time Christmas was over and we were all getting ready to leave, Gloria had decided she was damned if she would leave the elaborately decorated Christmas tree behind with those she felt, no matter what their reason, had betrayed her. She organized the project of launching the tree, fully decorated, into the sea. We made quite a ceremony of it, and our English friends laughed a lot. So did Jim.

When Jim and Gloria lived briefly in London, we went to Glyndebourne with them to hear *Falstaff* and to see the Moscow Art Theater do *Uncle Vanya.* The actors were thrilled to meet James Jones whose books were famous in the U.S.S.R., best-sellers from which Jim—along with other U.S. authors—received nary a ruble in royalties. And once we went to Hampstead Heath to a carnival where the fortune teller insisted that the couples were Jim and me, and Steve and Gloria. She became furious when we tried to tell her otherwise. Her insistence puzzled us a great deal; we were all so happy with the couples we were.

In 1974 the Joneses returned home from Paris. Jim had not been in good health, and after suffering from heart trouble, he decided to listen to the doctors and try a warm climate. They moved to Key Biscayne, where Jim was writer-in-residence at a college. Jim was allowed only certain foods, and Gloria became an expert wok cook. When we visited them, Steve taught Jamie tennis, and I held a class one day on musical theater for Kaylie and her contemporaries at her high school. Florida never seemed right for the Joneses, and soon, nontropical though it was, they went out to the South Fork of Long Island where so many of their friends had settled: Irwin Shaw, Willie Morris, Peter Matthiessen, and us, among others. Steve and I were perennial renters in one Hampton or another over many years, but the Joneses rather quickly decided to buy a house, and Jim continued his work on *Whistle,* the book he never finished. He wanted to, he struggled to, but his heart sadly failed him before he could quite get to the finish line. It was to be the last book of his war trilogy: *From Here to Eternity, The Thin Red Line,* and *Whistle.* I remember evenings at the rented house in Sagaponack before they were in their own place, where Steve, Jim, and Gloria played poker with their French friend Monique. 159

Jim had given me parts of *Whistle* to read, and I sat in the other room reading while bilingual curses and epithets drifted in from the card game. Jim's friend Willie Morris completed writing the book after Jim died, having discussed the contents in detail and following the outlines Jim had written.

At the service in Bridgehampton, his friends spoke, Kaylie spoke and recited Edna St. Vincent Millay's "I Am Not Resigned," and a young army bugler in uniform blew taps the heartbreaking way we all knew Prewitt must have sounded. Gloria was bereft beyond consoling. She still is. Theirs was a mutually fierce and loyal devotion. Back in the '50s, Jim had indeed found *"The* Girl—for life," America had found its great contemporary war writer, and Steve and I had found a treasured friend.

Jim presented a macho picture to the world: gruff, hard drinking, cigar chomping, rough talking, iconoclastic, belligerent. He was all of that, but he was not *only* that. He had been small as a boy, with poor eyesight. When Jim was young, his father committed suicide by shooting himself. Jim grew up covering much of his deep feelings but was sensitive, kind, gentle, easily moved, in love with poetry. His most famous hero, after all—the lead character in *From Here to Eternity,* Private Robert E. Lee Prewitt—was not a macho army man but the opposite: a misfit, a musician, an artist who refused to box when ordered to by his superiors because he had once blinded a man in a boxing match. This was a character Jim loved and admired and, I think, one who expressed a great deal of what Jim was like himself. He hated brutality and injustice and any system that was dictatorial, like the army, but at the same time he appreciated the friendships and loyalties, the male brotherhood, that can exist within that system. I had the feeling that in his aggressive, spoiling-for-a-fight persona he was playing a part.

Jim's inscriptions to us in his books read as follows: *Some Came Running,* February 1958: "To Steve and Betty, and Susanna and Alan, To the Old Ones, Two of the dearest friends Mos [Gloria, from Mosolino] and I have had or will have. For the Juniors: Two of the children we'd like to have."

In *The Pistol,* August '62: "For Steve and Betty, who have no need of this autograph since they already have the #2 copy of the original, signed, sealed, thumb-printed and religiously farted upon. Love, Jim." And in *The Thin Red Line,* "For Steve and Betty, who are just the best fucking friends in the whole fucking world. Period. Jim."

There is a nice continuity in the friendship of our daughters, Kaylie Jones and Susanna, and just as Jim would show me his work in progress, from time to time Kaylie reads to Susanna whatever she is working on. As of this writing, she is completing her fourth book and is teaching creative writing both at a Y in a posh Manhattan neighborhood and at a school in a tough district in Brooklyn. Her brother Jamie is married, and he and his wife Beth live in Washington where he works for a U.S. congressman. Jim would love it if he could hear me say, "They are two of the best fucking young people I know."

Random Memories
of Penelope Gilliatt

P enelope Gilliatt was a woman of letters, a woman of wit and warmth, and a woman of outstanding redheadedness. I remember her and her hair coming at me during a movie opening party in New York in the late sixties, and how special she made me feel by telling me how much she liked what my partner Adolph Green and I had written for the stage and for the screen. She—this perceptive and knowledgeable critic who had alternated with Kenneth Tynan on the *Observer,* covering movies and the theater, she who admired Harry Langdon and Jean Renoir and Samuel Beckett—also admired us. She wrote stunningly about "movies." She never seemed to be writing about Film with a capital *F.* At first I was in awe of her—she who could converse fluently in Latin and Middle English, she who not only owned a harpsichord but could play it. Somehow our friendship flourished.

She and my husband Steven Kyle adored each other, and with her reserved and whimsically funny and charming little girl Nolan, she would visit us at the country houses we used to rent in one Hampton or another. And there were many dinners in town, at our house or at hers, and later in a West Side apartment. She was a great cook. Weekends she would arrive in the country, but weekend or not, and disregarding the demarcation between day and night, she seemed

to be always writing. She often dressed in orange, which was great with her hair, or red, which was not but still looked terrific, and she carried a small case for clothes and a huge, monstrously heavy leather bag crammed with books—books she was reading and leather-bound smallish notebooks in which she wrote with pen, covering page upon page with small flowing script.

The books that she sent us, with inscriptions to both Steve and me, fill a large shelf. I seem to have two copies of *Unholy Fools* (1973), her collected movie reviews and profiles written for *The New Yorker* (as well as other publications), and two copies of one of her books, *Nobody's Business* (1972), a collection of short stories. Her writing in both the anthology and the stories is clear, economical, beautifully balanced, and filled with insight and sometimes quirky, trenchant observations. On Jean Renoir, of whom she also wrote a complete biography:

The sight of his own gestures as he was talking made me remember one of those fugitive shots which can break through his films so piercingly—a shot in his 1939 picture *La Règle du Jeu* of the plump character played by Renoir himself, the fortunate, poignant stooge, who has just idly let loose the fact that he would have loved to be a conductor. In a shot late at night, on the terrace steps of a grand country house, he can be seen for a second from the back in an image of the clown sobered, conducting the invisible house party inside to the beat of some imagined musical triumph. His big shoulders droop like the withers of a black pig rooting in the dark. Recently, after I had spent some time with Renoir, it struck me that the character perhaps embodies a little of the way that he thinks of himself, and that this great, great master of the cinema, who has an amplitude of spirit beyond our thanks, actually sees himself as a buffoon.

An elegant writer.
Her last collection of pieces is called *To Wit* and subti- 163

tled *The Skin and Bones of Comedy.* In this she discusses and dissects what comedy is and what makes it last, with her own witty perception. Over centuries and continents she looks at everything from Shakespeare and Oscar Wilde to John Cleese of the silly walks and Eddie Murphy and, of course, Buster Keaton. A lot about Keaton.

She preferred Buster Keaton to Charlie Chaplin, which almost led me to challenge her to a duel, but it never came to that. After she wrote the beautiful award-winning film *Sunday, Bloody Sunday,* she tried very hard to get another one floated based on her short story "Fred and Arthur." It kept almost happening, and then not, a source of great disappointment to her. The story is included in *What's It Like Out?* (1968) and is about an oddly paired vaudeville team, one of whom started out on stage as a tiny tot being tossed about like a football by his vaudeville team parents in much the same fashion as Buster Keaton.

Her years at the *The New Yorker* were filled with hard work, fun, mishap, and an abiding friendship with the editor William Shawn. She told me that one time a story she had handed in was returned to her from one of the checkers with a curious note on it. *The New Yorker's* checkers are famous for their attention to the minutest detail and fanatic protectiveness of *The New Yorker's* standards, akin to guarding the Grail. In her story a husband and wife are in bed, and the husband says something like "Dear, let's go downstairs and have some toad-in-the-hole." English readers will know that to be a meat savory. The checker wrote in the margin, "A bit racy for *The New Yorker,* what?"

Although Penelope lived in America for many years and loved it, she never relinquished her intrinsic Englishness. A truck remained a "lorry"; she never called, she "rang up"; and in response to a remark she liked, she was apt to reward the originator with "you clever sausage."

What a glowing further career she might have had and what beautiful, inventive, never-to-be-written pages this cleverest of all sausages might have produced we will never know. When she was forced out of denial about the alcohol blight

164 that ruined her life and made gallant attempts at recovery,

they never worked. It is hard to picture her joining anything resembling an AA group and "sharing" with others whom she undoubtedly viewed, compassionately but objectively, more as possible subjects to write about than fellow sufferers. I can just hear her saying with a smile crinkling the corners of her candid brown eyes, "Chaps ought to be able to pull themselves together on their own, oughtn't they?" Yes, they ought, but it doesn't often work that way. Most tragically, it did not for her.

Penelope loved music. As I walked into her funeral service, I heard Bach, and, later, Schubert, followed by one of her favorite parts of *Così fan tutte,* and I remembered what it was like to go to a concert with her or to the theater. I would be looking at the stage, naturally, but Penelope would be watching me. She did this with everyone, I learned. She wanted to share in how you were enjoying it.

Penelope Gilliatt was an original. She enriched my life. She was my dear friend, and I shall never forget her.

Chaplin's Leading Lady

F ault!" yelled Charlie triumphantly in his reedy voice, face split by his blinding grin, corners turned up, half-angelic, half-clownish. My husband Steve, on the other side of the court, was doubled over with laughter. Just as he was starting to serve to Charlie, this silver-haired person in perfect tennis whites suddenly transformed himself into the Little Tramp, doing a tiny hilarious dance, and Steve fell apart. Advantage, Chaplin. The others in the doubles match might have been Norman Lloyd and Sydney, Charlie's son, as outrageously funny as he was handsome. Most of the time Charlie played serious tennis, but there did come moments, usually crucial ones for him, when he would do a little something that would reduce the other players to helpless laughter, and a point was won by his side.

This highly competitive spirit in Charlie never died, as I had occasion to learn personally a few years later. Perhaps all great stars, having had to compete so intensely to get where they were, carry this spirit into everything they do, even when the stakes are meaningless. Steve told me Bogart was like that on the croquet field. Even when they were partners, if his ball rolled up against Bogart's, partner or no, Bogie could not resist whacking it off the field.

At the Chaplins' I looked down at the tennis game from the overhanging porch with Oona Chaplin, Adolph, and a few other guests. The children were playing somewhere on the lawn near the swings. Their third child, Josephine, was the same age as our first, Susanna, and this was a peaceful Sunday afternoon long ago on Summit Drive, way up above Hollywood, when the Chaplins could still live there. Steve and I were in the neighborhood because Adolph and I were working on a movie. When that happened, I would rent a house in Beverly Hills, once on Camden Drive, twice on Rodeo, once on Roxbury, and once on Beverly, and Steve would come out from New York as often as was possible and practical. There were several of those Chaplin afternoons over the years; sometimes we would go out to a restaurant with them, and on several occasions they came over to Camden, Rodeo, Roxbury, or Beverly for a dinner party in my rented nonsplendor.

Later on came the disgraceful event of Chaplin being denied reentry into the United States after he and his family had sailed to Europe. From then on they stayed there, until this country shamefacedly came to its senses and allowed Chaplin, an old man by then, to come back and be honored in New York and in Hollywood by the industry and art form he had done so much to create.

Sometime in the '70s we all found ourselves in Ansedonia, Italy. The Chaplins were at the Hotel Il Pellicano in Port'Ercole, just down the road from the villa that Leonard and Felicia Bernstein had rented for the summer with their family. And right next to them were John and Jane Gruen: Jane the painter, John the writer. He was next door because he was writing a book about Leonard, and here in the blazing Italian sunlight he could observe his subject, a friend to begin with, in his nonhabitat and bring along a photographer, Kenneth Heyman, to prove it was all true.

At lunch at the Pellicano, Oona was her serene and beautiful self, and Charlie was twinkling and mischievous except when he spoke of his latest film, *A Countess from Hong Kong*. "It's the best thing I've ever done," he said solemnly, "the best of them all." With *City Lights* and *Modern Times* flashing across our brains, we all sat in skeptical but respectful silence, but Oona tried to demur quietly. "Oh, Charlie . . .

Really . . . it's—well, it's . . ." "No, I mean it," insisted Charlie. The picture had opened to a total lack of acclaim, a failure. Oona smiled. "Oh, Charlie, you always say that about the last picture you've finished." Charlie laughed and looked at her with love beaming out of his eyes. He took her hand, and they seemed to be on their honeymoon. I remember his having told me, a long time before, the story of their courtship and wedding. After the ceremony they had driven out to a hotel in Santa Monica using assumed names, and Oona went in first. Charlie thought she'd be more comfortable if he hung back a bit fussing with the driver about the bags or something. As he got to the hotel door, he heard the clerk saying to Oona, "And now, young lady, where is the young man?" Telling the story, Charlie smiled. "That was the line I had to make my entrance on."

We spent a great deal of time at the Bernsteins' swimming, reading, and doing nothing. Each day was perfect. The villa was on the water, which was always a bright metallic blue under a ditto sky and the sun a hot metallic yellow. I remember elegant, beautiful Felicia each morning scanning the scene with dismay, under shaded eyes. "Oh, God, another perfect day!" she would cry. "Why won't it ever rain or even get cloudy? I can't stand this!" Jamie, the older daughter, was there and having a fine time, and I know Alexander, their son, was about twelve and a half because every day at some point he would have to give up the aquatic life and go off to study with Leonard for his bar mitzvah. Leonard was, among many things, a Talmudic scholar with a deep knowledge of Hebrew, both ancient and modern. I know no kid likes to get out of the water, but I know this joint study brought Alex and his father very close that summer.

Lenny is deservedly known as a great teacher, but he met his match trying to teach me how to snorkel. He and Alexander, first cousins to the fish, could not understand my deep-seated fear of the water. Simple terror might describe it. With my fins and mask on plus a rubber tube, and both of them holding me, I would lie down with my face in the water for only a brief few thrashing seconds, then come up spluttering while Alex hooted in disbelief. My shame lives on.

Leonard had ordered a Maserati that year, and when it finally arrived at the dock in Port'Ercole, we went down to inspect it and were promptly whisked off for a drive. Steve and I sat in the backseat, which really doesn't exist. We perched on some sort of ledge, and as Lenny zoomed off at what felt like one hundred miles an hour, we clutched the back of the front seat in white-knuckled desperation. Lenny swerved blithely around the curves of the corniche, turning his face back toward us, all the while talking away, expounding on the virtues of the car and the scenery, and life in general—not one word of which we could hear in the rushing wind. The gorges fell off precipitously on either side of the road, and our own gorges rose accordingly.

The evenings were a bit calmer. But there was one evening when the Chaplins came to dinner that was headier for me than any death-defying ride in a Maserati. I played opposite Charles Chaplin. There are only a few stills to prove it, but I swear it happened. Two of the Chaplins' daughters, Josephine and Victoria, both in their teens, were with them. Josie eventually married a businessman, and Vicky met and married a performer. Together they created a marvelous little circus that tours all over the world, and by now their two small sons take part in it. She is breathtaking and beautiful on the trapeze. That night in Ansedonia the two girls sat quietly with their parents, and talked charmingly. The two older ones, Geraldine and Michael, were already actors, although Michael did not stay in the profession. Those four are the California children. The next four were all born in exile in Switzerland.

When dinner was over, Charlie and Leonard began a kind of Gaston-Alphonse routine about playing the piano. "Please, Charlie, you play, you're my guest. I want Charles Chaplin, the greatest star in the world, to play on my piano!" "No, no, maestro. No, *you* are the greatest musician in the world, and I cannot play the piano in front of you!" "Yes, you can," said Leonard. "No, I can't." "Yes, you can." And Char- 169 lie did. He improvised a bit, then played "Smile" and other great songs and scoring music he had composed for his films. He started to branch into an improvised operatic-sounding creation, I hit a high soprano note or two, which became a duet, and at some point when things were getting unbearably dramatic, Charlie rose to join me. Leonard slipped into his seat at the piano and started making up a highly turgid, violent, and romantic opera that Charlie and I seemed to know because we sang along perfectly in a three-way instantaneous collaboration. Our small but select family audience was laughing and clapping and urging us on. Josie and Vicky were saucer-eyed in astonishment. I did not know this until later, but Oona said they had never seen Charlie do anything like that and could not believe that that was their autocrat-of-the-dinner-table father up there. They had seen his early films, of course, and had had the odd experience of joining their school friends in the ball-bouncing game of "Charlie Chaplin went to France to teach the ladies how to dance," not quite knowing who they were chanting about, but they had never seen him clown and carry on like this at home or in any other living room. Suddenly Charlie was singing, "But now, I must go!" and I sang back imploringly, "Don't go!" Charlie wept, "But I must go!" I entreated, "No! Don't go!" This sorrowful leave-taking and entreaty to stay continued to grow to a climax, and at some point I did something, I don't know what, that got a big laugh. I could sense that Charlie wasn't terribly amused as he swept in front of me, outdoing me in volume, height of register, and breadth of gesture. Of course he was brilliantly funny, and we continued on to an apocalyptic ending equal to the immolation scene from *Götterdämmerung*, with Charlie well in front of me. This great man, this acknowledged genius, the world artist, felt he had to compete with even the likes of me at a family dinner in a friend's living room.

Just being in the same living room with this adored comic image of my childhood and this revered cinema artist-magician of my adolescence and adulthood was enough of a wondrous event for any lifetime. But to have actually gotten to know him was the unexpected fulfillment of early impossible wishes. He had high personal standards and was generous about the work of others but quick to sniff out pretentiousness. His yardstick of whether something was good comedy or pathos was "Is it effective?" Making something, whatever it was, "effective" was the director's and the performer's mission and the measure by which it succeeded or failed. And if he said an actress had "charm," as he would say of Emily Stevens, a not widely known actress he admired greatly, he was giving the greatest compliment he could give. Oona may have grown overfamiliar with his stories through the years (even in their marriage that must have been a given), but to any of us, hearing him tell about almost anything at all that happened to him, accompanied by gesture and movement, was a spellbinding experience. When he performed impromptu, he became in every detail whatever he was portraying. If he was imitating an opera singer, he suddenly made you feel you were hearing Caruso.

When my children were small, five and eight, the big Chaplin revival, the reissue of all his work, had not yet taken place. There were no theaters playing his films and no TV programs showing his two-reelers and chronicling his extraordinary life and work, as we later saw in Kevin Brownlow and David Gill's series *The Undiscovered Chaplin*. I was sorry my children did not have the opportunity to live what I had lived, discovering Charlie. Then one day a small ad in the paper for a theater way out in Brooklyn announced *The Gold Rush*. Steve and I bundled the small ones over there and had the joy of seeing this remote, dilapidated old theater filled with laughing, screaming kids, ours among them, reveling in their first Chaplin immersion and rocking the theater with their glee. Our kids sat by turns mesmerized, collapsed with laughter, or sobbing with tears. Upon getting home, the first thing Alan, five, did was to reach for paper and pencil to draw a quick, accurate impression of the same Little Tramp I had discovered at around his age, a single, sure line limning baggy pants, turned-out, turned-up shoes, and hat and cane, with a few extra dashes for eyes and mustache. That was a never to be forgotten trip to Brooklyn, which is, of course, where I, too, first saw Charlie Chaplin. And there I was some years 171 later in Ansedonia, Italy, having one of the most transcendent experiences of my life competing for the living-room spotlight with him. Let us say I played not quite opposite, but slightly behind, Charlie Chaplin.

My Garbo

"So you are the Betty Comden and Adolph Green I've heard so much about!" These words came at us in a throaty, softly accented voice and out of what must have been the most glamorous, tantalizing, desirable pair of lips in history —Garbo's. *She* had heard about us?! I remember staring at that Face, speechless—that dazzling, mysterious, disturbing face, incandescent above a beige cashmere sweater and pants. We were in Gene Kelly's living room in Beverly Hills, and we had been summoned as if to a command performance for a royal. It was the way of things out there at that time, for a gathering at Gene's—informal, sweatered, floor-sitting—to wind up with everyone who felt like it getting up and performing, not to be "on," not to impress anyone, but out of sheer exuberance and just for the hell of it. We might sing some Gershwin, Porter, Arlen, Rodgers and Hart, and Rodgers and Hammerstein, and Gene might sing and dance "The Old Soft Shoe" and perhaps throw in a few acrobatic steps from his early nightclub act. Judy Garland would sing, and we'd all cry, with Saul Chaplin, composer, producer, and superb musician at the piano, playing superbly. The two of us needed no urging to get up and do a brace of numbers from our nightclub days with the Revuers, plus selections from an ill-fated show we had written with terrific music by Solly (Saul), plus assorted bits of indescribable cuckoo non- 173 sense. This kind of thing happened at many gatherings out there in different homes. I gave a birthday party for my husband Steve at a house I had rented on Rodeo Drive, across from Gene's, while I was out there at MGM working on a movie with Adolph. Steve had come out to be with me for a while, and I wanted to give him a nice birthday party. I had run into old friend Leonard Lyons, the *New York Post* columnist, and had invited him, saying a few people would be dropping in. During the evening he had watched Judy, Lena Horne, Ethel Merman, Ray Bolger, Milton Berle, Gene, and Frank Sinatra perform, and had seen a belligerent Beverly Hills cop who thought there was too much noise withdraw with a beatific smile as he realized it was Humphrey Bogart who had met him at the door with "Anything wrong, officer?" Lenny muttered to me, ashen pale, his eyes dancing, "A few people dropped in, huh?"

How can I apologize for this egregiously name-riddled paragraph? I can only say we were all friends and enjoyed those evenings together, and Steve did have a nice birthday party.

Cutting back to "Garbo night," we were at dinner at the home of friends in the San Fernando Valley, and suddenly a frantic call came from Gene saying that Garbo was there, he had told her all about us, she wanted to meet us and see us perform, we must come at once, and our friends would surely understand. After all, it was Greta Garbo. Our friends did understand and insisted they would have done the same, and so, shamelessly, we left in mid–main course and sped through the night and the canyon from the Valley to Beverly Hills where we were met with Garbo's unforgettable greeting.

She sat on a couch, and we took our usual places near the piano and did many numbers, goaded on by requests from our friends on the chairs and the floor; and, as always, standing and watching in the doorway was the couple who catered the party, Marcel and Renée. They did many different parties in many different homes in Hollywood, and we would see them watching from many different doorways as we played the living-room circuit. They knew our material

174

well. In fact, one night Steve announced, "Tonight Marcel and Renée will do the numbers."

I could not look at Garbo while performing, but I could hear her laughing, and after we finished I felt shy but did go up to her and let her words of praise roll over me. One would think I would remember every syllable, but somehow I remember only a kind of drunken glow. And looking into that face, I felt oddly embarrassed. I could not believe that some people actually thought I looked like her. But when I hit my early twenties, it began to happen. An occasional person would squint at me and say, "Did anyone ever tell you you look like Greta Garbo?" A shiver of nonrecognition would shake my frame, and I would rush to the mirror imploringly. What I saw was a forehead slightly narrow at the hairline, not low enough to be called cretinous but certainly not the sweep of marble that was *her* brow; wide, high cheekbones, yes, but somewhat dwindling in the chin department; eyes longish and deep-set, yes, but much closer together than the Divine One's. I would toss my head back, flare my nostrils, pull down the corners of my mouth, and peer out from under lowered lids, or I'd roll my orbs heavenward in an attempt to convey the throes of consuming passion. I could not see it, although occasionally, glancing at a photograph of her, I would catch something that—dare I say it?—reminded me of me.

What do you say to people who say you look like her? If you pooh-pooh the whole thing, you seem to be protesting too much, and if you say, "Yeah, I know," you are an affront to all that is sacred. In time I learned to get through the moment by saying, "There is nothing more wonderful you can say to man, woman, child, or beast," and move swiftly on to something else. I never knew how to react when, playing in vaudeville with the Revuers, the group I started out with, the great Henny Youngman, who was on the bill, would greet me with "Here she comes, the Jewish Garbo."

I had always worshiped the Swedish one. As a little girl, every Saturday I went to Loew's Kameo on Eastern Parkway, a few blocks from our Brooklyn apartment, and saw whatever was playing. Up to a certain age a child had to be 175 accompanied by a grown-up, and sometimes strangers would respond to a tug at the sleeve and the plaintive plea, "Hey, mister, will you take me in?" But I was forbidden to do that. My mother took me, or my father or brother or my aunt Rose, and I saw silents that were full of sin. But I suppose they assumed I would not know it if I saw it. I remember Garbo in *A Woman of Affairs* and a scene in which she reclined on a couch deep in the embrace of a man who was clearly not her husband.

The camera moved in for a close-up of her hand languorously hanging over the side of the couch, and as the embrace deepened, we saw her beautiful long fingers loosen her wedding ring and let it drop to the floor. What did that mean, do you suppose? Watching *Flesh and the Devil,* I knew it was not right for her to come between two great friends and cause them to fight over her, but I could not believe that this thrilling creature was actually a "bad woman." Years went by, and I was thrilled when she first talked and thrilled when she first laughed, then sad when she failed because they messed up her last picture. And then I missed her on the screen, but not too intensely because by then I was deep in my *Potemkin–Alexander Nevsky* period. Oh, *perfidio.*

To say that our paths kept crossing after that heady evening at Gene's and that a beautiful friendship developed would be stretching the truth a wee bit. In fact, I never met her again. I never even spotted her on the street, as everyone else seems to have, and I never looked up at Bloomingdale's to see that it was she who was fingering the same scarf I wanted. But in a curious way some connection was made just a few years before she died. I got to play her in a movie.

My friend, the director Sidney Lumet, whom I deeply love and admire, asked me to play Garbo in the film he was about to make, *Garbo Talks.* I was stunned and full of apprehension, but Sidney is a great director and I knew this was a glorious opportunity. He began by telling me there would be a lingering close-up of me near the end, and I said, "Sidney, I could never get away with it."

He said, "What do you mean? You look just like her."

Then came the question of billing. He said, "You can't

176

have billing. I want them to wonder, 'Is it really she? . . . Yes, it must be she.' "

Again, I protested: "But Sidney, everyone will know it isn't Garbo. Even if they don't know she hasn't done a film since *Two-Faced Woman* and has turned down everything offered her over the years, I don't look enough like her. I feel presumptuous, silly. Please let me have my name on the picture."

Sidney was adamant.

Everyone in New York, it seemed, appeared in a mob scene shot at the Museum of Modern Art, and each had one line apiece, if that, and each of them got billing, but not I. The mystery had to be preserved. I still loved Sidney.

I read the script and liked it. There were several scenes in which the Garbo character appeared, some distant, long shots, some with back to the camera, and near the end the close-up in the park and one spoken line.

The story is about a young man (Ron Silver) whose mother (Anne Bancroft), who has worshiped Garbo all her life, is dying of cancer. He makes it his mission to find Garbo and ask her if she would visit his mother in the hospital before she dies. He finds Garbo (me? . . . well, not exactly), and she (me? hmmmmmm) visits the mother and makes her dying wish come true. The young man, Gilbert, and Garbo pass each other in the park later on, and his girlfriend is astonished as Garbo (me? . . . we-e-e-ll) speaks to him. I was scheduled for only one day of shooting; I thought it rather strange, but I knew Sidney had a reputation for working fast. Excited, I went to my first wig fitting and costume conference. There Sidney introduced me to a tall young woman named Nina who was getting exactly the same wig.

Sidney explained that in the long shots, where she is seen from the back—getting on a boat or standing in a flea market—he wanted someone tall (taller even than Garbo in real life) who would stand out so that the audience's eye would fix on her immediately. And in the hospital, where she does not speak but listens to the mother with her eloquent back to the camera, the angle demanded a taller-than-life figure. Nina. I began to see why I was scheduled for only one 177 day. But I still loved Sidney. I was given a perfect slouch-brim felt hat and a perfect silk shirt to wear under my perfect polo coat and pants. After various tries I wound up wearing a beautiful camel's hair and vicuña coat that had belonged to Steve in the happier days a few years before when he was still alive.

On my first and last and only day of shooting, we all met in Central Park. In the makeup van, the person making me up was working reverently from a ravishing photo of the Divine Garbo herself, which I decided looked sorrowfully and somewhat accusingly at me. I looked at myself in the mirror and felt, as I had felt all along, that this was something of a mistake. But I still loved Sidney.

I was to be discovered under a spectacular cherry tree heavy with blossoms and was then to pull thoughtfully at a branch or two, then stride down a slight incline to a path where I would pass Gilbert and his girlfriend.

Looking at me through the finder, Sidney called, "Pull down the branches more to cover your face. Yes, that's better," as I all but obliterated myself in foliage and pink petals. "Turn your back a little." I still loved him. Then I strode right up to the couple, trying to look long-limbed (an acting problem for me) and to approximate her free, sailing stride, and delivered my line with what I felt was the right deep, musical, slightly accented husky tone she would have used and the casual yet strongly felt concern I thought the moment required. I moved past the camera. It was all over so fast—no lingering stares out to the horizon, Queen Christina–style, no tossing back of the head with a throaty Ninotchka laugh. That was it.

Sidney seemed very pleased, but, you know, he started life as an actor, and a very good one, too. He is also famous for making his actors feel terrific. I loved him.

A short time later Sidney called to say there had been some weird outside noises on the soundtrack during my line, and he would be calling me to come in and dub it. I never heard from him. Going to the screening of the film sometime later on, I said to Sidney, "I didn't hear so I guess you cleaned things up . . . I mean, the line came out OK?"

Sidney said, "Oh, didn't I tell you? We were so rushed —didn't have time to get you in. I said the line myself." Do I *still* love him? Well, of course.

And many's the compliment I have graciously accepted for all the feeling I conveyed in just some small, eloquent moves of my back and shoulders as I listened to my dying fan in that hospital scene. (Sorry, Nina.) And a modest thank-you has been awarded all who tell me I sounded just like her in my short but effective scene. I know I've been dishonest and I will be punished, but it's such a long story.

There was another evening involving Garbo at the Kellys that I missed. Someone selling Revere Ware for cooking had convinced Betsy Blair, then Mrs. Kelly, to let him come and prepare a dinner at her home, thereby demonstrating the marvels of his product. She invited just a couple of close friends who would understand, including George Cukor the director. When she opened the door for him, he said, "I hope you don't mind . . . I've brought along a friend." It was Garbo. Betsy could not but feel flustered. What a way to entertain a *Queen*—a Revere Ware demonstration. But of all the guests Garbo was the only one fascinated by it, standing in the kitchen and marveling at how little water was needed when cooking with Revere Ware. Or is it none? She asked many detailed questions and ordered a whole set of the stuff.

But I don't like to think of her standing in some kitchen being deeply absorbed in the properties of Revere Ware. She is gone now, and I would rather think of her slipping that wedding ring off her finger, seducing entire World War I armies, renouncing her true love through racking coughs. But never mind her magic, her artistry. Selfishly, my favorite memory is of her sitting in the Kelly living room, honoring the performance with her inimitable laughter and telling this bedazzled worshiper that she had heard so much about her.

Chronicles
and Lamentations

Roddy McDowall took this while I was out in California working on an ill-fated show. My serenity belies my true feelings of teeth-gnashing frustration and despair.

RODDY MCDOWALL

EDWARD OZERN

Ah, "the glass of fashion and the mold of form." Modeling at a Pauline Trigère tribute at the Fashion Institute of Technology.

With Alex Maguy in the suit he made me in Paris in 1951. The suit has held up better than I, as you can read in the pieces about my physical deterioration, for which I have no pictures (none I care to show you, anyway).

In an odd corner of the dining room in the house on East Ninety-fifth Street, which I had to sell, reluctantly, for financial reasons. Odd collection of stuff there: Moroccan screen, gold goats, samovar, modern sculpture, and a primitive painting by Steve's father, Leo Schutzman, who never painted until he was seventy-five and then had two one-man shows on Madison Avenue before he died at eighty-five. All the oddness wound up being a terrific room in a terrific house. I hated moving.

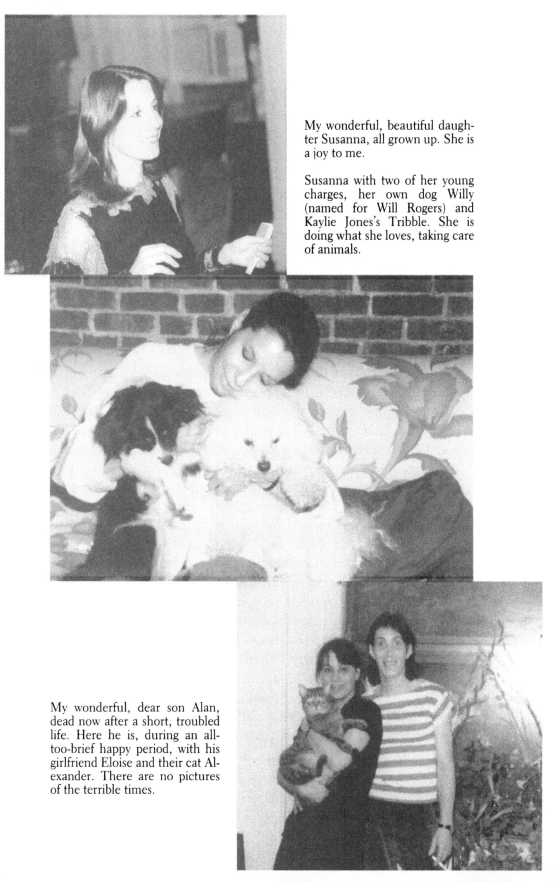

My wonderful, beautiful daughter Susanna, all grown up. She is a joy to me.

Susanna with two of her young charges, her own dog Willy (named for Will Rogers) and Kaylie Jones's Tribble. She is doing what she loves, taking care of animals.

My wonderful, dear son Alan, dead now after a short, troubled life. Here he is, during an all-too-brief happy period, with his girlfriend Eloise and their cat Alexander. There are no pictures of the terrible times.

No More Fat Hair

*M*y back is strong and well. It gives me no pain. It is there when I need it to help me lift the Sunday *New York Times,* propel me up my stairs, and bend over, not to the floor, for God's sake, but at least to somewhere between knee and ankle. Friends hiss enviously, "She has a back as supple as Hiawatha's and as sturdy as Arnold Schwarzenegger's." It seems everyone is in spasm, in traction, in agony, or in debt to orthopedists. "How come she isn't?" they keep hissing. I don't know how come. I only know that everything else is crumbling away gradually like the Parthenon. Sections of that great structure are now being carefully sealed up somewhere in Greece, but I don't think storing me away indoors can possibly halt the relentless progress of my erosion.

A few months ago I was awakened by a wild pain in my left arm and shoulder plus lesser but still sincere pangs in the other arm and both legs. Then a raging attack of pins and needles, more like stilettos and scissors, seized my right hand. After a moment or two of total disbelief, my quick diagnosis was that I was coming down with some exotic form of flu. I hauled myself up, and, amid stifled moans, hobbled to the medicine chest, where, although I could raise my arms only a few inches without screaming, I managed to reach for some medicine bottles. First, however, I had to journey back to my bed to find my glasses, and after a good deal of peering, I was able to make out which was Coricidin and which was aspirin. If I ever have to read directions in an emergency, the moment will be long gone by the time I get the glasses, locate the magnifying glass—because emergency directions are always in fine print—and place myself under a light bright and searing enough for brain surgery. This dimness of sight is the result of something called Fuchs's corneal dystrophy, but I had a cornea transplant operation that improved the right eye enormously for a while, but cataracts started forming and . . . But that's a whole other story of a whole other crumbling.

Losing faith in aspirin, I took my body, all aching and racked with pain, to my regular doctor, an internist who diagnosed my trouble as "tension" and asked, "Why are you so tensed up?" Since he was one of three persons I had encountered that morning, I, like the Ancient Mariner in the Ancient Rime, stoppethed him, and holding him with my good eye, began to tell him why. But when it began to look as if my tale would be even longer than the original Ancient Mariner's, he stoppethed me and forthwith sendethed me off to a rheumatologist.

Much blood was drawn and many tests made. On the phone a few days later the rheumatologist informed me, "You have one of two things . . . the symptoms are much alike. It is either a muscle thing, polymyalgia, or an arthritic thing. We call it 'elderly rheumatoid arthritis.' " He must have heard me turn pale on the phone because he quickly added, "Don't let the name upset you. It's the only kind we have other than 'juvenile rheumatoid arthritis.' "

"Haven't you anything in between?" I gasped, voice hoarse with rage, pride, and terror. "Let us say 'mature arthritis,' or, taking a cue from television, 'prime-of-your-life arthritis,' or perhaps something imported like 'arthrite d'un certain âge,' sold in the one- or two-ounce size with or without the spray?" I made a fairly good fist, only the third elderly arthritic finger refusing to join in, and shook it at the phone.

All the doctors I went to agreed that, although it might not cure my condition, it would help me feel better if I took regular exercise. Three times a week now, a comely sprite with the most gorgeous exercise outfits has been coming to 185 my house and putting me through a series of body maneuvers. I am planning to buy exercise outfits as gorgeous as hers, but for the moment am working out in a ravishing set of old thermal underwear, my other things being too loose for her to see exactly what is going on with me and my body. After about twenty minutes of working out, she takes me to Central Park and walks me, not keeping me on a leash exactly, but under sharp-eyed scrutiny, so that she can correct my posture as I go slouching towards Bethesda Fountain.

Sometimes on our walks my depth perception is faulty, and my exercise lady has to serve as my seeing-eye dog as well, which thought returns me to the saga of my eyes. It began with the appearance of the creeping corneal dystrophy of which I spoke, but at the cry of "transplant!" from the lips of the first doctor I saw, or dimly made out, I decided to shop and consulted with eight others, all of whom joined in the cry of "transplant!" The ninth one, however, prescribed eye drops, and I fell in love with him. I tried to hurl myself into his arms in gratitude but missed completely and wound up hugging his standing scale. But after a while even he came to agree that my cornea should be set out to graze and that I needed someone else's. I got on a list and waited, rather like waiting for my number to be called in a bakery, but when the delay became too long, my doctor sent me off to Pittsburgh, where apparently the cornea crop is as high as an elephant's eye, and I got me one. I asked my wonderful Pittsburgh doctor why this was so, and he told me that a great deal of the "material" came from Johns Hopkins. "Lots of crime around Baltimore," he explained cheerfully, leaving me much to fantasize about under my bandages. It was a marvelously successful operation. It is no one's fault that the demon cataracts commenced.

Recently, I sat in a lovely seat in row H at the New York City Opera's production of *La Rondine* and was enjoying it thoroughly, slightly fuzzy though the figures on stage were, until the intermission. In the lobby some friends asked how I liked the English subtitles, and I recalled that, indeed, this innovation of Beverly Sills's had been a huge success but I had forgotten all about it, and wherever the subtitles were,

186

they had completely escaped my notice. There was much shaking of heads as my friends explained to me gently that the titles were there above the proscenium for all to see. When act two started, I looked up and discovered some pale green patterns traveling across the top of the proscenium. But it all reminded me of a Henny Youngman line: "I went to the ball game yesterday. From where I sat, the game was just a rumor." Dear Beverly, for me your subtitles were just a rumor. Nothing will do but a large clear strip projected on the back of the seat in front of me. Until that is perfected, I will have to content myself with simply reading the argument in the program and happily drowning myself in the music.

Then there is my hair. Recently, the top started flopping over unmanageably, and a sensation like a stone plummeting to the bottom of my stomach told me that my hair must be getting thin. We used to have a joke in answer to that news: "Who wants fat hair?" Well, I do. I remember how years ago a girlfriend of mine and I laughed when we saw an article in the paper giving advice to balding men, which suggested they make a low part and create a "judicious arrangement" of hair across the pate. We shrieked with all the cruelty of thick-skinned, thick-haired youth. "Judicious arrangement!" Now as I comb carefully each morning and while preparing my evening toilette, I can see these words burning as clearly as I can see faint suggestions of pink scalp beginning to peep through my once crowning glory. No one is aware of this as yet, of course, but this is only because the arrangements I create are pretty damn judicious.

In contrast to all this, one thing about me is flourishing: my fingernails. I could never grow them past the cushions of my fingertips, and short as they were, they were full of ridges and edges. But suddenly they are long and strong and opalescent, and I lose much time just staring at them in incredulous admiration. This is all because a little magician at the hairdresser's has been applying some new potion. I have decided that when I go, I will have put in the tomb with me my bottle of this precious fluid to take on my journey, just as the Egyptian pharaohs took along their priceless possessions. But I understand that nails continue to grow under- 187 ground, and so perhaps it won't be necessary. Is it possible that soil is the best thing for growing fingernails?

But I am not speaking of the Grim Reaper here. It is the Gradual Reaper with whom I am engaged in constant battle. Each night when I go to bed, there is the excitement of not knowing what new infirmity I may face with the dawn. It is a kind of game, really, a sort of Rusk-ian roulette. What may be next? Not my back. Not that. Why, my back is as supple as Hia—, as sturdy as Arn—. Will my back be next? Now I lay me down to sleep. Age cannot wither nor custom stale my infinite anxiety.

Wanted: The Runaway Slave of Fashion

*". . . the new leg is a little girl's leg.
. . . This isn't a skinny leg. It's
delicately round, but with absolutely
no calf."*

—EUGENIA SHEPPARD,
New York Herald Tribune,
February 8, 1965

After I finish packing away my little white Courrèges boots in tissue paper, I'll be ready to leave. I've already stored my gaily printed jersey tops with the gaily printed stockings to match, and also my kindergarten dresses and my natural unpadded, unwired, marvelously droopy brassieres. Anyone can see from the above that I stay pretty much up there with the "fashion firsts." Fashion means a great deal to me. I subscribe to *Harper's Bazaar, Vogue, Town and Country,* and *Queen,* and hardly a *mois* goes by I don't glance through *Elle.* And, of course, it must follow as the night the day that I read Eugenia Sheppard daily in the *Herald Tribune* and twice on Sundays. That's why I'm going away for a bit. It's just a small operation. I'm having my legs cut off.

There's really nothing else I can do. Eugenia had this column the other day entitled "Little Girl Legs." After looking at the European mannequins at the fashion showings there, she says that American legs—the long-stemmed beauts with the swelling calf—have had it. They are "out" this year, and what *they* are wearing are little straight-up-and-down ones like "polished little poles," such as little girls have, and legs with any noticeable calf now look "too full-blown and over-ripe." In fact, she says, to be caught with calves this season is "just too crass for words."

Now, I have a pair of legs on me that men have been 189

saying for years are knockouts. I've never been able to see it personally. They are viable for all everyday purposes, of course. They never give me any trouble, and they take me where I want to go. But talk about your "overripe": they look about ready to roll off the vine. They are, if anything, a bit too curvy, if you will, somewhat on the order of well-developed dancers' legs. In fact, countless are the times people have asked me, "Do you dance?" To repeat, I don't see it myself, yet they have been known, literally, to stop traffic. They don't anymore.

On Sunday, I was crossing the street and there was, as usual, the screech of brakes and this truck driver leaned out, gaped at my gams, and yelled, "Wow!" On Monday, Eugenia's column was printed. I read it, put the paper down shakily, gave up my breakfast, and tried to find an excuse not to go out that day. But I had to, and so I uneasily prepared to venture forth. I scanned the column carefully once more for some ray of hope and saw that "the new ideal leg is a round little pole. Actually, it looks as much like a forearm as a leg. Legs and arms seem to match."

Clutching desperately at this straw, I pulled a pair of stockings up over my arms and slipping my hands deftly into a pair of boots, did a handstand in front of my mirror and tried walking up and down on my palms. After all, my arms are not quite as Rubenesque as my legs. But I got dizzy, and anyway, my Adolfo turban didn't look too convincing pulled on over my feet.

So I went out, right side up, and it happened. A truck drove right by me without stopping. The driver had a disdainful sneer on his lips as his pig eyes swept down the length of my leg, and at the moment he rounded the corner, running over my toe, I distinctly heard him mutter, "Crass."

Safe at home once more, I experimented with an old leftover wheelchair I have around the house, working out an attractive arrangement of various jackets and matching or contrasting lap robes. But your wheelchair is a tricky beast, and I couldn't maneuver it up and down stairs without standing and walking, and then, of course, the jig was up. You
190   could see THEM.

I then toyed for a while with the idea of hiding out someplace till the whole thing blows over. But where could I go? Appalachia? A favela in some teeming South American capital? No, no place is really safe. They smuggle *Tribunes* everywhere. And suppose something should happen to me— a fatal accident, for instance? I mean, let's face it: This pair of legs I've got I wouldn't be caught dead with . . . not this season. I can just hear the police sergeant looking me over as I lie there: "Say, this must be an old body. Why didn't you report it sooner? It ain't no circa 1965. Get a load of those crassly curved calves! Why, this year all the bodies we pick up got those well-bred little girl legs."

So I'm off for my operation. And I've got the most marvelous leg man designing me a divine new pair. His name is Dr. Geppetto. You can't do better, if it's "polished little poles" you're after, and they come with a year's supply of scented sandpaper.

You can tell this was written a while back. Truck drivers do not yell "Wow!" at females anymore. Harassment. There are probably quite a number of females today who would like to yell "Wow!" at passing truck drivers, but they wouldn't. Harassment again. Fashions have changed in so many areas, not just in what you put on your back. *Plus ça change, plus ça change* a lot, I think.

I have slipped egregiously behind in my devotion to fashion. I saw in the magazines recently that there was a brief flare-up of cutting the sleeves out of jackets and attaching them at the shoulders with one casually placed safety pin. I resisted this. Maybe it is some ingrained revulsion at the idea of an exposed safety pin, dating back to my childhood when I wore mittens on a wool cord that wound around my neck and through my sleeves, where it emerged at each wrist and was attached by safety pins to my dangling mittens. The pins showed. It was a device to keep one from losing one's mittens, but it was also a device guaranteed to mortify one. To avoid the exposed safety pin, perhaps they could simply sew the sleeves into the armholes. No, I don't think I could suggest anything so deconstructivist. Not today. And I have not 191 climbed up onto the new high-platform shoes, the kind I used to wear in the 1940s both on and off stage. Perhaps instinct tells me the altitude is not good for my heart at this point. They used to say in those old war movies, "Don't send that boy up in that crate." I say, "Don't send me up on those shoes!" Also I passed swifty through a movement to have underwear acceptable as outerwear. A friend of mine caught me in my nightgown one evening and said, "Hey, I didn't know we were going dancing at the Rainbow Room!" and changed swiftly into his collarless, sleeveless leather dinner jacket and short baggy trousers with the fly in the back, and off we went.

I did not really enjoy dancing around publicly in my nightgown. It seemed more appropriate for me to wear it in bed, look up, and, as in the old song "Dancing on the Ceiling," watch my lover dancing overhead.

Shortly after that song was written in the early 1930s, I began to be aware of magazines like *Vogue* and *Harper's Bazaar*. Opening the pages in those days was like plunging out of the chaos of daily life into an oasis of serenity, beauty, and quiet good fortune. It was like sinking into a cushion of soft velvet where women with names like Mrs. William Rhinelander Stewart III reigned supreme, elegant and distant, perhaps fingering a long string of priceless pearls or clutching a small precious fur close under her perfect chin. I loved the smell of *Vogue* before they began dousing every page with some unwanted scent. The paper itself smelled lovely.

Of course, it cannot be said that at that time, even though I read the magazines, I became "the glass of fashion and the mould of form." I was allowed $2.98 for a brown hat for school and $3.98 for a black one for "good," and the same for shoes; school, brown, and black "good" ones at the same prices. I remember my awe while shopping one day with a more affluent school friend who saw a burnt orange felt bag. She fancied it. It cost $5.00. She bought it promptly, without hesitation. Would I ever be in that queenly position, I wondered. As that position became somewhat more possible, I started spending more than $3.98 for the "good" hat and tried to keep up with what was going on. At one point, because

Judy Holliday's father had a girlfriend who worked there, Judy and I had the run of a store called Wilma's on Fifty-seventh Street. This place was not exactly known as a bastion of good taste. The windows were full of neon daytime satins covered with sequins and provocative outfits trimmed with pink fur and marabou, setting a kind of "lady of the evening" tone. But Judy and I had entrée to the back room where there were some really good clothes. I recall once, while wearing a simple black crepe dress with a plain round neckline, I was approached by a friend who asked, "Where did you get that lovely dress?" "Wilma's," I replied. Her eyes widened in disbelief as she said, "You must have stayed up all night taking the sequins off." Wilma's was good to Judy and to me. I even got my wedding outfit there—a dusty blue wool dress and jacket. Not one sequin.

Being chic does not necessarily depend on how much you spend, runs the saying. There is always the myth about the little shop girl (now shop person) who can do such wonders with a snippet of lace placed just so, or a perfectly arranged artificial flower, that you would think she had spent millions. I once read that the impeccably accoutred Gloria Guinness, another of the goddesslike ladies in my early Vogues, in her pre-Guinness days made her own lingerie, sewing each rosette and satin binding with a fine artistic hand. Later, she did not have to do that.

I feel money helps. I have watched myself from decade to decade spending varying amounts, teetering along with the trends, sometimes under protest, stamping my foot over the "New Look" in the '50s, cinching my waist above very full skirts, then suddenly letting the belts fall away as the shapeless "sac" emerged and "waistline" became a dirty word, as I "sac"-ed it along with the madding throng.

Today I am no longer au courant. I do not sport a single tattoo. Nor do I wear little rings in my nostrils or nipples, or even a tiny pearl in the crease next to my nose. I find myself persistently clinging to a longish skirt, although the hemlines are climbing higher and higher again even as you read.

When all this plus the general chaos of life gets to be 193

too much for me, I just make a dive for my old unscented *Vogues* and spend a little soothing time with Mrs. William Rhinelander Stewart III. Listen, today I wouldn't have my legs cut off for anyone.

A Moving Experience

Death and divorce, it is said, are the two most devastating disasters a person can experience. Running a close third is moving, particularly if you do not want to do it at all but are forced to do so by circumstance.

Tennessee Williams's Blanche said she was dependent on the kindness of strangers, and I, like Blanche, found myself dependent on a total stranger in a time of crisis in my life, my moving day. After months of nightmarish preparations, the day had unexpectedly arrived when I actually had to move from my four-story-cum-basement East Side Manhattan town house, stuffed with the accumulation of several lives, into a 2 BR, wraparound LR apartment high up in a tall, incomplete tower to the sun on the West Side. It was like dropping my loosely layered, elaborate life into a car-crushing machine and slipping the flat, compact, supposedly manageable result into one of hundreds of identical shelves, stacked one above the other, forty-eight stories high. Mine was a high shelf in the G line, but really not quite identical with the others. A talented decorator had helped, and the minute I staggered into my new home a split second before the movers and saw it fairly empty except for the few reupholstered pieces that had already been delivered, I only cried a little. It looked pretty. In total exhaustion I flopped down on the beautiful paisley chaise longue, once dark blue in my bedroom upstairs 195 in the long-beloved house, and lay there as the movers methodically piled cartons around me, forming a kind of Great Wall of china, and glass, and books, lamps, clothes, utensils, linens, bric-a-brac, paintings, and work files—all the trappings of a life.

After hours of unpacking and pushing things around, still barely scratching the surface, the work being done mainly by a strong devoted friend, Ralph Roberts, and my tireless loving cousin Mu, while I groaned and looked pathetic, I was alone. Emotionally and physically drained, I was filled with one all-consuming desire: a hot bath. Oddly enough, my small apartment boasts three bathrooms, but two of my tubs had been commandeered for extra storage space. After turning the faucets of the third, or master, bathtub, I faced a sickening reality: no hot water. In fact, no cold water.

Enter the Stranger: handyman/engineer/angel. Very apologetically he explained that nothing could be fixed until morning. Feeling as dainty as Jean Valjean after being chased through the sewers of Paris, I really needed that bath. I wept. The Stranger, wings sprouting through his overalls, said, "Don't cry. I've got an idea. There's a vacant apartment right across from you. I'll give you the key, put on the lights"—and here's the angel part—"and scrub out the tub for you nice and clean. And you just leave it when you're finished. . . . I'll scrub it out again tomorrow." I wept even more. He left me, and soon I was in a vacant apartment, sitting naked, naturally, in an unknown tenant's bathtub across the hall from my new home, having my first West Side bath through the kindness of a stranger. (*Two* strangers, if you count the tenant.)

That night was the culmination of a period in my life comparable only to the Perils of Pauline combined with the Labors of Hercules. The problem was that the great prize awaiting me at the end of it all was moving, which I didn't want to do in the first place. Selling the house found me showing people through, flashing ambivalent smiles of encouragement mixed with "Do you notice the huge apartment house going up in the back garden?"—knowing I must give it 196 up, yet hoping secretly for some last-minute reprieve. But finally my bluff was called in the shape of nice people who made the unrefusable offer and who did not mind the looming structure behind or the listing of the elegant staircases. I faced my gloomy financial situation and went to the aptly named "closing"—the closing forever of that period of my life.

After my husband died I did not want to budge. I wanted to stay wrapped in the ambiance of the home we had created and to cling to the sights and scents of all we had shared for such a long time. Of course his clothes were given away, except for some great sweaters and ties and shirts and vests I'm still wearing. But I left his dressing room sink right next to mine, just as it had been, with a few snapshots stuck in the mirror and his colognes and shaving lotions all around. I did not want to part with that whiff of him I would get as I walked through.

I played many roles during the four months I had to prepare for the move, starting with being a plucky yet somewhat schmucky widow of six years who had never had to decide what kind of space to live in or what to put in it, since a beautiful and much-missed husband had done all of that over the years. I had pictured living in a handsome prewar edifice reeking with tradition, fireplaces, and a magnificent terrace on the park—and, to ease the pain, located in an old familiar neighborhood, the Upper East Side. The agents descended and the fruitless frustrating quest was on. When about two months' worth of torn-off calendar pages fluttered past my eyes, I found myself settling hastily for what I'd sworn I'd never live in: a modern monster, not even finished, on the opposite side of town, with nubby wood doorknobs on the closets and nary a fireplace. The men in my life—that is, my lawyer, my accountant, and my investment advisor—had warned me passionately not to buy. "Cash flow" was the desired state of grace. I was to rent, and so signed a lease and prepared to leave the land my house stood on with all the dignity and pride of Jane Darwell forced off her property in *The Grapes of Wrath*. One role I did not play was Scarlett. I did not scratch, facedown in the dirt of the only plant salvaged from my old East Side plantation, swearing, "I'll never   197 go hungry again!" Brooding over my rent, I just hoped I wouldn't.

Inundated with the responsibility of emptying my huge house and preparing a new couch for myself in the presence of who knows what West Side enemies, I assumed yet another role, that of the efficient executive Rosalind Russell, and in the interest of "getting things done," I acquired a decorator, Nancy Muir. I got my decorator through my therapist. Doesn't everyone?

I proceeded to divide my time among several grueling activities, eliminating every possession from my old life that would not fit into the new, trying to figure what of the old would look good in the new, and agonizing over swatches and colors to give the right background to and disguise the old on its way to the new, plus deciding what structural changes should be made in the new. Every object I handled, from my piano through my mother's courtship letters, down to a pair of pink socks stuck in the back of a drawer, had to go through a six-way decision process: Do I take it with me? Do I put it in deep storage? Do I put it in accessible mini-storage? Do I sell it? Do I give it to some worthy cause? Do I throw it away? That's not quite true. I never thought of throwing away my huge piano. In fact, it was a controlling factor in what size living room I could comfortably consider.

Making all the decisions in my cellar alone was the "Labors of Hercules" part. Hercules would have been delighted with the Augean stables after an hour in my cellar.

But some of the things I found down there were lovely, like those boxes of letters. I recall one night sitting in my dining room lit by shadeless torch lamps so I could see what I was doing. The room was piled chaotically with books, clothes, and assorted objects collected for a donation pickup, and the table was covered with a sheet and some newspapers, some of my mother's letters in one pile and some of mine in another. The phone rang. It was my daughter. I had given her a few letters she had written to me while on a teen trip, and she was calling up to read me a passage, exclaiming, astonished, "I never knew I told you things like that!" She had sneaked out of a concert at the Fillmore in San Francisco to join some friends and go wandering, and almost got sent home. I then read to her something I had written to her father while I was away working in California, about her when she was a baby—what she was doing and what miraculous changes were happening daily. And then I reached into the other pile and read her a letter my mother had written years before from the country to my father in the city, describing baby me, in much the same marveling-new-mother way. Three generations had a conversation that night. I arranged to take and keep those boxes of letters forever.

Early on, the movers, two warm and hearty brothers, had come to see what they had to move, and they were both encouraging. As I got closer to the final day and decisions had been made and much was cleaned out, the brother who did the actual physical part came over again. I was distraught, dirty, and discouraged, but he looked admiringly at the disorder and the packed piled-up cartons marked with sticker dots: red to go, green to store, blue to mini-store, black to donate. He said, "I must compliment you. When I first saw this place, I never thought you'd ever be ready in time. You've done a great job." I glowed. Had it come to that? A compliment from my moving man had given me the same thrill as winning a Tony.

I try not to think about the last sorry scene as I left my not-quite-empty house. There seemed to be a lot of uncategorizable stuff left over after all the packing, and I had arranged to have a "yard" sale on my living-room floor, run by a peculiarly depressing mother-and-son team I had discovered in the yellow pages. There they were, putting demeaningly low price tags on all sorts of objects and impersonally handling possessions, perhaps not cherished but still they had belonged to me and my family, and meant something to me. I did not feel I could bear to hang about while strange folk wandered into my house and picked over our stuff. My cousin Mu came to my rescue, as always, along with her sister Inez. They shooed me out of the place and remained behind to cope with the sordid scene. The pitiful amount made from the sale was hardly worth the agony, and I'm sorry I had ever allowed myself to think it might have been a good practical 199 idea. My gallant cousins spared me the details of what happened; somehow it was over, and I never had to go back into what had once been my castle.

The morning after my first bath on the West Side I looked around and felt good. My apartment has a wee terrace, the one feature I had clung to through the battle and all the attendant compromises. I had lived for years with a garden, and my soul required access to the outdoors, someplace where I could open a door and step out into the air. There it was, with a view south, east, and west, including a stretch of the Hudson. It was glorious. On the Fourth of July I could see the fireworks all the way down at the Statue of Liberty. I awoke one morning not too long after, and there was something in the way, a fat structure getting taller and taller, blocking the open lane through which I had seen those fireworks. My heart dropped to the sidewalk below. I realized the significance of what I'd been seeing for a few days, tall cranes reaching up into the sky like ugly long-necked dinosaurs. I remembered that Virginia Woolf knew that when she saw a vision of a black shark's fin reaching up from the water, she was about to go mad. That's the way I felt at the sight of those cranes: I shall go mad. But I decided not to. There is still a lot of view, more than enough for me to be able to go out on my terrace and, as in the movies of yore, scan the panorama, fling my arms out wide, and shout, "New York . . . you'll lick me yet!"

I like living on the West Side in my three-and-a-half-room apartment up in the sky. In Jane Austen we read of how people in those times always sought an abode with a "pleasing prospect." Without "the radio [and TV] and the telephone and the movies that we know," and the theater a goodly distance away in London, viewing, enjoying, and commenting on the "pleasing prospect" made up a fair share of one's entertainment. Well, in addition to all the contemporary distractions mentioned above, I have a truly pleasing prospect. To the south, my huge windows and tiny terrace look out over Lincoln Center (handy for a last-minute decision to hear and/ or see something), and still, in spite of new buildings in the way, present a spectacular panorama. On the west is my piece

200

of the winding Hudson River, sun blazing like gold on it by day and setting like fire by nightfall behind New Jersey. Toward the east is a cut-up view of Central Park (more cut up now by another upstart skyscraper), and the imposing East Side of my former life. Light streams in even on a gray day, which is a good thing when you live alone, and at night the stars and moon over the lighted buildings all around and the sparkling trees at Lincoln Center make me think it's still the best place to live.

When I am not staring outside, I look in and see the beauty that my wizard decorator created for me as I wept and got in her way. She arranged my life neatly and charmingly in this limited space which she made feel spacious. From a cherished hanging of mine, a paisley with stripes, mainly muted reddish orange, reddish rose, and reddish red, she chose the colors for the whole place: a warm indescribable shade (this is not my field) for the walls, similar colors plus browns and beiges to cover the furniture. Where the walls meet the ceiling she has placed a border of the same colors following all the contours of the somewhat L-shaped living room, the window-covered walls, the alcove of banquettes (the perfect place for dining created by removing a closet), the bar (created by converting a bathroom), the floor-to-ceiling bookcases, the kitchen door, framing everything up to the passage to the bedrooms. The chaise, now an inviting paisley refuge, lords it over the living room, and even my huge piano fits comfortably because Nancy told it to. She did not plan this, but my Chagall has just the right colors for the room. I think I would have kept it anyway.

My bedroom is a warmly welcoming rosy nest, the walls and drapes all in the same color and carrying out the living room scheme. My old chests, an even older desk, and a Venetian mirror make up the rest of the room surrounding my queen-sized bed (no room for a king), and another tall, smoky Venetian mirror glows at the end of the hall.

But I do not only dine, hang out at my bar, look in the mirrors, and sleep in my home, I also work there. And it takes a heap of filing to make a home an office. The second bedroom has a pull-out bed in black, a round table for a desk, an 201 upholstered swivel chair, and walls lined with shelves and closets to house all the books, records, tapes, CDs, record player, speakers, TV, VCR, and miles and miles and miles of files. Apart from these which are black, it is all a gorgeous blue: blue walls, blue closet doors, blue Pierre II window shade, and a blue, red, and black rug coordinating the whole damn thing. (Hey, maybe this *is* my field.) It is to this blue grotto that my partner Adolph Green and I repair daily to go to work.

My home is beginning to bulge at the seams as I do more work and get more letters and collect more programs, scripts, contracts, notebooks of ideas, magazines I *must* keep, old tax returns, and the thousand everyday bills that flesh is heir to. Yes, I had more room in my house where I lived so many happy years with my husband and our children. Sometimes when I am visiting at someone's town house I look a bit wistfully at the garden, but then I remember when I lived in the house alone, the heavy rains at midnight that would flood my cellar because of the leaf-clogged drain, leaving me in high boots and dudgeon, running from cellar to kitchen, up and down, pail in hand trying to bail out. And the sight of a block of town houses covered with snow, looking like a Currier and Ives, can bring a tear to this old eye until I remember how my back felt after shoveling my steps when no boy came by to perform that favor for a king's ransom.

When you have a husband who loves you, he'll take care of all those things. But he's gone. There is a time in life for a certain kind of living, and then there is the time for a change to something different. I have my "pleasing prospect," including a piece of the Hudson River. But there is a change and even an unpleasant scent in the air that will take my river away from me. Donald Trump is planning a city named after himself to be erected on the Hudson shore all the way from Fifty-seventh Street up to Seventy-second Street, and my home, my street, Sixty-seventh, is right there in the middle. His original plan for buildings over one hundred stories high has been thwarted, but I understand that he is getting approval for the slightly cut-down version, and when it is built, no more sunsets on the Hudson for me. The sun will set much earlier behind a high-rise. The streets around me will be darkened by shadow and will be more congested and more full of fumes than they are now, and traffic will be an oil painting of a still-life. As that other tower rises to the east of me, fifty-six stories high, with a plan that includes ten movie theaters, I must face the fact that this city which I love so much has a city-planning scheme that could only have been designed by the Alfred E. Neuman of *Mad* magazine fame. If he did not actually draw it up, he was surely consulted. Of course there is *no* plan; it is all disastrously haphazard. I have made this complaint personal—*my* river, *my* view, *my* light, *my* air—but of course there are a couple of other people who will suffer along with me. Let the river wend its way. Donald, *you* stay 'way from my door!

My Body Revisited

*I*n six years anxiety has given way to *que sera, sera.* Having taken stock of my body situation at that time, I concluded that each dawn's awakening would inevitably bring the unknown and perhaps not altogether delightful discoveries that come with the relentless march of time, and I would lay me down to sleep with a gnawing anxious feeling. I would toss sleeplessly trying to think up substitutes for the appellation "senior citizen," which for some reason I loathe, although at this writing it still gets me a sixty-cent ride on a bus, and could only come up "time challenged." I am a time-challenged person, just as someone who was once referred to as disabled is now rightly called, I think, physically or mentally challenged. I mean no disrespect. I like the new appellation. It tells you that here is someone who is still a viable human being, capable despite some rotten thing that happened, something beyond that person's control.

Then what about the passing of the years? Is that not a rotten thing beyond my control? And am I not determined to do great in spite of it? Ha, ha. "Time," I challenge you! And having made that decision, I have passed from anxious to insouciant. I am a veritable Pippa passing through life singing "God's in His heaven, all's right with the world!" The dawn's awakening is replete with optimism in place of dread, even though I find it hard to sit up quickly in bed or put my weight smoothly and equally on both feet as I hold on to the bed table and feel for the floor. Is it now OK to cut the euphemisms, face the facts, and use the word *old?* Not yet. To paraphrase Eliot, "I grow time-challenged, I grow time-challenged, I shall wear the bottoms of my blue-jeans rolled."

Pulling out my chart and starting this review from the top, I note that my hair is not "fat," but then again, it is no thinner than it was six years ago. With frequent enough perms and back-combing, it is no crowning glory in the Julia Roberts sense, to be sure, but it is still a serviceable cover for the scalp and frame for the face. Frivolous bangs do wonders to camouflage the relatively new deep furrows between my brows. It has not been the most carefree of six years, and as for the rest of my face, as stated above, *que sera, sera.*

Moving briskly south, we come to the eyes. What has gotten thinner are the eyebrows, the outside curves of which seem to have vanished after some diligent face scrubbing one day, or is it just plain balding? What is now required is the judicious application of eyebrow pencil. Since I use kohl black even in the early morning, one can often see, when I've been in a rush, a brow divided against itself: one half hair, the other a black crescent, and the two not necessarily connecting. As for the eyes themselves, that is a saga that has gone on for years, and the last six are no exception. In addition to the original cornea transplant I had in one eye because of something called endothelial dystrophy, known around the club as Fuchs's, I've had a second transplant and two cataract operations. When I feel like laughing about it, which I must remind myself to do, I repeat Groucho's line: "I've got Bright's disease, and he's got mine." A simple reworking . . . well, you get the idea: "I've got Fuchs's dystrophy, and he's got mine."

When this ailment first made itself apparent, I consulted many doctors to avoid the inevitable transplant. A few of them were eminent Spanish surgeons very skilled in this field. Could it be because they make such sharp knife blades in Toledo? One of them said to me, "People do not get this disease until they are in their seventies." Since I was a mere growing girl of forty-eight at the time, I asked, "Then how come I have it?" His answer was "It is the will of God." At the 205 time I wanted my money back, but I have since come to see the wisdom of his words. A man of science, he had long given up the idea that science had all the answers, and in the last twenty-five years we have become aware that his explanation may be as good as any for the random, inexplicable events that interrupt people's lives. For example, a small extra blight caught my eye, literally. A tiny stroke in the optic nerve deprived a blood vessel of its supply, leaving me with a black opaque blot right in the center. I see around it. But the right one is chugging away at almost full capacity since a small procedure opened a window of opportunity in the area where the cataract had once lodged. Before this magic casement had been opened, however, I had an experience that almost made me want to stay at home permanently.

I was on my way to see *Waiting for Godot* at Lincoln Center's Vivian Beaumont Theater, a short walk from my home. It was pouring seriously, but I had told my friend I'd just walk the couple of blocks and meet him there. Umbrella in hand, I set forth. I was rather enjoying my wet walk protected by boots, raincoat, and umbrella and climbed the Sixty-fifth Street stairs to the level of the Opera House and made a right turn toward the Beaumont. On the way there is a large beautiful reflecting pool complete with sculptures and benches; and I started to walk alongside it—I thought. At this point it was raining furiously and there was a lashing wind, so I had to keep my umbrella way down in front of my face. It was dark, and my depth perception is none too good even in blazing daylight, and I could barely see my feet. As I struggled toward the theater entrance beyond the pool, I was suddenly up to my thighs in black water, walking on the bottom of it. How I stepped off the edge of the pool without breaking my leg (which I did on a later occasion, but not by trying to walk on water), I will never fathom, but there I was.

I was so astonished, I started to laugh as I stood two and a half feet deep in the water. There was no one near enough to see or hear me, but far off in the lights outside the theater I could see a bunch of dry people. With difficulty I pulled myself up and out, my boots heavily full to the brim 206 with water, and knelt there on the stone side of the pool panting for breath. If someone had asked me, "What are you doing here?" would I have been quick enough to answer, "I'm waiting for Godot"? I had no chance to try my wit since no one was around and it was getting toward curtain time, and I was soaked. I had a choice. I could hurriedly run home again, change my clothes, and hurry back, or just brazen it out and slosh to the theater soaking wet. I opted for the latter. I knew that in the heart-pounding, exhausted state my experience had left me, I would try to rush and wind up slipping on the wet street or in my foyer or over my own foot and have a terrible accident. Having made my decision I sat there in a puddle, rain pouring down, emptied my boots, pulled them on again, and dripping umbrella held high, went slogging through hell toward the lights of the Beaumont and civilization.

My friend stared and said, "What happened to you?" But I just rushed to the ladies room, where I wrung out the lower half of my drenched pants and my hat, and mopped my face and hair with woefully inadequate paper towels. We rushed to our seats, and I sat there wet to the bone, loving the play and repeating to myself over and over again Beckett's line expressing what life is all about: "I can't go on, I'll go on." I don't like to brag that I come from terrific Russian stock, but I did not sneeze once. However shaken I was by my immersion experience live at Lincoln Center, I decided not to stay at home forever but actually braved the outside world again the next day, more wary of open manholes than ever. Yes, we go on.

But obviously I do not see very well. On a recent African trip, I had distance glasses and field glasses to help me, but to take a picture I had to center the animal first in my vision, then drop the field glasses quickly and raise the camera swiftly and shoot. In a moving vehicle, impossible, and I have many shots of bushes, tree tops, and the backs of my companions' heads, but still I got some beauties, and they give me great pleasure. Imagine being able really to *see* Africa!

Moving right along the body, I mean down, we come to the tongue. This is a new area of devastation, not tapped six years ago. A bump on the side of my tongue was wrongly 207 diagnosed at first as something to do with the salivary gland, so I went off on a fabulous trip to Venice, but shortly after my return the lump was still with me and growing, and before I could get it out of my cheek (I made lots of nervous jokes about what was happening to me), I was in the hospital having my tongue operated on for a malignant tumor. I was a bit nervous. It is only that part of my livelihood is derived from performing, a pursuit that requires a certain agility of tongue, and no one would tell me whether or not I would ever be able to speak again, let alone sing fast lyrics. And it is nice to be able to converse with people you like. I summoned my brother Nat, the doctor, to come from California, and he and my surgeon, marvelous Dr. Elliott Strong, were at my bedside when I came to. I heard them talking. Dr. Strong was explaining to Nat that during the operation he had to decide whether to do a vertical or a lateral cut and why he decided on the one he chose, and I don't know which one won. I did know that there was a pad and pencil right there to enable me to communicate with the world, but I was having none of it. I spoke immediately. Words poured out, and I threw the pad into the trash.

What if Dr. Strong had decided on the other incision? I ponder this from time to time because although I felt at the beginning as if there were a pillow on the side of my tongue, my speech was pretty clear, and I was even able to give a performance not long after. It was decided that I needed no radiation or chemo even though a string of lymph glands had also been removed. All I did was repeat lots of tongue twisters like "Moses supposes his toeses are roses," and gradually the old tongue magic came back as good as new. Of course I have to go for checkups (it is cancer, after all), but they are required less and less frequently, and anyway, as I think I said before, *que sera, sera.*

We now skip from chin to knee. In between there is some lingering arthritis in arms and hands, to be sure, but I do not care to give it the time of day. My center section is perfect, do you hear, perfect. Oh, yes, a mitral valve prolapse somewhere in the heart, but they keep telling me it's nothing, so I'll tell you it's nothing.

The knee thing, however, was one of life's unneeded interruptions. Whether it is fair to categorize it under results of the "time-challenging" process, I am not sure, but it came about because my vision is poor and I am not as sure-footed a mule as I used to be, so I guess it qualifies. Out in the lobby of the Palace Theatre, at a meeting of the creative team of *The Will Rogers Follies,* for which I am co-lyricist, I tripped on a hunk of rolled up carpet and crashed my right knee on the concrete floor. It was bare concrete because the Palace was undergoing renovations in preparation for our grand opening, and the carpet obviously had not been laid yet. I had picked my way among these hazards without mishap before, but this time I caught my unsure hoof and went down in agony. If the leg was held out straight, it was bearable, but if it slanted toward the floor, it hurt so screamingly I would have gladly betrayed my country and everyone else's just to get the pain to stop.

I was carted out of there to my director Tommy Tune's doctor, Dr. Richard Bachrach (how the word *doctor* keeps dotting these pages). X rays followed by being wrapped in something called an Immobilizer (not a Schwarzenegger character, just a sort of brace), and I was wheelchaired home. I had fractured my pet patella, the right one. Pain, ice packs, round-the-clock attendants, visits to the doctor, my loyal, unbelievable cousin Muriel doing service beyond the call of duty or love, became my life, with the almost immediate addition of therapy. Lift that leg! Flex that knee! Get a little drunk on your vitamin C! The wheelchair had an extension on the right side that held my leg out straight, but for getting in and out of it, or changing position in bed, Muriel brilliantly devised a kind of sling that could be slipped under the arch and heel at one end and held like reins in my hand at the other. It probably saved my sanity if not my life.

The next day it was back to the theater for rehearsals, where I sat in my wheelchair at the top of the center aisle conferring with my colleagues and having cinnamon bagels sent in. Suddenly we were in preview, and to see the show I had to be wheeled into the ground-floor box, stage left. From there I could see only about one-third of the show. Picture my thrill and surprise when I graduated to a walker and could sit in a seat like a grown-up in the center of the house and see the full panoply of the truly gorgeous sets, costumes, and staging. For a while it was a seat on the aisle with my right foot stuck out into it, raised if possible; then after what seemed a lifetime I graduated to a cane with the help of the doctor, Carolyn my therapist, my day and night helpers, my daughter, my housekeeper, Mu, the people who wheeled me, including Adolph, and the doorman at the hotel next door to the theater. All through this I kept working on the show and healing quickly, helped, I am sure, by some magic concoctions sent me by nutritionist-chiropractor supreme, Dr. Alan Pressman.

My darling brother is a truly great doctor but a very conservative one, and I'm afraid this last sentence will send him into a violent rage. I just hope he never reads it. "Time-challenged" though I may be, I did make a stunning recovery, and although I cannot think of anything very positive to say about breaking your knee, at least I can say it did not kill me. And to quote the stirring Sondheim, "I'm here, I'm still here!" And my dentist tells me I have the jawbone not of an ox but of a twenty-year-old.

There is a story, apocryphal perhaps, about W. Somerset Maugham giving a lecture on "The Beauties and Recompenses of Growing Old." Apparently when the hall was filled to the rafters, Mr. Maugham, a man well along in years by then, entered and sat in a chair. He paused. He stared out at the audience. The pause took on epic proportions. Finally he rose and said, "I can't think of any," and walked off the stage. As I reflect, I just want to say, "Move over, Willie, I agree with you." Even so, somehow I keep trying to stick to my premise that I have come through many things and will come through a lot more, and although "time-challenged," I want to try to be insouciant, optimistic, Pippa-Passes-ish, and dedicated to the proposition *que sera, sera*. That is how I feel right now. In another six years' time, perhaps I will undertake another top-to-toe checkup. That is, unless I've already checked out.

Her Second Chance

While I was out shopping for the perfect shade to dye my old hair shirt, it suddenly occurred to me that I should quit troubling "deaf heaven with my bootless cries" and face the fact that I have had a long and rewarding career. People sing our songs, know our shows and movies, and even watch us performing now and then. Still, I wish I could get another crack at it, but, of course, that is impossible. By "it" I don't mean a show that faltered, I mean bringing up my children, particularly my boy Alan.

Would I be any more talented at it now that I have lived it once? The roads not taken remain untaken till the end of time, as anyone knows who has ever experienced an ounce of regret or remorse. In a bad movie I could get a "second chance" and, depending on the screenwriter and what They think They want in the front office, things could either wind up as before (the producer is a fatalist) or everything could be different, better, maybe even glowingly glorious (the producer believes in the perfectibility of man and moms).

My daughter Susanna, well and beautiful, now happily divorced, walks and boards dogs for a living. She is and always was crazy about animals and loves what she is doing. She is gifted, with a strong, original decorative sense; she studied at the School of Visual Arts to be a fashion illustrator and worked for a while as a kind of gofer/observer at the atelier 211 of the distinguished fashion and costume designer Donald Brooks, who, as a great friend, gave her this enviable opportunity. She worked in a boutique or two, then at some point realized that she had no interest whatever in the world of fashion. For a while she created delightful collages in small hand-painted frames, little scenes made of cut paper and cardboard and sparkles and paint, which she sold in a friend's specialty shop. But now at last she is where she wants to be. She explained to me that walking a dog is far more than taking him out to perform his bodily functions. It is, more important, providing him with his exercise time and his social life, where he gets necessary fresh air, hard to come by for city dogs, and an opportunity to meet and mingle with others of his species in all shapes, colors, and sizes. Susanna tells me that she has nothing to complain about; she is enjoying herself and looks forward to every day. That is not a bad thing for a mother to hear, that her daughter is happy with her life. My son, on the other hand, is dead. In the movie *Her Second Chance,* which I fantasize about, it would not be so. Alan would be living, filling the world with his brilliant off-center art and beguiling all who came near with his charm and wit. Why isn't he? Screenwriter, tear up that last page and go back to the beginning.

HER SECOND CHANCE
(First Draft)

MEDIUM SHOT: A DELIVERY ROOM . . .
MAY 23, 1953

A mother, BETTY, is delivering a baby with the usual groans and grunts. A DOCTOR and NURSES are assisting.

MEDIUM SHOT: BABY EMERGING
(NURSE'S P.O.V.)

NURSE
(enthusiastically)
What a nice round head!

SECOND NURSE
And what a sweet expression! Pure sweetness!

DOCTOR
Ah, it's a boy!

CLOSEUP: MOTHER

MOTHER
(through her grunts and groans)
Well, at least Steve and my father-in-law won't set
fire to me the way they do in India. . . . I have *one* girl
already. Two, and it's more dowry money or the gasoline
and the match!

(ME, reading the script:
I never said that. My head was too full of beautiful
thoughts. I was not about to come up with schneppers or
comments on the weird practices of faraway lands. I felt
joy, pure joy. Speak to scriptwriter.)

NURSE
(puzzled)
Oh, Doctor, why does he have purple splotches
here and there?

DOCTOR
There was a mild infection. I painted the mother
with gentian violet just to be sure. It will fade shortly.

MEDIUM SHOT: MOTHER AND CHILD

MOTHER sees her boy, who has come through
what must have seemed to him something akin to the
Blue Grotto in Capri. He does have a splotch or two, but
he looks dear and is smiling.

CLOSEUP: MOTHER. She hugs the baby and
cries with pure joy.

(NOTE: Possibly a song here if the mother is not
too tired to get on the phone with her partner and write
one.)

SHOT WIDENS TO INCLUDE ENTERING FATHER

FATHER STEVE and MOTHER BETTY embrace and kiss. He hugs the baby.

(NOTE: Maybe the song comes *here* . . . a duet. No, Steve never liked to sing; loved music but never sang.)

SUSANNA toddles in and is allowed to greet her baby brother.

LONG SHOT: TUTTI

SUSANNA
He is pure cuteness!

(They all hug.)

MOTHER BETTY
(voiceover)
Of course I realize I have not had a "baby." I have had a "person," something my friend Stanley Donen always tells his friends who are expecting. This adorableness will grow up, and along the way I must be vigilant and aware, protective yet independence-friendly . . . and—
(A glow of all-seeing militant motherhood creates an aura around her.)

(NOTE: ME: I thought no such thoughts. I was tired and fell asleep. But after all, this is the rewrite.)

From the earliest moment, Alan was entertaining and smart, and willful, and looked like a rounded elf or Eskimo (Arctic American?). He made us laugh so much I'm afraid we often forgot he was a little child, we were so busy enjoying the show. At four he built a tree house at one of our rented places in Ossining, decorating a fork in the tree imaginatively with leaves and bits of cloth and colored paper signs; he peopled it with his toys, and he would strum a toy guitar and make up songs, which he delivered in a surprisingly grown-up hoarse voice. The opening line of one of them, as I recall, was "I could love you the way I should, but anyway, darling . . ." There is really nothing brilliant about it, but he performed it with so much performer's conviction and style that it *seemed* brilliant. What I was never told was that, also at four, he was apt to lie down on the sidewalk in the city, refusing to budge even though Tillie and his sister and many a passerby tried to convince him to get up. Those things I was never told. Tillie was given full responsibility. She was a wonderful large, pretty woman, African-American, born and raised in St. Croix but with no accent whatever, and she had come as Susanna's nurse when Susanna was about a year and a half old. When Alan arrived, I asked her to take on the two of them. I was away working, either physically distant out of town or in California, or just mentally removed, around the house but oblivious. I was told that when Alan was about four and Susanna saw him trying to figure out some words in a book, she said to him, "Don't you dare learn to read." She was mad at this intriguing interloper and was feeling threatened.

I have a photograph of Alan lying on the floor, drinking, with his bottle in one hand and holding the book he was reading with the other. I remember we were in New City at the time, visiting Norman Lloyd, the director, and his wife Peggy, who were staying in producer John Houseman's house. It was then that Norman, who was directing a production of *The Taming of the Shrew,* got the idea of putting Alan in it as one of the child ragamuffins in the theater box with Christopher Sly at the beginning of the play. Norman said Alan looked just like a Shakespearean clown. Alan was tremendously excited at the idea, and we all went down to the rehearsal. Alan wanted to know what he was going to wear. Norman showed him the brown raggy tatters he would be dressed in, and Alan's disappointment was epic. He had seen pictures of kings and queens and nobles in splendid robes, and I had held him on my knee at a show of mine where he was dazzled by the color and excitement. He must have pictured himself looking resplendent in his stage debut. He refused even to touch the ugly costume. It was "see-my-agent" time. We left with him crying bitterly.   215

Steve had a lot of the responsibility for running the family as I went about my business, loving my children but feeling inadequate, and happy to let others take over. I felt I had no gift for mothering at all, and was bewildered and scared by the daily problems that came up. Letting others make decisions and calling in doctors became my pattern. When she was eight, I started Susanna with a therapist. She was very shy and quiet at school and not doing well. When he was nine, I started Alan. He was brilliant in art class but willful the rest of the time and was having learning problems. I say "I" did this rather than "we" because I truly don't think Steve would have done it without my urging.

Sending a child to an analyst is not a criminal act, I realize, but I know I did it to shift responsibility, hoping if I closed my eyes, ears, nose, and throat and tiptoed by, all the pieces would fall into place and things would be just swell. Years and years later Alan told me, when I visited him at one of the many hospitals he frequented, that only one other kid in his class was going to a doctor, and that he felt Steve and I must have thought he was crazy. We sent Alan to school at Dalton, where Susanna was, because it was convenient having them both at the same place, disregarding the advice of their warm and wise pediatrician, who thought Alan would do better in a more structured environment. I always listened to doctors except when their advice seemed to cause me inconvenience. It was also convenient to treat The Children more as a unit than as individuals, although there was a difference between them of three and three-quarter years. We did things together almost all the time, all four of us, and bedtimes became the same. Susanna had none of the privileges of seniority, and Alan's precocity and sense of importance got a boost. Later he displayed that combination of low self-esteem plus grandiosity so characteristic of addicts.

216

HER SECOND CHANCE

LIVING ROOM: THE FAMILY

MOTHER
Whoops! Seven o'clock! Off to bed, Alan! Susanna, your bedtime is eight o'clock, so you and I just have time to knead the bread dough once more before we let it rise overnight!

ALAN
OK, Mom, I know I'm younger and it's only fair.

MOTHER
Alan, I'll come up and sing you a song. . . . Now scoot!

(He laughs and goes happily to bed.)

SUSANNA
Oh, what fun, Mummy! I feel so grown up and womanly!

FATHER
(calling up to ALAN)
Alan! . . . You and I will go to the Town Tennis Club tomorrow . . . just the two of us! I'll give you a lesson!

ALAN'S VOICE floats down.

ALAN'S VOICE
(o.s.)
Swell, Daddy! Wheeeeeeeee!

SUSANNA
Sleep well, Alan dear.

When he was only two and a half, Alan announced that he wanted to go to "cool" because that is what his beloved Zoozanna did, and we looked for a place that would take an untoilet-trained kid. The French Lycée, which takes them that young, asked imperiously, "Ees he clean?" and so he 217 wound up at Temple Emanu-El, where his little problem was widespread. Taking an unusual approach to the situation, Steve started telling the children a story about a little boy like Alan. I never listened to it. I was too prissy and was not sure it was a good idea. But the children clamored for it, and Steve obliged behind closed doors. It was about a small boy, I was told, who insisted on "going" in his pants, much to his father's chagrin. The father would take him to a baseball game at Yankee Stadium and it would happen. Steve started by saying people simply moved away from them in the stands, but as time went on, he elaborated. The stadium emptied out completely, and soon the repercussions of the boy's behavior began to take on international proportions. I would hear the kids shrieking with laughter behind the door. Alan was cured. He simply stopped. Once in a while the kids would demand a nostalgic replay of the story, and although therapy was no longer needed, Steve would come through for old times' sake. All through these early years, Alan's talent was astonishing— his drawing, his use of words, his ability to grasp a whole concept from one detail. He was fascinated by things that were dark—the scariest books, the most terrifying pictures of snakes, dinosaurs, and monsters—and his drawings tended to be macabre, as later, in his teens, he was obsessed with the works of Aleister Crowley and other occultists. Were those signs to be picked up as significant?

HER SECOND CHANCE

MOTHER
Alan, dear, why draw all those nasty snakes and monsters?

ALAN
You're right, Mama. . . . How about this cherub?

(He draws a perfectly beautiful cherub. Closer inspection shows it has a devil's horn and tail. But look, the MOTHER *tried* in the rewrite.)

I'm not sure exactly when Alan began smoking pot. He was having learning and behavior problems at school when he was twelve, and was on his fourth or fifth analyst, a woman who was really wonderful. But when she learned he was smoking marijuana, she said she could not continue with him because she was not equipped to deal with drugs. Nobody was. Nobody knew what to do at that time. Do they now? This was new then, and baffling.

I had to embark on a long, long stay in Hollywood shortly after this. Alan's new analyst begged me not to go. He said something like "This is a most unusual boy. He knows he is a 'much-prized' child but does not know his place in the family, and it would be better if you stayed around, because he might be on the verge of something serious." Financial pressures were heavy. Hollywood meant instant money. I felt I had to go.

H.S.C.—Rewrite:
She did not go.

I made a point of coming in from the coast, taking the "red-eye" every other Friday night, arriving Saturday morning and going back early Monday morning. Later, the mother of one of Alan's friends told me that Alan had said he wished I would either come home and stay or not come home at all. It's true, those weekends had a feeling of unreality about them, all of us trying to act as though everything was all right, following the rules that we mustn't spoil Mummy's time at home. We never really talked anything out, but Steve and I were up all night every night, talking, talking, talking about what to do and never knowing. Alan changed schools and was at a perfectly awful place; I also hated his friends. They all smoked pot and took other kinds of stuff. My chronology is fuzzy in through here, but when Alan was fifteen it was recommended to us by a doctor that he go to a group that two psychiatrists were putting together over the summer. It 219 sounded helpful. At the last minute this could not be accomplished because they could not get the backing together. The summer was looming. As an alternative the doctor (whose name shall live in infamy) advised us to send him to a branch of New York Hospital in Westchester somewhere, and that is what we did. Steve and I were leery about it but drove him up there and left him. It was a locked facility. Alan told us later how he felt that first night, locked in a small dark room and finding himself the next day with some contemporaries on drugs, but also with genuine loonies. We visited him there every week, sitting around the grounds with very little to say, two of us hopeful, all of us miserable.

After a while they felt Alan had made progress, and he was granted an outing. We had investigated a place at Yale and were going to look it over as a next step. We went back to our house from there, and the time was approaching when we were to drive Alan back to Westchester. We lived in a house and were sitting in the kitchen on the ground floor, having coffee. At one point Alan said he had left something in the living room above us and went up to get it. After a few minutes it seemed odd that he had not returned downstairs, and then it became clear that he had let himself out through the door on the floor above. We couldn't believe it. Steve, in a panic, rushed up the stairs and out and ran down the block but, of course, Alan was nowhere to be seen. Steve rushed back. We looked at each other, paralyzed. We made some calls.

Later, Alan called from the house of one of his friends. I asked him how he could have done such a thing. Where was his sense of honor? He laughed incredulously. "Honor?! To get out of that place I would have done anything." We tried to negotiate, but he would not come home. Steve got ready to go over there. He ran up the stairs. He was suddenly stricken with incredible pain in his stomach and turned white. I called our doctor, who said to get him to emergency at Mount Sinai, and I got in touch with Susanna to meet me there. Steve was in the hospital for nearly five months and came very close to dying of pancreatitis. He was a well-filled-out six feet tall, but after two operations he was down to 125

220

pounds and looked eighty years old. Visitors used to ask me how my grandfather was. But he survived, and brilliantly.

When I called Westchester to explain why we had not dutifully returned Alan at the appointed hour, they told me it was essential to get him back there and I should use *any means* possible (their emphasis) to accomplish this. I was in torture. Steve was close to dying and Alan was out roaming, doing God knows what. I had my orders. Before I did what I did, I called a dear friend and asked his advice: "Should I lie to Alan to get him back to the house so he can be picked up?" I knew my friend had been in a similar quandary once about an unstable relative. He said I must do it. In his case, the relative thanked him for it afterward and said it had saved his life. Reluctant, and knowing it was a betrayal of trust but clinging to the rosy end result and doing it anyway, I called Alan at his friend's house the next day or so, told him his daddy was sick in the hospital, but it was safe to come home. He came home at the arranged time, and I had someone pick him up and take him back to the hospital. When I called the hospital and told them Alan was on his way, they were very disapproving of the way I had accomplished what they had urged me to do.

Trust is a precious thing between a parent and a child. I knew that, but the hospital had said to do "anything." So much for trust.

       H.S.C.: She does not lie to her child. He decides to go back because it is the honorable thing to do.

Alan stayed at the Westchester facility for a while, but not long. Friends smuggled drugs in to him. Then one day he climbed the impossibly high wall and escaped. I remember my mixed feelings when the hospital called me. I knew what he had done was awful, but I was full of grudging admiration. That took ingenuity and courage. He called me shortly thereafter, from where he would not exactly say, but he had hitched a ride and was OK.

I saw him a few times, but he was in increasingly bad shape, stoned and a bit wild. Steve was desperately ill. I tricked Alan into coming home once more and had him taken to St. Luke's, where there was a locked drug rehab, another blow for truth.

H.S.C. I did not do it.

My days were spent in large part commuting between St. Luke's and Mount Sinai. I was horrified to find at St. Luke's two of the druggie friends I was hoping to get Alan away from. Later, Alan was in several other "places": Gracie Square, Mount Sinai, the Hartford Institute of Living, Su Casa, to name a few. Alan seemed to want to do something about his drug problem himself and, in fact, he had put himself into Gracie Square. At one point, suffering from a deviated septum, he asked if he could have it operated on, to which I agreed. The father of a friend of his (a user, of course) was a plastic surgeon, and Alan arranged to have a slight straightening of his nose accomplished at the same time. After the operation he began using heroin. He spoke of having defiled his body by trying to change it, that this had been a wrong act, and he wished he could undo it. I found I needed the help of a therapist myself at this time, and it was she who told us of a residential place in Manhattan, an unlocked facility where young people lived and worked hard and seemed to come out having conquered their addiction. There were strict rules and a lot of group therapy, and once a week the parents also had to go to a group session. Even Alan's friends were astonished at the extent of Alan's drug activity, and it took two of them to round him up somewhere and somehow persuade him to go to this place and live there. The man in charge, Dr. Casriel, now deceased, also ran a group therapy empire in the same building, while the young people lived upstairs. I admired him. I thought he was warm and smart and had a good idea, and although things did not work out in Alan's case, Casriel had many successes. After almost

222

a year of living there, working hard cleaning and scrubbing, doing kitchen work, cooking, building repair, and progressing higher and higher in the structure, Alan was about to "graduate" when he suddenly walked out the door. The unlocked facilities work on the premise that if you want to leave, you can leave; you have to want to be there. Some clamoring brought him back for a confrontation with the staff, the other residents, the other parents, Susanna and us, all exhorting him, several of us in tears, but Alan just said he didn't care: Taking drugs meant more to him, and he would just keep doing it. We never threw him out. (That came later, when I was alone, without Steve.)

Alan and two of his friends wanted to go to Nepal, supposedly to set up a hand-painted T-shirt business. By this time Alan was going around asking all our friends for money, depleting my jewelry box, and taking checks from the back of the checkbook, but we did not have him arrested. We knew he wanted to be in Nepal because drugs there were plentiful and accessible, and we reasoned (?) that maybe he could find a better kind of life for himself there. (Read: "We were at our wits' end and needed peace.") We financed the trip, and his letters were at first ecstatic. Relations with his friends worsened, however, as his excessiveness grew to the point where they did not feel their money or their possessions were safe. One of the young men, in fact, stayed in Nepal and did find a good life. He married a Nepalese girl, had three children, and tried to help Alan, but he was hard to help. There were two trips to Nepal, with rehabs in between, and the second time Alan went, he continued on to Bangkok, where he lived quite a long time. Phone calls for money came, and I, in shreds, was too cowardly to take them, but Steve took them, and the same pattern was played out: first the yelling and scolding, and then the giving in to Alan's requests, which were usually backed up by the news that if he did not get the money he would be thrown in jail. He always got the money. My head under the blanket, I hoped Steve would stay firm, but was relieved when he agreed to send the money. Alan was also thrown into jail, which over there is a dungeon. A friend who had been inside the place, too, called us and told us what 223 it was like; he also said that when he last saw Alan, he looked as though he was dying. Calls to Senator Jacob Javits and a lot more money got him out. This happened twice.

H.S.C.
No Nepal trip? Let him stay in dungeon?

In 1979, when Steve had a second attack of pancreatitis, it never occurred to me that he could possibly die. Alan was twenty-six, living in Bangkok, and working for a friend of his as a "mole," someone who smuggled drugs into the United States. My golden lad was working in the Golden Triangle.

With Steve so ill, I hoped Alan would not come home. I feared it would be bad for Steve. But the friend, his boss, financed Alan's trip, and he arrived at the hospital looking like a model citizen, with a short haircut and a conventional light tan suit. That is the way "moles" have to dress. Nothing attention-getting, nothing bizarre—and Alan had had such a penchant for the bizarre in hair and in dress. Seventeen days later Steve died. Susanna, who had been living with someone for about five years, came home to live with me, and I was very glad she was there.

Alan never left the country again. What followed was a round of stays in various hospitals as his health started to deteriorate. I stopped giving him money and, desperate, he wandered into a methadone center and began the best couple of years of his life. He met a terrific girl, not in the program but through a friend. Eloise and he fell in love. After he got out of Bellevue, where he had had pneumonia, he moved in with her and began something touchingly close to a normal happy existence. He was drug-free except for the methadone, and he was diligent about taking it. Throughout everything, all during the years, he had never stopped drawing. Some of the work was psychedelic, as there was a lot of LSD along the way. He told me once when he and I were discussing his first trip to Nepal, he remembered seeing six of me at one time.

224

Good idea for musical number?

But now he had lovely subjects to draw . . . Eloise and her big beautiful cat, and the cozy apartment. She encouraged him to go back to school. "Go back to school" is not exactly a realistic way of putting it, since Alan had not been to school since "graduating" from some rip-off tutorial "high school" that gave him a diploma but was hardly a school at all. He had always remained curious about everything and read a great deal about art and philosophy. He read Edgar Allan Poe, Dostoyevski, De Quincey, and, of course, the writers of the occult. He wanted to study art therapy and, with Eloise's guidance and encouragement, enrolled at the New School for Social Research, undertaking a full program of four subjects. It seemed to me too ambitious, but I was so thrilled at what was happening, and so burstingly happy, I decided to believe all would turn out perfectly. We did things that normal families do: I visited them for lunch. We had dinner together. They came to see a show I was involved in. When Eloise's parents came from California, they took us all to La Grenouille for a gorgeous feast, and there were daily calls and inquiries about the cat.

H.S.C.: No rewrite here.

The problems were not over, however. Alan had been away in a deep sense. And he really had no foundation to come back to. The schoolwork was overwhelming to him. He had never developed any work habits, did not know how to study, and had lived a totally undisciplined life for so long. He tried, but it was too much for him. Emotionally, addicts remain at the age when they began drugging. Alan and Eloise loved each other very much and he tried very hard, but he began slipping. The second term he wound up taking just one course, in film noir. And he began to smoke pot. Just that. 225

But things got out of control. They tried to plan a trip, but the money Eloise put aside for it was suddenly missing, and after a drawn-out struggle, she had to tell him it was over.

Back to desperation, his and mine. He was out in the street. I found Alanon, which is where you go when your life is involved with an alcoholic (who should be in A.A.), and through those meetings I discovered that there was something called Naranon, where all who gather are involved with addicts (who should be in N.A.). I learned the three C's: I didn't Cause it, I can't Control it, I can't Cure it. Detach with love. I tried to explain it to my darling friend Gloria, happily remote from this experience. At Naranon a group of people, all of whose lives are being deeply affected by someone on drugs (a child, a husband, a wife, a lover), get together around a table, or on chairs in a circle, and feel safe to talk. Everyone is anonymous. No one who has not been there can quite grasp what having a drug addict in your life is really like. The tyranny of the sick, it rules your life. You are obsessed; you think you can change him and you try every way you can, but you learn that it does not work. You cannot change the person, you can only change your own attitude toward him and the actions you take concerning him. Learning all this is meant to help you. It *may* help him. There is no teacher, no authority in charge. Anyone can lead the free meeting. You just exchange experiences, offer comfort, not advice, and give one another the feeling that you are not alone. It is safe to cry.

I know the configurations of many a church cellar in New York because that is where most of these meetings take place, but I found my home base around a table in a conference room at Gracie Square Hospital. I learned about "enabling." With the help of a sympathetic, intelligent, wise stranger who became my "sponsor," I did the twelve steps. I was not consistent and sent Alan many mixed messages, but in spite of the criticism leveled at these programs now and the fun made of the oft-repeated clichés and the boring group jargon, I feel these meetings are the best answer so far. Gloria would still ask me, knowing it would make me laugh, "Well, what did you learn in Drunk School today?"

I also had a therapist. Both she and Naranon were helpful. I did not always do what I should have. I tried to get Alan to go to various rehab places—Su Casa, Hazelden—but nothing worked out. I paid for hotel rooms, food, clothing, toilet articles, but sometimes I didn't. I was not consistent. Sometimes he was in the street. He panhandled. He never landed in jail, but he was sick more frequently. Several pneumonias, many hospital stays. It seems to me I must have visited him in every hospital in the city. Wherever he was, everyone was charmed by him, loved to come and talk with him, got mad at him because he did not want to change.

His downward progression continued. He tried to keep up with his daily methadone, which meant getting to a clinic. He took other drugs as well. It was hard for him to follow through on applications for assistance, getting to the right offices. His health deteriorated horribly, and he really wanted to be in the hospital because there he was taken care of. It was hard to watch and feel so helpless. Then he learned that he was HIV positive from a dirty needle long ago. I saw to it that he had a room to live in and expense money (knowing where a lot of it would go), and I met him at least once a week to have coffee and talk. I refused to hear the death knell. Surely they would discover something . . . ?

Soon the last pneumonia struck and he was in his last hospital, Beth Israel in New York. But in the rewrite:

HER SECOND CHANCE

FULL SHOT: HOSPITAL ROOM IN WASH-INGTON, D.C.

ALAN is in bed, MOTHER sitting at bedside.

MOTHER
Alan, darling, keep the oxygen mask on . . . it's easier.

ALAN
(removing mask and smiling)
But Mom, I don't need it, I'm not sick!

A DOCTOR enters.

DOCTOR
How are you feeling, Mr. President?

ALAN
Totally good, Doctor! I'm fine.

DOCTOR
You gave us quite a scare with that infection. It looked like HIV.

ALAN
It was all a mistake, Mother. A wrong diagnosis.

(MOTHER and ALAN hug.)

Because of your awareness and vigilance bringing me up, I was a smart, maybe a little eccentric, but happy kid, and your extraordinary instinct for mothering gave me the best start a boy ever had. So is it any wonder I wound up as President of the United States?

MOTHER
It's every mother's dream!

SUSANNA enters, and they all embrace.

CLOSE SHOT: The THREE

MOTHER
Alan is going to *live!*

They are laughing. ALAN grabs a guitar from under the bed.

ALAN
(singing)
"I could love you the way I should, but anyway, darling . . ." Remember, Mom?

TIGHT SHOT OF ALL THREE

They are all so happy.

                    ME
              (voiceover)
But this is the rewrite. In life, there are no rewrites.
I'll never get that second chance.

Holiday Moods

*E*veryone who has been there knows that the loss of someone close gives holiday times a special poignancy. To make things easier for myself, as is my wont, I decided on Christmas Day, 1991, to visit the cemetery. There were three new stones I had not seen, and I felt a need to complete something by going and assuring myself that everything was all right—or as all right as things can be at a cemetery.

The first stone was my husband Steve's, who had died twelve years before this visit. At the unveiling I noted through blurred eyes that the inscription on his footstone read "eighty-six years." Steve had died at sixty-six. My first reaction was shock and outrage, quickly followed by helpless laughter because Steve would have thought it was funny. I only wished he had been there to laugh with me. The monument people promised to fill in the "8" and make it a "6," but when I visited again, I got a lesson in the true meaning of "carved in stone." The "8" shone defiantly through the cement "6," and there was nothing for it but to order a new stone.

The second was Aunt Rose's, who had died two years prior to this visit, just before turning 101, and the third stone belonged to my son Alan, dead a little over a year. All the stones were perfect now, no mistakes, no typographical errors. Everything else looked swell, too.

The plot, accommodations for twelve, had been

bought through his temple by my grandpa, at the old Mount Carmel Cemetery in Queens, and there they all were, grandpa and grandma, my mother and father, and my aunt and uncle, the parents of my cousin Muriel, who had accompanied me that Christmas Day. In keeping with the old tradition, we collected nine assorted pebbles each and placed them on the footstones, as witness to our having been there. Then for a few minutes we sat on the stone bench. The cemetery people had told us it would be cheaper for us without the bench because then their mowers could zoom through from plot to plot with no obstacle. A plot with a bench, like a room with a view, is more expensive. But our grandpa had asked us to keep the bench always, and so we did. I was glad it was there. The December day was beautiful, quite cold, and I felt shaken, particularly by the sight of my son's name so clearly cut into the clean stone. ALAN KYLE, it said. Was it possible? Again I learned the meaning of "carved in stone." It was inarguably there, final and forever, forever. It was Christmas, and there he was. But it is not as if just the Christmas before we had been laughing and celebrating together. Many years earlier, Christmas had become for him just another nameless, hopeless piece of time to be filled entirely with the pursuit and the consumption of drugs.

When the children were young, Christmas at our house was just like Christmas in any other normal Jewish-American home: The big beautiful Christmas tree stood in the library near the fireplace, where hopeful stockings were hung, and the night before, miraculously, the space around the base of the tree was piled high with presents. Steve and I would rouse ourselves sleepily after a late night out. Steve would put on his long red underwear, stuff a pillow in the front, don a five-and-dime cap-and-beard arrangement, and we would go down to the library, Steve "ho-ho-ho-ing" all the way. The children, Alan and Susanna, who had been waiting impatiently since dawn, would scream with delight, and although they knew it was Daddy, there would still be a slightly wondering doubt, even apprehension, in their eyes until they pounced on him and pulled off the hat and beard.

Steve's family had celebrated Christmas, but it was a 231

ritual I had never had as a child. We observed Hanukkah with a family dinner at my grandparents' home, lighting the first candle with our aunt and uncle and cousins and our unmarried aunt Rose. We received generous checks from our grandpa and exchanged modest gifts, usually of our own devising. My upbringing was not particularly religious, but my mother lit candles on Friday night, we went to temple on Rosh Hashanah and Yom Kippur, at least to visit our father there, and my mother kept a kosher kitchen with two sets of dishes (one for dairy product meals, the other for meat-based foods), along with two sets of silver to match. Years later when I got married, my mother gave me a few leftover pieces of silver from the long-past broken-up sets. It was a while before I could see butter on a "meat" knife without feeling a slight frisson akin to nausea, even though I'd been eating bacon since high school.

I was either dumb or there was some important human element lacking in me when I was a child because I have no memory of being jealous of kids who had Christmas. Or maybe our parents did something that made me satisfied with what I had. Aunt Rose told me that one night when I was a year old, she had come over to babysit because my mother and father were going to a formal dinner. It was Christmastime, but their event had nothing to do with that, of course, and was probably concerned with Hadassah or the Child Study Association, two of my mother's big interests, or maybe the Beth Moses Hospital.

While I lay drooling in my crib, my brother, four-year-old Nathaniel, had been invited to go across the hall to our lovely neighbors, the Olivers, to see their Christmas tree. Daddy was in his tuxedo and Mom in a long pale pink satin gown, ready to leave, when Nat came running back to our apartment bursting with joy, waving a tree-shaped branch the Olivers had given him, and shouting, "We have a Christmas tree! We have a Christmas tree!" My father gently explained to Nat that we did not have Christmas trees and that he would have to give it back, whereupon Nat exploded in torrents of tears and clutched his "tree" with an iron grip. Having a tree was not seemly in our kind of Jewish home. Symbols can stir painful echoes in anyone who has been through a pogrom, a concept not easy to get across to a four-year-old.

Our parents were already late for the dinner, but my mother put down her bag and her wrap, peeled off her long white gloves, sat little Nat on her pink satin knee, and rocked him. She explained that different people believed different things, not that one belief was better than the other but they were different. She said the Olivers were Christian and of course they believed in God, only it was God divided in three: the Father, the Son, and the Holy Spirit. We were Jewish, and we believed in God, too, but to us God was One, one all-powerful loving God. Hear, O Israel, the Lord our God, the Lord is One. Jewish people did not have Christmas trees, but they had this One Wonderful God. Miraculously, said Rose, Nat's tears stopped. He jumped off Mother's lap and ran over to the Olivers, Rose following. Exuberantly thrilled for some reason that we had this one swell God, he explained to the Olivers that they believed in three but that we had *One* God, thanked them for the "tree," returned it, took a candy cane instead, and ran joyously back home. And Mummy and Daddy went to the ball. It seems to me my mother could have taught Moses a thing or two about selling monotheism.

At the Brooklyn Ethical Culture School we celebrated differences. The school was not very big on Christmas. It was big on Yuletide. We had no Christmas pageant, we had a Winter Festival and a Spring Festival, marking the fact that of course there were Christmas and Easter but that all cultures throughout history had had their own unique ways of cele-brating those magical changes of the seasons.

Greeks did it, Celts did it.

Even Visigoths in pelts did it . . . etc., etc.

Every Christmastime, in the big hall of the Knights of Columbus building near the school, we put up an evergreen tree plus a candelabra, and sometimes we were Roman vestal virgins and warriors, and sometimes we were medieval lords and ladies carrying around a big tray with a papier-mâché boar's head on it, singing *"Caput afri defero . . ."* We ac-knowledged Christmas, but we had no crèche. Who knows? There might have been a sensitive Visigoth kid at school.   233

We learned Christmas songs like "Deck the Halls" and "Jingle Bells" and even "Good King Wenceslas," but not the ones with Jesus in them. I learned all those later, and I find them beautiful. But although I know a lot of lyrics to a lot of songs, there are still some big gaps in my knowledge of this field.

Remembering how exciting our Winter Festivals were, as well as how considerate and democratic, when my daughter Susanna started going to the Dalton School at age three, I plunged into action. I heard they were having a Christmas pageant. I made an appointment with the headmaster and confidently began my pitch about dropping it and having a nice nonsectarian W.F. instead. "After all, the children are from all kinds of backgrounds, etc., etc.," I began with fervor. The head of the school looked aghast. "But Mrs. Kyle, our Christmas pageant is an old Dalton tradition, as old as the school itself. It's famous." I really could not quite understand why she did not see the logic of my sensible suggestion. A year later I was in London in connection with a show. The work was just about finished. I was planning to stay a couple of days to see some theater when I got my daily call from Steve in New York. He assured me all was well and as an afterthought said, "Oh, by the way, Susanna is going to be in the Christmas pageant playing an angel." I exploded. "What! 'By the way'!!! You almost didn't tell me that!? She's in the Christmas pageant! How thrilling! Oh, my baby . . ." I was furious I had not been told sooner. I canceled my plans to stay and booked the next flight back, arriving just in time to catch the show. There she was, my four-year-old angel Susanna, as an angel in pink gauze with a gold halo and gold wings, kneeling, partly visible, by the crèche. I beamed and cried. What a great idea—a Christmas pageant!

Around Eastertime one year Susanna came home from the fourth grade at Dalton and asked "Why don't we have a seder [the ritual feast on the eve of Passover]?" They had been studying the ancient Hebrews in class, and she had made a most beautiful illustrated book of the lives of the Hebrews in Egypt and the Exodus. Old secular Dalton with

234

its Christmas pageant had awakened her interest in her past. From then on for several years we had a seder, though I, a woman, had to lead the service with my meager knowledge of Hebrew remembered from tiny tot Hebrew school.

But all through my life the holiday that pulled most strongly on my insides was Yom Kippur, the Day of Atonement. When we were children we would drop in briefly at the temple during the long day of fasting, which we were not supposed to do until we were thirteen. It was easy to visit Grandpa because he went to the reformed temple, Shaari Zedek, right across from us, and Mother and I, along with Nat, could walk in and mingle and find him. But with Daddy it was quite different. He was at the orthodox Jewish Center, and women had to sit up in the gallery. In my teens I would walk over there with my cousins or a friend and wait around until my father took a break and came out for a few minutes. Yom Kippur always comes in the early autumn, usually hitting the hottest day of the year. But we young ladies were in our fall finery, wool dresses or suits, hats and gloves, enduring the broiling heat because we felt it important to be in our holiday best. After my father died I lost track of the whole thing.

Years later, then an actively working woman, wife, and mother of two, I felt that ancient pull. I wanted to hit my roots, surround myself with that old-synagogue-in-Brooklyn atmosphere. Conveniently, there was an orthodox shul on Lexington Avenue and Ninety-fifth Street, down the block, and the rabbi lived next door to us. Steve said he hoped I would enjoy my roots if I found them and wished me luck as I started down the street with Rabbi Langer and his wife. I followed her up the stairs to the balcony, recalling the look and sound of the old Jewish Center. When we got to our seats, I was greeted by a barrage of elegant French from a twittering group of chicly dressed and deliciously perfumed French women. I had forgotten that during the war the Upper East Side had become an enclave of French Jews fleeing Hitler and that the Langers were themselves French refugees. It did not look or sound or smell one bit like my 235 childhood in Brooklyn, and I realized the truth of *"On ne peut plus rentrer chez soi,"* as Thomas Loup (Wolfe) once wrote.

The year Steve died I again felt the need to be in a synagogue on Yom Kippur, and a friend took me to a service. The next year my friend Leonard Bernstein asked me if I'd like to accompany him and his son Alex on his usual Yom Kippur route, dropping in at various synagogues around town. He called it "shul hopping." Sacrilegious as it sounds, it was in no way disrespectful. It just meant that Leonard would visit a few different places of worship during the long Yom Kippur day, arriving at different ones for different sections of the service. He was of course greeted warmly by the officials of each synagogue, quietly and ceremoniously given his prayer shawl and yarmulke, and taken to a place of honor to pray. I was seated somewhere near him when it was a reformed or conservative synagogue but went upstairs at the orthodox ones.

At one very beautiful and luxuriously appointed temple, I looked down at the elaborate main floor where the Ark, which holds the sacred scrolls, gleamed with gold and silver, and all the men wore white satin yarmulkes and white prayer shawls. There is a point in the service where the rabbi and the other celebrants prostrate themselves for a few seconds before the Ark, spreading their arms out on the floor. From above in the balcony it was a breathtaking and moving sight. I told Lenny I had had a better view than he—the overhead, or "Busby Berkeley," shot as in the early musical movies. That day Leonard took good care of me, making sure we got to another beautiful temple in time for the memorial service that he realized meant so much to me because of Steve.

Now Leonard is gone, too. The first Yom Kippur after his death, his sister Shirley and I decided we must go to shul. I told her that for the past few years, since I sold my house and moved to my West Side apartment, I had been going to the Kol Nidre service, which takes place on Yom Kippur Eve, at the orthodox synagogue right behind me but that since I was not a member, I could only get into the "annex"—a vast

characterless space on one level where the men and women

are separated by a cardboard partition, something like a large bundling board. We suddenly thought of Marshall Mayer. He was a friend of Leonard and Shirley's brother Burton at Dartmouth and was now a rabbi with a congregation quite near me, B'nai Jeshurun. Years before, just after he was ordained, instead of settling for a cushy Westchester post, he went to Argentina where he built up a huge following and worked secretly with Jacobo Timerman in the dangerous pursuit of helping families locate their loved ones in prison and getting information back and forth.

When Shirley called to arrange for us to go, Marshall said, "Of course you know you will have to come to the Lutheran Church of St. Paul and St. Joseph."

"A church?" Shirley asked.

He explained that during the past fall, just as he and the cantor at B'nai Jeshurun had stepped away from the altar while preparing a service, the ceiling of the synagogue caved in—over the exact spot where they had been standing. They praised the Almighty for saving their lives, and as they were wondering where they could continue to hold services during the extensive repair period, the minister at the church a block away contacted them and invited them to worship there. The two congregations met and prepared a workable schedule together, arranging also for a beautiful banner to be draped over the crucifix at appropriate times.

Now the High Holidays had come, and Kol Nidre was to be held at the church. Rabbi Mayer made us welcome. The day was, true to my old memories, a scorcher, and the church had no air-conditioning. It was packed to the top of the choir loft. The minister and his family occupied a row. We squeezed in with Marshall's wife and his family. The service began with Kol Nidre played on the cello. The cantor, who comes up from Argentina every year to sing this service, repeated the moving opening cadence in his magnificent voice, and I wept. Kol Nidre is done three times during the service. The emotion built. At the end of the prayers Marshall said because of the heat he would take pity on his flock and deliver no sermon. Instead he spoke with gratitude to the minister and his church, and presented them with a silver 237 chalice, mentioning that although Lutherans do not use wine in their services, it would serve as a decoration and reminder of the close friendship between the church and the synagogue.

That year the memorial service was a hard one to get through; Steve, and now Leonard, and that impossibility, Alan.

I still celebrate Christmas, holiday of my adult years, in a way. There are tree-trimming parties to go to that include carol "sings" where I have to fudge the Jesus lyrics. Susanna and I exchange gifts, and my friends and I still seem to give each other presents, a dwindling number as time goes on and children grow older. There are other changes. The Christmas card that Leonard and Felicia Bernstein sent every year—a photograph of them with their three children, Jamie, Alexander, and Nina, growing and changing every year—is now supplanted by a Christmas photo from Jamie and her husband David and their two cherubs, Frankie (a girl) and Evan. The arrival of this card the last few years has been both heartbreaking and reassuring. And sometimes on Christmas day I visit friends who have grandchildren, and the room is a sea of colored paper and ribbon, and boxes and toys and sweaters and kids piled up in happy confusion, the way our library once looked.

Sitting on the stone cemetery bench I realized that Alan's last Christmas was spent in the hospital, one of many hospital stays during more than twenty years of his turbulent, tragically wasted life. When I visited, he asked if he could have a guitar as a Christmas present. He was in a wheelchair, very weak and emaciated, and still sneaking cigarettes. By then he was no longer merely HIV positive. The disease he had contracted from a dirty needle, who knows where or when, was marching on. I told him I would think about it since I knew he could not manage it until he was stronger. It did not occur to me that he was dying. The ravages of the drug life are such that although Alan looked alarmingly pale and thin, I had seen him looking that way before and he had always come through. Later I was sorry I had not gotten him

238

the guitar immediately. That was just one of the things to feel sorry about.

About a month later, Susanna called and in a stricken, anguished voice asked, "Why didn't you tell me Alan has AIDS?" I said I had not known how she would react. They had been estranged. She had not wanted to see him for several years, a situation not uncommon in a family where one child is an addict. I asked her how she had found out. It was one of those crossings of paths that seem so impossible but aren't. Alan had been living at a Y and taking part in a program called Momentum. At a different church or synagogue every weekday, Momentum welcomes over a hundred HIV or AIDS victims, providing a hot dinner, a free store where clothing and food are distributed, pastoral care, psychological counseling, housing and drug rehabilitation information, and music. There is always someone playing the piano at dinner, or flute and piano, or sometimes a singer, sometimes a group. One evening Alan wandered over to the piano to talk about songs with the pianist and mentioned some of my songs and his connection with them. The woman playing was the aunt of a close friend of Susanna's, and she related where she had seen Alan. Susanna was shaken. I told her where Alan was. I merely gave her the information, making no demands, no suggestions. A couple of days later she called and said she had been to see Alan. She described her horror at how he looked and how sad she felt. They had both said how much they loved each other and had a warm, loving talk. I was glad she had gone, and so was she. By the end of the next day, Alan was dead.

Earlier that day, before going down to the hospital, I asked my friend Cynthia O'Neal if she could meet me there. She had been working with AIDS victims and other terminally ill people, and I wanted some kind of reading from her on how Alan was doing. He had called me the day before in a state of panic and told me his doctor had frightened the hell out of him. The doctor had said to Alan that it was hospital procedure to get a signed paper from me stating whether or not life support systems should be used if needed. In other 239 words, they let him know that he was so close to death, there might come a moment soon when he would not be able to answer the question himself, and he had to tell me what he wanted me to do. This was the first moment he had fully realized he might die. And it was the first moment I realized it, too. But not really. I still did not accept the fact.

I told Alan not to panic, that I would come right down and we would talk about it. I was furious that the doctors had done this, but they insisted they had to do it. I could see the results as soon as I walked into Alan's room. He looked as though he had truly given up. He lay prone and faint, his eyes almost transparent, and he was rigged up to an oxygen mask that he kept tearing away from his mouth. Cynthia came in, and he lit up at the sight of her. He embraced her and immediately wanted to draw her. He ran his finger along the outline of her elegant cheekbone and chin, and reached for the paper and pencil I gave him. But he was too weak.

While he lay back, Cynthia and I walked toward the door, and I asked her what she thought. She thought he looked like someone who had partly crossed over already and that life for him, even if it could go on for a while, would be increasingly more horrible. She had watched it so many times. If he wanted to go, he should be allowed to go. I still did not quite grasp this. I asked Alan what I should do; would he like them to keep him going as long as possible or not? It was up to him. We tried to joke about it. Earlier he had apparently told the doctor he wanted them to do everything. But a short time later when the doctor came in with the paper for me to sign, Alan had changed his mind and said he should be allowed to go when the time came. Not the easiest paper to sign. I signed it. Cynthia left. Alan showed me the cards he had gotten from visitors to other patients in the four-bed room and from social workers and other hospital staff people who had apparently formed relationships with him and who obviously loved him. I looked at the latest drawings he had made, taped to the wall behind his bed. They were beautiful, particularly one delicate illustration for the Dostoyevski book *White Nights.* It was a picture of a man smoking opium.

240   We talked quietly of the past. Alan told me how won-

derful it had been to see Susanna and how they had cried together. He said he was sorry—sorry about everything. I told him no matter what had happened, no matter what troubles we had all been through, his father and I would not have wanted a life without him. His ravaged, sensitive face lit up in an incandescent smile. I sat by his bedside holding his hand and watched him gradually slip away, not realizing what I was watching.

I sat with him as long as they would let me, then took his drawings from the wall, packed up his few belongings, and finally, at the orderly's gentle suggestion, went out of the room. I could not reach Susanna, but left word for her to meet me at my apartment. When I called Adolph, he volunteered to come down and take me home, but I wanted to get away from there as quickly as possible and told him and Mu and a few others I called just to come to the apartment. Alan's last doctor put me in a taxi.

Susanna came, and Mu, and the Greens and Cynthia, and I remember Betty Bacall bearing huge bags of food from Shun Lee West. Heartache is not a poetic euphemism, it is real pain. Your heart actually hurts. The intensity diminishes with time, as does the number of hours a day and night you live with vivid memory plus hopeless yearning. But it doesn't go away. I feel it still, and hardly a day goes by that I don't think of Alan; the pictures are disturbing, but I'm so glad to see him.

All through the grisly stuff that everyone must go through, Susanna was my anchor, and when I expressed a desire to have some kind of service, she said, "Not at a funeral home . . . in your living room." I also expressed a wish to hear Hebrew, and after thinking despairingly of what kind of rabbi I wanted, I realized that I knew one: Isaac Stern's daughter Shira. Our friends gathered, people who had known Alan all his life, had tried to help him, had been exasperated by him, had been saddened by the way he had chosen to live —people who loved him. Shira arrived, perfectly beautiful with her startling blue eyes and wearing a small round embroidered skullcap and shawl. She asked everyone to form a circle of comfort and gave us prayer books. The men were 241 given yarmulkes. I held on to Susanna's hand. Then Shira stood and began to sing the service in Hebrew. I will never forget the sound of her pure sweet heartbreaking voice filling the room. She then asked each one to read a part of the text. There was such a deep feeling of community, I was truly surrounded by love and comfort. Gloria told me later that she felt part of something almost tribal: the circle, the music, the men in skullcaps, the intense uplifted feeling. Shira had told me before that she would ask me to speak about Alan. I was not sure this was such a good idea, but she felt it was important for me to do it. It was hard. I tried to talk honestly about him and what our lives had been like, and I thanked everyone for caring so much all along and for having helped, none of us ever knowing what might help and what might not. I described some of what Alan had told me about his last days in the hospital.

Apparently he had had some good talks with a priest named Father Connor who visited him in his room. No rabbi seems to have come by. Alan told me he had been comforted by the young Catholic. Later, after the service, I remember Steve Smith, himself a Catholic, who was sadly to die later that year, whispering to me mischievously, "I think we got him in the end." Whatever comfort Alan received, and wherever it came from, I am grateful.

As the wind began to bite more bitterly at the cemetery, I was thinking I no longer needed to worry whether or not Alan had a coat or whether he was huddling in some doorway somewhere without the coat.

Now, at the time of this writing, it is early spring, and Easter and Passover are on their way. On Christmas day I made things tougher for myself by visiting the cemetery. What can I do to myself for the spring holidays? Run all the movies of Steve and me with the children? Look through all the albums and boxes of pictures never mounted? That might be a step toward undoing myself fairly completely. But I draw the line at the cemetery. I have not been there since, having found everything in order there, the date, the planting, the stone bench. There is no need to go again. The holidays will remain as difficult as ever, I'm sure, a mixture of sweet memories, pain, and regret. Yom Kippur is still the worst, I think. Steve went into the hospital on September 30, which happened to be Yom Kippur Eve. But because of the vagaries of the Hebrew calendar, Yom Kippur falls on a different date each year, so I get hit twice: September 30 and whatever day Yom Kippur happens to be. Or is it Christmas that is the worst? I want a lot of things this Christmas. I want a world that is one big Winter Festival like the ones we used to have at Ethical. Every culture, go do your own thing. And let everyone else do his or her or its own thing, even the Visigoths. I want everyone to have food and a place to live. And I want . . . I want no one to have to come to a program like Momentum because there won't be any drugs or AIDS. And I want music and moonlight and love and romance. And a few more terrific books to read, and outfits to wear. And I want my son back. And . . . and . . . Merry Christmas to all and to all a good night. And God bless us everyone . . . the God that is three and the God that is one, and the God with seven arms, and all the rest of you Gods. Bless us. Bless us everyone! Happy Holidays!

Proverbs
and Revelations

On a landing at the Louvre. Not the first time I saw Paris
but one of several, each a renewed joy and excitement.

Being "painted" by Moïse Kisling at his studio in Paris on our first trip.

London, 1965—we meet the Beatles, an event that I think thrilled me even more than the children. Here is Susanna with Ringo, who along with his mates dissuaded her and Alan from going to Liverpool.

Out of Africa and into the lion's mouth. On safari with a bunch of strangers. We came out of the bush good friends.

Ever incredible Venice: on the balcony of our gorgeous suite at the Grand Hotel
—a lucky find.

Isn't it romantic? Yes, it was.

Political involvements and commitment. People I admired and campaigned with and/or for: Mrs. Eleanor Roosevelt, a big influence in my life; Adlai Stevenson, who I still think could have been a fine president; the Kennedys (here are Teddy and Jean Smith)—I worked for John for president and Robert and Teddy for senator; Bill and Hillary Clinton—I support them all the way.

I never wanted pictures taken at the New Year's Day gathering. It changes things when people know there is a camera around. But we often wound up around the piano, so here are some of us at a smaller party: Adolph and Phyllis are next to me and Jerome Robbins, longtime friend and colleague, is seated next to Jule Styne at the piano. How I miss Jule. Not only did we work together often, but he was a dear, hilarious, irreplaceable friend.

My brother Nat with me on the porch of my recently acquired Bridgehampton house. At the beginning of this book there are pictures of us as kids—the way we were. Here is the way we are, still close.

The First Time I Saw Paris

Our friend Kiki, the superb painter Moïse Kisling, a colleague of Picasso and Modigliani, looked bewildered and disappointed. It was 1951, our first trip to Paris, and we were sitting with him, at his invitation, in the famous old Paris landmark Le Moulin Rouge. Kiki had said to us in his charmingly accented English, eyes twinkling, "I will take you to the *real* Paris, the Paris I know so well." He looked around the place in disbelief. It was a shabby, rundown sort of hall where a desultory line of aging, heavily made-up ladies were performing a ghostly echo of a cancan of long ago. When they lifted their ruffled skirts flirtatiously and shook them at the ceiling, you wished they wouldn't. The music was tinny, and the only food available was ham or cheese sandwiches wrapped in wax paper.

"Well," said Kiki, finally laughing ruefully, "I haven't been here for about thirty, forty years." He apologized, and we all laughed and moved on to La Coupole, the big, brightly lit meeting place for artists like Kiki and anyone looking for good food and company, and there we fell upon heaping plattersful of tiny crisp frogs' legs.

We had known Kiki in New York, where he had spent the war years and was intimately involved with our old friend Snow Paltridge, a girl Steve had met while she was a model at the Art Students' League. She was a warm, somewhat exotic woman, and beautiful, although she resembled her dachshund, and was most helpful to Steve and me by lending us her apartment in Tudor City when she could, complete with sandalwood soap and incense.

Excited, we visited Kiki in his atelier, which had been Modigliani's at one time. It was up a curving wrought-iron stairway and looked out on a leafy courtyard. The food at lunch was delicious, although what tasted to me like very fine tuna fish turned out to be brains, and the salad oil and vinegar cruet that I admired as an interesting piece of sculpture was actually a graceful glass penis, at the base of which the oil and vinegar were decoratively and naturally in the glass balls.

After lunch Kiki made me pose (fully clothed) on his platform, arranged a large empty frame around me, and, holding palette and brushes, pretended to paint through the frame. The series of snapshots Steve took of this scene, with me in various positions, looks as though Kiki is actually painting my picture.

Kiki introduced us to his friend Alex Maguy, a well-known couturier of the 1930s who was just reopening his salon and insisted I have something designed by him. Alex, energetic and very self-confident, had served in the Maquis during the Resistance, and his hatred of the Germans was so intense he not only would not buy a Mercedes, he refused even to get into one and he spat whenever one passed. He made me a stunning suit of mixed brown-gold wool with brown velvet lapels, a suit I have to this day.

The reopening of Alex's salon did not work out so well, and by the time we returned to Paris in 1958, Alex, already a collector himself and a great friend of Chagall, Picasso, and other painters, had opened an art gallery. It is there that Steve and I were able to buy the beginnings of a collection: a beautiful Chagall in rather atypical colors, some drawings, a Matisse, a Pascin, a tiny Picasso, a Derain, and a very faint Degas back of a horse. There was also a Picasso poster oddity from a 1956 exhibition in Vallauris: on one side, the beautiful poster itself, and on the other, the same poster but with extra painting added by Picasso, plus his painted signature.   251

It was all glorious then and it still is, courtesy of the hit show I had running at the time, *Bells Are Ringing.* Somehow we were never able to add to our collection after that. The truly big hit remained elusive for a while. When there were some successes, obligations of a not-so-happy nature loomed and had to take precedent over art collecting. We did have some rare Indian paintings and a beautiful unfinished Kisling —the head of a girl with red hair and blue eyes, a gift from him, which looks finished to me.

The Victory of Samothrace poised for flight at the top of the staircase at the Louvre was the thrill one hoped it would be, and the Mona Lisa, which you come upon so casually, is smaller than I had pictured it, but seeing it, the real *it,* was another incomparable moment.

We had arrived in Paris with a few names and telephone numbers given to us by Ruth Dubonnet, lady love of our close friend and composer of many of our shows, Jule Styne. Ruth had lived in France a long time while married to her third husband, André Dubonnet, a friend, unfortunately, of Hermann Goering. It took a special act, made law by President Eisenhower, to get her passport reinstated. Actually, during the war she had driven an ambulance for the right side, ours, and had been a patriot all along, no matter what her then-husband was up to. Ruth was a handsome woman with short dark hair, and she had been somewhat of a femme fatale in the 1920s with a star-studded roster of admirers. Humphrey Bogart once told us that when he was going up Ruth's stairs, he was apt to run into Fred Astaire coming down, and Chaliapin, the great opera bass, might be waiting on the landing.

Steve and I felt shy about it, sitting in our rooms at the Raphaël, but we finally decided to call the top name on Ruth's list, Charles Gombault, the editor of *France-Soir,* the very fine leftist newspaper, and his Canadian wife, Elaine, publicist for Dior and others.

Elaine, an effulgent redhead, as we later learned, immediately invited us, sight unseen, to spend the next day and night with them at the old farmhouse they had bought a short distance from Paris. I told Elaine just to look for the best-looking thing coming off the train, male or female, and she spotted Steve at once. A long friendship ensued, in Paris, at their home where people from the worlds of politics and the arts gathered at marvelous dinners, and in New York when they came here. The Jeu de Paume and the other galleries and museums, shopping, the Ritz, eating, La Méditerranée, Maxim's, Brasserie Lipp, Le Relais Bisson, Lucas-Carton, Pré Catelan, and walking, just walking and looking, just *being* in Paris . . . There is still a song to be written called "The First Time I Saw Paris." The first time we saw London and then Florence and Rome should have songs, too.

In Venice I remembered the pictures of my mother on one of her trips, circa 1910, standing in the Piazza San Marco in a long skirt and jacket buttoned up to the neck, feeding the pigeons, many of which were roosting on her immense hat. How hot it must have been in those clothes in August, and it must have been August because that is when schoolteachers took their vacations.

San Marco is a great first-time sight that never dims no matter how many times you see it. On the 1958 trip while sitting at a table in San Marco, we suddenly saw a blazingly beautiful vision at one corner. Entering the plaza were a stunning blonde and an equally stunning brunette, who turned out to be people we knew: Stella Adler (the blonde), renowned actress and acting teacher, and her daughter Ellen (the brunette), who became a fine painter and is one of my closest friends, and is still beautiful. In a town used to ravishing women, heads whirled and people gaped.

I remember our getting a little lost trying to find our way back to our hotel and asking for help in a shop. Our Italian obviously needed work because the shop owner looked puzzled, then eagerly said to us, "English! English! I go!" and went off in search of his friend who spoke English. The friend who spoke English came and, after listening to where we wanted to go, told us, "First you go on your right, then you go on your wrong." We found our hotel.

The beautiful Grand Hotel became our home because when the gondola dropped us at the Danieli, where we had been booked, we found our tiny room looked out on a wall. 253

Despair. I suddenly recalled that a friend of mine had said, "If you ever go to Venice, ask for suite 29/31[?] at the Grand." Back into the gondola for a breath-held sail down to the Grand, where by some miracle "our" suite was empty. There is no point in being in Venice, it seems to me, unless you can walk out onto your balcony (we had two), lean on the stone balustrade, and gaze into, across, down, and up the Grand Canal. Darkening gilt furniture, tapestries on the walls, a huge, elaborate bed with a headboard of scrolled wood and upholstery—everyone wanted our suite.

Florence uplifted us so much that after we had been in Rome a few days and had seen the Colosseum, the Forum, and the Sistine Chapel, we went right back to Florence. You need a lot of time for Rome, so we took the time on a later trip, but on this first trip we simply had to spend a few more hours at what I'm afraid I first called the "Pizza" Palace when asking directions and the Ponte Vecchio and the Michelangelo David and the Masaccios.

There were many other trips, and we added Spain, Lisbon, and later Israel and Greece. Previously we had visited London while a number of friends still lived there, and we saw spectacular theater.

We were there the year Laurence Olivier and Ralph Richardson did *Henry the Fourth,* parts one and two, and the double bill of *Oedipus Rex,* with the Olivier anguished howl heard "round the world," in combination with Sheridan's hilarious *The Critic.* Later these unforgettable programs came to New York, where, of course, we saw them again and were able to say when someone remarked on how incredible they were, "Yes, we caught them out of town."

Then in 1965 we made a particularly world-shaking visit to London. We took our children and we met the Beatles. Steve and I interrupted Alan, eleven, and Susanna, fourteen, during their nightly ritual of rock 'n' roll record listening by telling them we would take them to Europe for their Easter vacation. What ensued was the kind of golden moment that makes all the vicissitudes of parenthood suddenly worthwhile. The children, cool characters both, reacted with spontaneous, uncontrolled emotion and actually wept for joy.

We had only ten days and were planning five in London and five in Paris. As I pressed their dear wet faces close, they looked across at each other and with one breath sobbed ecstatically, "At last we can go to Liverpool!"

Liverpool! Not exactly a must on the average traveler's itinerary. Then I realized our children were not to be "average travelers." They were pilgrims. If you're hung up on Mozart, you want to go to Salzburg, and if you're hipped on Wagner, you want to make the scene at Bayreuth, and if you were a record buyer between ten and sixteen in 1965, you wanted to walk barefoot to Liverpool. We reluctantly agreed to make the pilgrimage with them, but first, in London, the Tower, St. Paul's, the Houses of Parliament, the changing of the guard at Buckingham Palace, Hampton Court, and Brown's Hotel, where we stayed and where everyone in the lobby at tea looked like Dame May Whitty.

Then the miracle happened. We visited the movie set at Twickenham where the Beatles were shooting their second picture, *Help!,* under Richard Lester's brilliant direction. The scene involved Ringo falling through a trap door into a small compartment occupied by a tiger while the others give him helpful escape suggestions from above. A climax is reached where they all sing to him the "Ode to Joy" from Beethoven's Ninth Symphony.

Walter Shenson, the producer, had driven us to the studio, and it was he who introduced us to Ringo and Paul. We later met George, briefly, and John, too, but he was being interviewed and no deep bond of intimacy was established. But Ringo and Paul talked to us and the children most freely. The kids showed it more, but I was completely thrilled.

The conversation sailed lightly from Murray the K, the disk jockey, to Leonard Bernstein to American crowds, to groups and boots and haircuts, and finally I asked them if they ever went home, up to Liverpool. "Not if we can help it" was the good-natured reply.

They explained to the children that what they were looking for, the music, excitement, and the people, was all in London by that time. The kids exchanged one of their famous looks and said, "If you say that, then we don't want to go." It 255 seemed to me that a shaft of light streamed across that set in Twickenham, and I could hear a hundred mixed voices belting out the "Ode to Joy."

When we were leaving Brown's for Paris, something arrived for the children, not from the Beatles but from our friend Sidney Bernstein, whose Granada offices were in Manchester. Learning that the kids were not going to Liverpool, he arranged to send them a rare piece of wood. The paint was worn off, and it bore an inscription stating that it was part of the floor of the Cavern in Liverpool where the Beatles were born. The planks had been sold piecemeal to the Faithful, and this plank was signed by the Cavern's owner, Ray McFall, so we knew it was indeed a piece of the True Floor. We never got to Liverpool, but somehow a bit of Liverpool came to us. The children carried it reverently to the United States.

If asked, Susanna and Alan would never have had any trouble picking out their favorite trip. I cannot pick mine, but somehow I keep remembering most fondly our stay in Naples and then our drive up the Amalfi coast, seeing Amalfi, of course, Sorrento, Herculaneum, and finally Capri. The things disdainfully called "touristy" are often the very best things to do, so we went off one afternoon in a little boat to go through the famous Blue Grotto. Hundreds of boats like ours were idly making their way toward the entrance. I lay back in the golden sunlight and ran my hand through the cool water as our boatman manuevered us along. Steve and I exchanged looks of pure joy, contentment, and love. Suddenly a man a few boats away seemed to be calling over to us. He stood up tall in his boat. As he neared I realized he was actually calling to me. I looked across several boats at him, puzzled, and clearly heard him saying "Bellissima! Bellissima!" while staring right at me. I looked at Steve, feeling flattered and a bit uncomfortable, then heard him calling in Italian and pantomiming, "Would you mind terribly if I took your picture, you are so beautiful?" I looked inquiringly at Steve, who shrugged and pantomimed that it was all right. I thought to myself, "This is really very sweet." And feeling rather set up about myself, I tried to look unselfconscious and poised while the man took my picture. He called across,

256

thanking us both profusely, said what a privilege and an honor it was and how beautiful *la signora* was, and rowed off. Steve and I laughed, and soon, along with many others, entered the grotto. It is indeed a beautiful blue sight, the curved ceiling reflecting the extraordinary blue of the water, until it is an experience of entire "blueness" all around. Feeling pleased with the beauty of it all, and with myself, I saw that we were emerging from the grotto. As we were disembarking, the man from the other boat to whom my picture was as needful as food or drink, I thought, rushed over to us, waving a fan of the pictures he had taken of me and shouting hoarsely, *"Cinquanta mille lire! Cinquanta mille lire!"* He offered the pictures to us with one hand while extending his other with open palm and toothy grin. Many other similar photographers were rushing around yelling and collecting their due. Steve paid him at once. I turned a becoming beet red after all that blue and wondered how I could have been so dumb, so easily suckered. Ah, flattery! Ah, conceit! Ah, vanity! Before I go off into my aria, I must hasten to say that it didn't take long before we were laughing. I looked at the pictures. Actually, they were nice snapshots: me in a white skirt, black top, and pink linen hat (black and white, of course, but I remember what I was wearing). I did not think *la signora* looked so beautiful, but then, of course, neither did my personal photographer.

It is impossible to pick the favorite trip. Each one had something special in a different way: Greece, running up what felt like a mountain on Cape Sounion to be stunned by the sight of the Temple of Poseidon looming black against the early evening sky—or the first mysterious encounter with Delphi, or the Alhambra, or Masada, or walking up the Via Dolorosa in Old Jerusalem, or visiting Richard Burton and Peter O'Toole shooting the film *Becket* outside London. There were trips with the children, too, to Niagara Falls, Mexico, St. Thomas, and Jamaica.

About two years after Steve died, I was in Majorca with my partner at director Hal Prince's house working on a project with him, and just before leaving for New York, I decided 257 this was the moment I must take the plunge and travel some-where by myself. Barcelona was not far, and when Steve and I had been in Spain and spent glorious days in Madrid, Se-ville, and Granada, we had regretfully missed Barcelona. Un-easily I made the reservations, and Hal advised me about hotels and restaurants. I asked him to make the dinner reser-vation for one (Dinner for One, Please, Jaime) at an elegant place and to find out if they would take A Woman Alone, and whether pants were acceptable. Spain had been a very formal country still when we were there in 1958, requiring the black dress and pearls, at least, for dinner. At the Ritz in Madrid, I recall, Steve and I had lovely rooms. I was a writer and travel-ing under my married name, so there was not the slightest whiff of decadent, unreliable show business emanating from my person. But actors were verboten. The Humphrey Bo-garts, members of that riff-raff set, mummers, were not ac-cepted and had to stay in another hotel along with such low-lifes as John Gielgud, Laurence Olivier, and Vivien Leigh.

My flight was a short one. The hotel looked agreeable, but I had a painful pang knowing I was alone. Of course I had made business trips on my own, but this was different. This was for pleasure, and thinking back on the great exciting romantic journeys we had made together, I was not sure how much pleasure it would be. A walk through the streets and over to the newly opened Picasso Museum made me feel elated and reassured. But then I returned to the hotel, changed, and got transportation to the restaurant, being sure to take along a book and a notebook. As I walked in and sat down, a feeling of downright abandonment engulfed me. I sat there trying to look composed and sophisticated and won-dered how I would ever get through all the way to dessert, six courses away. The food was delicious, the pace stately. I did not smoke, and envied those who did, because at least it is something to do. In the long waits between courses, I pulled out my notebook and wrote in great detail about the Picassos I'd seen and the period clothes in the Costume Museum and the fantastic Gaudí buildings I had passed, to be seen in detail the next day.

I was there only three days and learned that as long as I was out seeing new and fascinating things, and even ducking in somewhere simple for a solitary lunch, I was fine and having a marvelous time. But nightfall, bringing with it an equally solitary dinner, depressed me, and I found the solution in room service and a book and so to lonely bed.

That's the way it is. Whatever happens to you, you have to keep twirling. I think. Since Barcelona I have been on my own to East Berlin (on an International Theater Institute conference trip), to Vienna at Hal Prince's invitation to attend the opening of *Turandot* which he directed, Salzburg with Lenny, on the *QE 2* doing my *Singin' in the Rain* comments for a free first-class passage, to Ireland to celebrate friends Bob and Kathy Parrish's fiftieth wedding anniversary, and to Africa with twelve total strangers.

All of it has been pleasurable. It is not the same as traveling with someone you love, who incidentally could turn out to be someone who can take care of the tickets, the baggage, the reservations, and the little airport horrors that are the maddening incidentals of travel. Did I mention that one also misses the love and companionship? What would I have done, I wonder, if I had been alone when the Paris airport went on strike?

Steve and I were on our way to Tel Aviv, the first stop of our Israel trip, to stay at Rehovot with the dynamic head of the Einstein Institute, Meyer Weisgal. At the Paris airport there was a great deal of milling and shouting, but Steve calmly got on the long line at the car rental window. To pass the time we started chatting with a French couple behind us and decided that we two couples should rent a car together and head for Brussels, where we could make our Tel Aviv connection and they could make theirs to Hong Kong.

We shared a pleasant drive with them and later a marvelous dinner at one of Brussels's famed restaurants, all the while assuming, from the easy old-shoe relationship, that they were a married couple. Not at all. He was in the wood business, and she was a café singer. Several years before this they had shared a flight out of Paris to the East. On the way they found they liked each other and that their routes coincided 259 exactly: Hong Kong, Singapore, Bangkok, Ceylon, he buying teak, mahogany, and other woods, and she singing her heart out in cafés in just those same cities.

He was French, dark, thin, dapper, and married; she was from the Canary Islands, curvy, blond, still looking around. They arranged to rendezvous every year at the same time and place (there is a play in this somewhere, I'm sure), and share a happy clandestine jaunt together. When she learned I was connected with show business, she whipped out her eight-by-ten glossy publicity shots, and we promised to keep in touch. I describe this happy couple only to make the point that things like this can happen. Perhaps one day I will be on a plane to London for my, I hope, annual feast of British theater, the best of the West End and the National, and the Royal Court and the Almeida, plus Stratford and Chichester, perhaps even including the Gate and the Abbey up Dublin way. There is this man sitting next to me and he turns out to be someone who is on the same route as mine, perhaps, well, let's say, uh—selling wigs and crepe hair for beards to the various theaters I have named, so that he makes the same stops I make, at the same time of the year.

This is far-fetched, you say. I say it's not impossible. Listen, Mr. Sandman, you don't have to make him "the cutest dream I've ever seen." It would be nice, however, if he could be, say, under eighty, giving us a chance at our romance for at least a few years more. Yes, I know I have been making a point of how well I am doing traveling alone, but is this asking too much? Hope springs eternal . . .

My Head: First Visit to That Small Planet in a Long Time

I have evaluated the state of my body on more than one occasion. Undertaking a physical update of where my body is now cannot be considered a challenging problem in investigative reporting: All I have to do is glance in the mirror. But where is the rest of me? I don't mean this in the Ronald Reagan–*Kings Row* "where are my legs?" sense. I mean my head, my brain, my thinking, my understanding, my feelings, my attitudes, my philosophy, my *weltanschauung,* if you choose, and I hope you don't, my "taking stock of what I have and what I haven't . . . what do I find?" (this quote appears here with the blessing of the Irving Berlin estate), my up-to-the-minute, hold-the-front-page thoughts about life in 1994.

What do I think? Well, I'm delighted to be alive in 1994. Ask who wants to live to be a hundred, and the answer is the person who is ninety-nine. Yet I am glad I was born in an earlier era, closer to the nineteenth century when there were still ice wagons and milkmen, buttonhooks, hair receivers, windup Victrolas, and trolleys. Just using the expression "hold the front page" is an indication of where one of my feet still is: next to Lee Tracy's, holding open the door of his editor's office as he yells he's got a scoop, in any number of old newspaper movies (Lee Tracy: actor, 1898–1968, played many reporters and press agents, distinctive nasal voice).   261

Way back then, before the media sucked up every last bit of air to spew it forth crammed with endless hitherto hidden goings-on, and before biographers felt impelled to dig into every corner of every room in their subjects' lives for dust balls under the beds and dead bugs in the chandeliers, there was an entity called discretion, and there were certain things that remained private and secret. I long for the days when people had less information. To expedite this I am starting a movement called "The People's Right *Not* to Know." For example, I do *not* want to know that Eleanor Roosevelt may have had a homosexual relationship. Today, being booby-trapped with politically incorrect land mines, I hasten to add that of course a homosexual relationship is a swell thing; I don't mean that it isn't. I just . . . How can I explain how I feel about Eleanor Roosevelt?

When I was a child in Brooklyn, Mrs. Roosevelt came to the Children's Museum across the street from where I lived at the time. Her husband Franklin D. was governor of New York State. The very tall governor's lady shook hands with a lot of us kids, and once I had looked up into those warm, twinkly, beautiful eyes, I was hers for life. Later on I had occasion to campaign with her and support causes with her, and I was there after Adlai Stevenson's defeat to listen to her exhort all us Stevenson people to join in with no dissension and work for the election of our exciting young candidate, John F. Kennedy. I would have done whatever she told me to, and I am glad I did it.

Although she has not been gone so very long, I cannot picture her here today where the daily soap operas bring every sexual and behavioral aberration in the book into your living room in the middle of a sunny afternoon, and the talk shows and the "behind the news" shows deal with subjects no self-respecting stevedore would have admitted knowing about a few years ago. (Are there still stevedores?) Reactionary, that's what I have become, and prim. After all, my mother would not let me say "hell" or "damn" or "bum." Maybe I'm getting more like her every day. But "reactionary"? No, that's not the word because that puts me in with the Helmses, and the

curtailers of freedom of speech and expression, and the crippling of the arts. There is a terrific line in a Shakespeare sonnet on this subject: "Art made tongue-tied by authority." No, I am not with the "tongue-tiers." I'm just old-fashioned. I still hear, ringing in my ears' memory, my mother's voice saying, "Life is not so short but that there is always time for courtesy" and "Never write anything in a letter you wouldn't put on a postcard." She couldn't have meant that second one literally; I've read courtship letters she wrote to my father whom she married in 1912. I guess she was just trying to teach my brother and me discretion. Those two statements are things I feel Mrs. Roosevelt might have said, too. I know she has helped to shape these 1994 thoughts I am trying to assemble . . . both social and political.

In my first political involvement I accompanied my mother to the polls, where she voted faithfully for Norman Thomas on the Socialist ticket. My father voted straight Democrat, and my grandfather, along with many of his generation who had done well over here, Republican. Every time I went with my mother, I listened hard to her murmured answers, trying to find out how old she was, but all she ever said was, "Over thirty." I felt very grown up being left alone when she went behind those mysterious curtains.

In 1934 some friends got me involved in the La Guardia campaign, about which I knew very little except the word *Fusion,* which was on all the posters. I am happy to remember that my first time out I had a winner. There was a period much later on when, having supported Walter Mondale and George McGovern, both wonderful men, I began to feel that if I put my name on a candidate's committee, it was tantamount to the kiss of death. Before and during World War II, having worked for Spanish War Relief and Russian War Relief as well as British War Relief, I wound up in a group lumped as "prematurely antifascist" but by sheer luck never had my life blighted by the House Un-American Activities Committee.

I feel I have always been on the right side, meaning somewhat to the left, but I never supported a candidate I thought Mrs. Roosevelt wouldn't like. I got somewhat carried away with Henry Wallace but at the last moment went for 263

Truman. The most disillusioning experience was campaigning for Eugene McCarthy, about whom I started out being excited and feeling I could make a difference, and by whom I later felt let down, even somehow betrayed. He is a brilliant and complicated man, but I guess he did not really want to be president.

Now where am I politically today? What are my "hold the front page" feelings? Still hopeful, I voted for Bill Clinton and I still believe in him, and I think Mrs. Roosevelt would feel that way, too. I also think she would join my People's Right *Not* to Know movement.

Of course I don't mean I should not know about and feel the suffering in the world: the cruel, hideous nationalist fragmentation with its age-old hatreds, self-perpetuating and seemingly eternal; the rise again—or did it ever fall?—of anti-Semitism; the injustice to minorities, among them women. As a woman I have been particularly fortunate because in my field I have encountered so little prejudice personally. That does not mean I am not on the barricades. Hell, "some of my best friends are women," and some of my biggest influences: my mother, my teacher Miss Stebbins, Edith Wharton, Beatrice Lillie, Billie Holiday, and Eleanor Roosevelt. In an age when Bosnians are being left to be slaughtered, a baseball star injures people by throwing an exploding firecracker at them, and children are tortured and go hungry every day, what are my thoughts about people? I am in no position to hand down laws. No person, no Great Power has had a rendezvous with me on a mountaintop to pass me a list of do's and don'ts, but I have decided what I like best about people and what I think people should be:

> Thou shalt be kind.
> Thou shalt be considerate.
> Thou shalt be courteous.
> Thou shalt be understanding.
> Thou shalt be forgiving.
> Thou shalt be truthful.
> Thou shalt be enthusiastic.
> Thou shalt be inquiring.

Thou shalt be fun.
Thou shalt be kind.
(You can't repeat this one too often.)

I am sure Eleanor Roosevelt was all of the above. If she had
been born a little later, she could have been president herself.
In fact, she *would* have been president. Of course, today as a
candidate she would have to undergo the excruciating third-
degree examination of her every thought and deed. They
might dig up that thing about the homosexual relationship.
That might keep her from being president, and that's what I
mean about everyone having so damn much information.

Clicking the remote the other evening, I came across
a nature program and learned that koala bears eat only gum
tree leaves, so where there are no gum trees, there are no
koalas. Now, that's my idea of a nice new thing to know.
The trouble is, I could turn to another channel and learn
something I do *not* want to know—that some prominent
screen star has sex with koala bears.

I guess that sums up where my head, my brain, my
thinking, my understanding, my attitudes, my feelings, my
philosophy are in 1994. Lee Tracy and I can remove our feet
from the editor's doorway because it is no longer necessary to
"hold the front page." Let the presses roll! You've got your
scoop!

The Old Order Changeth; or Waiter, Make That the Fin-de-Siècle Pudding, Please

Trying desperately to join the twentieth century before it becomes the twenty-first, I have bought a fax machine. It is thrilling. It is a marvel. However, as the century's days dwindle down to a precious few, I am still procrastinating about a computer/word processor, feeling somehow that of all the people in the world over two, I will prove to be the only one who cannot master it. I am still tapping away at my old typewriter, feeling daring because it is an IBM Selectric II, and very much reassured by knowing that Robert Caro, the author of many fat volumes about Lyndon Johnson, uses only nonelectric Royal portables. I was also fortified for a while by a piece I read by Nora Ephron explaining how much she loved all the rewriting she had to do on her old typewriter and how much she learned by changing and recopying all she wrote over and over again—until I mentioned this to her, and she confessed she had succumbed to the siren song of an Apple and was in love with her new computer.

It is all going so fast. I was born seventeen years into the century, and at this writing there are only six years left of it. I still can look up the Avenue of the Americas, which I call Sixth Avenue, and miss the old "elevated," and I still resent Fifth Avenue being a one-way street. When I talk to a salesperson, I have to remember there is apt to be a generation gap—often three generations wide. At Tower Records I was looking for a recent CD of a show called *Wonderful Town* for which my partner and I had written the lyrics. Yes, I do have a CD machine, and my old LPs form a pleasing permanent design up and down and across the walls of my workroom. It was only when I moved a few years ago from a house to much less space in an apartment that I allowed my old 78s to be wrenched from my bosom and put on the block. At Tower I asked a pretty young thing for the CD I wanted and told her it had originally been put out by Decca.

"Decca?" she asked. "Is that the name of the group?"

"No," I said, "that was the record company, and it was a show album called *Wonderful Town.*"

"Oh," she said, "you mean a sound track."

"No," I said, "a show album . . . a musical that played in a theater."

Looking at me as if I had rocketed in from Mars, she handed me over to someone else. He said, "You'll have to look it up in the computer."

I surveyed the machine he indicated, flung my arms around his knees, and, weeping piteously, pleaded with him to look it up for me.

Watching the young man punch in the information about my CD, those deft fingers rambling idly but swiftly over the quiet keys, I was aware that he was born knowing how to do that and understanding how those machines function. When my VCR in the country suddenly quit, my house-keeper's young daughter clicked a few clicks on the remote, and it worked like a dream. It seems the last two generations were born trailing not only clouds of glory but also of elec-tronic know-how as well. And their bodies move differently from mine when they dance.

When I first purchased the TV and VCR for the coun-try, I was anxious to tape the Kennedy Center Honors. We were honorees that year, and the show would be telecast while I was out to dinner. First I collected all the equipment I needed: the instruction book, my glasses, and a flashlight, these last two because I really do not see very well and to see at all I need bright, bright light, and the buttons are marked in such tiny print. Then I telephoned the helpful young man   267 who had sold me the stuff at the store and proceeded to try to beat the clock and get my machine set, but still be in time for dinner. With the phone cradled between shoulder and ear, my fogged-up glasses slipping off my nose, holding the flash in one hand and pushing buttons with the other, peering at the panels while straining to hear his instructions, perspiring heavily all the while, I was not a pretty sight. Trembling and gasping for air, I arrived at the home where I was to have dinner and, fortunately, watched the show there, because when I got back home, I had a blank tape.

We have seen so much change, and we have so much to learn—we who were kids when milk was delivered in horse-drawn wagons and then pulled up to the apartment in a dumbwaiter. Or must I say "dumb watron" since I understand that is the politically correct unisex term for whoever or whatever serves us.

Change can be both blight and blessing, of course, and this city, New York, comes in for constant criticism for having changed only for the worse. In the hope of being deemed hopelessly sentimental, and even with the sound of riveting in my ears as yet another monster building goes up cutting off my view of Central Park, I feel there is strong evidence that this is still a helluva town. The other day while doing some errands in my neighborhood I was walking up Broadway, and as I came toward the corner of Sixty-ninth Street I heard the sound of beautiful singing. It was a pure, clear soprano sound. Standing in the middle of the gutter, with some people passing and others standing to listen, cars coming dangerously close, was a lovely young woman playing a guitar and singing. She just stood there, poised, unselfconscious, singing away. People smiled at one another. There was an open basket near her for contributions. I then noticed that another girl stood by with a basket of cassettes. I bought one and moved on, her voice following me down the street. At home when I played the cassette, made up of songs she had written and produced, tears welled up. It struck me as such a gutsy thing to do: stand there in traffic and sing. The city was beautiful that day.

268   Another wonderful city afternoon I had was when I

went to the Matisse show at the Museum of Modern Art. I hit a time when it was not too crowded and wove my way through the magnificence and beauty of room upon room bursting with genius. Afterward, my soul well nourished but my stomach rumbling, I walked east in the cool autumn sunlight, crossed Fifth Avenue, and there was Paley Park, the small oasis where the Stork Club had once been. All that jockeying for the best tables and the white-powdered face of Brenda Frazier and the press agents hovering around the throne of Walter Winchell, the king of gossip, and the swooshing of cocktail shakers being shook had long ago been replaced by this pocket paradise with its waterfall cascading down the back wall and splashing delightfully beneath the muffled noise of traffic. I had not been a habitué of the Stork in those days, a couple of times in the '50s maybe, twice to the Cub Room with Judy Holliday. I am not nostalgic about it, but I relish this space in its present incarnation. People were sitting at the little iron tables, on the little iron chairs, some reading their papers, some resting, some eating. I decided to join the eaters and at the little food alcove got the best chicken sandwich I have ever tasted, and sat for a while, satisfying my hunger, listening to the water, resting my body, and loving my city.

I remembered how I loved the apartment Steve and I had had on Fifty-fifth Street, two blocks from where I was sitting. It was right after the war, and when my birthday came around, Steve said, "Let's get dressed up and go out and have a good dinner." We strolled down to Fifth Avenue, and Steve said, "Oh, that looks like a nice place across the street." We crossed Fifty-fifth and the Avenue and went into the restaurant near the corner. A somewhat roundish man with a florid complexion greeted us with a *bon soir*. Steve returned his greeting and explained that it was his wife's birthday and that we would like to have a fine dinner. The host bowed and ushered us to what we later learned was a most coveted table and proceeded to send us a bottle of gorgeous champagne. In our innocence we had wandered in where rich angels fear to tread, into Le Pavillon, where the Most Elegant Names in Town struggled to get reservations and where all were in 269 dread of the quixotic, despotic owner, Henri Soulé, the chap who had for some unreasonable reason welcomed us in. Out of that evening came a loving friendship. I would invite M. Soulé to whatever show I had running, and Steve and I would continue to dine there from time to time, even when we couldn't afford it, and kept up the tradition of the birthday dinner at the Pav.

We did not go in much for ritual, but another tradition we kept up year after year was our New Year's Day at Home. Continuity helps to make some sense of our chaotic and fragmented lives, and this event has been a kind of anchor for me.

Steve and I decided one year that people needed someplace to go after the rigors of New Year's Eve and that it would be nice if we just sat there and let them drift in, and give them shelter and sustenance and understanding only if they asked for it. There would be a long drinks-and-hors d'oeuvres period, and those who were going to the theater or who were appearing in plays or shows would go off knowing that everything would still be going on when they returned. We lived in a house, first one on Sixty-ninth Street and then a larger one on Ninety-fifth, and it was possible to serve a whole dinner for everyone with tables set up in the dining room downstairs, and people holding plates and sitting on the various flights of stairs or spreading out into the living room and library. The menu was always the same. After the cold shrimp, tiny hot dogs, and meatballs, with the drinks and the glogg, a lethal hot beverage Steve concocted from Swedish spices bought in a little bag and mixed into an imaginative mélange of liquors and served in a huge punch bowl, there would be the dinner cooked entirely by Tillie, our nurse/cook/housekeeper; it comprised stuffed turkeys; glazed hams; two kinds of kugel (noodle puddings), one with cheese, the other sweet, with raisins, cinnamon, and pineapple, both crusty on top; cakes; cookies; and real coffee, at least in the early days. Sometimes, when it got late, there would be music—Jule Styne would play, or Leonard Bernstein, or, later on, Cy

Coleman, and people would sing, Lena Horne, or Judy Garland, if she was in town, or people who were appearing in a show of ours, if one was on at the time.

In the apartment things have to be simpler. There is no organized dinner, and the party whose life span was once from five to two or three in the morning is now folding by around nine-thirty, but then, so are we. Every January first since the '50s a bunch of us have gathered, except for the year Steve died and the year Alan died. But continuity is a beautiful thing. The at-home that started well before she was born is now cooked and catered fabulously by Leonard's daughter Nina. Of course it has changed, but the party's not over and it has not changed for the worse. These are terrible times in many ways, but who says New York has changed only for the worse? Why, there are no more spittoons, for God's sake, no more horse manure in the streets, and no more goats on Eastern Parkway near where I lived as a little girl.

That girl came here as an immigrant from way across the river in far-off Brooklyn, where I had my little park across the way and my Children's Museum where they would not accept my doll and where I met Mrs. Roosevelt, plus my schools and synagogues and my mother and father and brother. Then, later, I had glamorous Manhattan, where the ladies wore hats and gloves and we had a sunken living room, and even later I had my husband and my children and my work. Did it all happen to the same person? I live now only two blocks from where I lived when I got married fifty-two years ago and where, in 1944, we started work on *On the Town.* Sometimes when I walk toward the park on Sixty-eighth Street and stop in front of 47 and look up at the third-floor bay window, I wonder if I am the same person who once lived up there. I find it hard to make the connection between Girl One and Girl (?) Two. It is true that along the way I changed my name a lot and my face and like everyone else I had good times and bum times. In fact, I have had a great deal of sadness. Is that what life is? A declivity between two mountains, the Before Life and the After Life? Is that why someone called it a "vale of tears"? Sometimes I ask myself if 271

I had known when I was young that it would be like this, would I have gone on with it? Well, of course. The alternative has nothing to recommend it. It is no good at all. And I wouldn't have believed it anyway, that life can be so full of wrenching sadness. I continue to love the husband who died, and I love my children, the one who is living and the one who is dead. And I have long-playing friends and a beloved work partner, and the work life goes on well past the fifty-year mark. And "time-challenged" though I be, I still like it here —on earth, I mean, and in New York and even in my skin, the outside covering I am at last beginning to feel more comfortable in.

I will be able to have only six more New Year's Day at-homes in this, the twentieth century. Now, feeling totally with it, *au courant,* up to date, and part of now, I can put my guest lists into my fax because it is also a copier and have neat copies for 1995. By then, who knows? I might even have those lists stored away in my new computer. I admit, in fact, at this writing, I have taken the plunge and bought one. Come on with your twenty-first—I've a smile on my face!

Lightning Source UK Ltd.
Milton Keynes UK
UKHW020329240919

350303UK00009B/2692/P